Date Due

People in Systems

A Model for Development in the Human-Service Professions and Education

Other Books by Gerard Egan

Encounter
Group Processes for Interpersonal Growth

Face to Face
The Small-Group Experience and Interpersonal Growth

The Skilled Helper
A Model for Systematic Helping
and Interpersonal Relating

Exercises in Helping Skills
A Training Manual to Accompany The Skilled Helper

Interpersonal Living
A Skills/Contract Approach
to Human-Relations Training in Groups

You and Me
The Skills of Communicating and Relating to Others

People in Systems
A Model for Development in the Human-Service Professions and Education

Gerard Egan
Loyola University of Chicago

Michael Cowan
St. John's University
Collegeville, Minnesota

Brooks/Cole Publishing Company
Monterey, California
A Division of Wadsworth, Inc.

Printed in the United States of America

10 9 8 7 6 5 4 3 2 1

Library of Congress Cataloging in Publication Data

Egan, Gerard.
    People in systems.

    Bibliography: p. 194
    Includes index.
    1. Maturation (Psychology) 2. Social institutions. I. Cowan, Michael A., joint author.
II. Title.
BF710.E33   301.11'3   78-25822
ISBN 0-8185-0320-3

Acquisition Editor: *Claire Verduin*
Production Editor: *Robert Rowland*
Interior Design: *John Edeen*
Cover Design: *Ruth Scott*
Typesetting: *Typesetting Services of California, Pleasant Hill, California*

Preface

As its title indicates, this book presents a model for people who are interested in human development and in the structure of the various levels of human systems that provide the sociocultural context or environment of this development. These systems might be small and immediate, such as the family, peer group, or classroom; they might be the larger organizations and institutions of life that affect us profoundly in both direct and indirect ways; they might be our culture itself. This model integrates these levels of systems in the form of a practical working knowledge of individual developmental processes and of the various ways in which the social settings of our lives, whether personal, institutional, or cultural, affect this development. The model weaves together the kinds of working knowledge and life skills that people need in order to face developmental tasks and crises resourcefully and invest themselves creatively in the culture of their lives.

We have written this book for anyone who would like to get a clearer picture of what it means to pursue his 'or her human development in the context of the social systems of life, as well as for individuals who are interested in careers involving the delivery of human services: psychology, medicine, nursing, education, social work, the ministry, and the like. Although it is intended primarily for students, this book is also addressed to professionals in the human services who may be familiar with many of the "pieces" of this model but not with the way we have integrated them.

This book, then, is both a primer and a primer. It is a primer because it is our first statement of this model, introduced with all of the hopes and hesitations of such a presentation. It is a primer because it is intended to be an open-ended model that will stimulate cross-disciplinary contributions to education and training for human development and foster change in social systems with people in mind. We hope that others will add to, emend, expand, and otherwise develop the model presented here. We find that what we have written in these pages challenges the ways we have been approaching the delivery of human services. We hope that it will do the same for others.

We would like to express a special word of gratitude to several individuals whose support and criticism have been particularly helpful to us: Dennis Kleinsasser, Carole Widick, and Kirk Lamb of St. John's University; Msgr. John Egan of Notre Dame University; James Bryer of the University of Delaware; and Richard McQuellon of Michigan State University. Thanks also go to Richard P. Albares of St. John's University, Robert D. Archibald of Ohio State University, Marvin Goldfried of State University of New York at Stony Brook, Clyde A. Parker of the University of Minnesota, Norman Sundberg of the University of Oregon, and Evelyn Whitehead of the University of Notre Dame for their reviews of the original manuscript of this book. The second author would also like to thank his wife, Cinny, and his daughter, Kristin, for their willingness to accept the strains of authorship on family life.

Gerard Egan
Michael A. Cowan

Contents

3
Life Skills: The Basis of Competence   42

4
The Social Context of Human Development— Level I: Personal Settings   65

5
The Social Context of Human Development— Level II: The Network of Personal Settings   80

10
Toward an Upstream Approach:
Applications of the People-in-Systems Model   163

11
Toward Mutuality in Human Systems   180

1

People in Systems:
An Overview

This book is ecological in the sense that it deals with the behavior of people in context—specifically, how people face developmental tasks and crises in the various settings of life. The model presented here emphasizes the kinds of life skills that are needed in order to pursue developmental tasks effectively and contribute to the systems that constitute the context of life. Such a perspective is designedly optimistic, for we see no value in the cultivation of pessimism. In the elaboration of this framework, however, it would be foolish to ignore the deficiencies of the world around us. Optimism needs to be tempered with the recognition of unpalatable personal and social realities. Let us begin by examining the demoralization that so often arises from our ineffective handling of the major issues confronting our world. Indeed, demoralization, at least at first glance, might seem to be a more realistic response to the world as it is than the guarded optimism we espouse.

Social Demoralization in the
Contemporary World

Events in our contemporary experience such as war, the denial of human rights, intractable poverty, and corruption in government have a powerful effect on a human quality that is absolutely essential to the survival of our world as we know it today—our collective capacity for hope. These discouraging situations take their toll on average people living and working in modern industrialized society, as well as those persons whose commitment is to an active involvement with the welfare of human beings. The following list speaks, although by no means in a complete way, to troubling realities that face all of us.

1

- The traditional values that have historically provided guideposts for individual and group behavior have in the minds of many people been seriously called into question, and their capacity to provide meaning and guidance in a simple, absolute way has been diminished.
- A sense of community, of belonging, that extends beyond our family and intimate friends has for many people been destroyed or diminished.
- With the rapid multiplication of bureaucratic institutions, the individual feels progressively isolated amid a bewildering array of social systems.
- Racial and cultural conflicts over issues of economic and social justice have made many people suspicious of others' motives and, perhaps more importantly, of their own.
- Our life-style is threatened by diminishing natural resources.

Mische and Mische (1977) spell out concretely the sense of powerlessness that pervades the lives of many people.

> The types of phrases that would complete the sentence "As a citizen of ———— I have power to ————" are declining rapidly in people's estimation of their own individual capacities as citizens. The types of phrases that would complete the negative phrasing of that sentence, "As a citizen of ———— I am not able to ————," are increasing:
>
> "Not able to ensure adequate food and housing."
> "Not able to ensure quality education for my children."
> "Not able to ensure clean air and water."
> "Not able to ensure a healthy environment."
> "Not able to ensure adequate medical care."
> "Not able to walk the streets safely."
> "Not able to get a good job."
> "Not able to trust our elected officials."
> "Not able to influence governmental policy."
> "Not able to control technology and technological processes" [p. 9].[1]

We believe that the cumulative effect of such realities on individuals can be described as a type of social demoralization (Frank, 1973; Mische & Mische, 1977, Chapter 1) in which individuals give up trying to cope with events in their world because they no longer expect to be able to cope effectively.

Sociologist Robert Nisbet (1969) has suggested that alienation, a day-to-day reality in the lives of contemporary people, is rooted in social demoralization:

> By alienation I mean the state of mind that can find a social order remote, incomprehensible, or fraudulent; beyond real hope or desire; inviting apathy, boredom, or even hostility. The individual does not feel a part of the

---

[1]This and all other quotations from this source from *Toward a Human World Order: Beyond the National Security Straitjacket*, by G. Mische and P. Mische. Copyright 1977 by Paulist Press. Reprinted by permission.

social order; he has lost interest in being a part of it. For a constantly enlarging number of persons ... this state of alienation has become profoundly influential in both behavior and thought.... For millions of persons such institutions as state, political party, business, church, labor union, and even family have become remote and increasingly difficult to give any part of one's self to [p. ix].

Novelist Joseph Heller (1974) brings us into the world of an individual who is experiencing the sense of alienation and helplessness that Nisbet has just described:

Something did happen to me somewhere that robbed me of confidence and courage and left me with a fear of discovery and change and a positive dread of everything unknown that may occur. ... I loathe conflict (with everyone but members of my household). There are many small, day-to-day conflicts with which I am unable to cope any longer without great agony and humiliation; a disagreement with the repairman who is cheating me out of service for a small amount of money or a conversation of complaint with one of those blankly illusive people who work in the business offices of telephone companies. (I would sooner let myself be cheated).... My wife is unhappy. She is one of those married women who are very, very bored, and lonely, and I don't know what I can make myself do about it (except get a divorce, and make her unhappier still) [p. 6].[2]

Alienation and feelings of powerlessness are not new problems in the history of the human race, but the complexity of our contemporary world makes them more complicated if not more intractable, and our relative psychological sophistication, combined with advanced communication media, makes us more intensely aware of them. The people-in-systems model outlined in these pages is an attempt to respond to these situations with hope rather than despair. It provides us with a framework to begin answering the following questions. How can we avoid or minimize demoralization? What kinds of practical knowledge and skills will help us fashion our own lives? How can we get at the roots of social demoralization? How can we equip others and ourselves to deal more effectively with people and with the social systems of life?

The Limits of Downstream Helping

A note concerning the word *downstream* used in the heading of this section: the story goes that a person walking alongside a river sees someone drowning. This person jumps in, pulls the victim out, and begins artificial respiration. While this is going on, another person calls for help; the rescuer jumps into the water again and pulls the new victim out. This process repeats itself several times until the rescuer gets up and walks away from the scene. A bystander approaches and asks in surprise where

---

[2]From *Something Happened*, by J. Heller. Copyright 1974 by Alfred A. Knopf. Reprinted by permission of Random House, Inc.

he is going, to which the rescuer replies "I'm going upstream to find out who's pushing all these people in and see if I can stop it!"

In our view, there is a need for a thorough reappraisal of the way we as a society have provided for the developmental needs of people as they move through life. Ask yourself this question: what are the most important influences on the person you are and on the quality of your life? Some combination of your family, your friends, your school, your church, and the places where you work and live is likely to head your list. Now ask yourself another question: what resources are available to assist these institutions to effectively accomplish their particular tasks while sustaining the development of their people?

Approximately 13% of federal funds allocated to community mental-health centers is currently earmarked for programs of a preventive or developmental nature (N.I.M.H., 1977). The remaining 87% is spent on the casualties of our culture. As a society, we have taken a largely "downstream" approach (see Hassol & Cooper, 1970; Carkhuff & Berenson, 1976) to human needs, waiting for people to develop severe problems in living and then investing enormous resources in attempts to rescue them, after which we send them back to the same human systems that were the source of their original difficulties.

Those who are professionally committed to the full development of human beings are vulnerable in a special way to the social-demoralization syndrome. Anyone who has worked in the helping professions for even a brief period has probably witnessed the "burned-out helper" phenomenon (Moore, 1977; Warnath & Shelton, 1977), in which an intense desire to help becomes an exhausted day-to-day coping with persons in difficulty that leads to discouragement regarding the helping endeavor itself. Most of us who are engaged in the helping professions would probably acknowledge such feelings from time to time.

The phenomenon of demoralized helpers has its roots in at least two factors: helpers spend a great deal of time in direct contact with the tragedies that signal failed human development, and they typically work "downstream," treating the casualties of ill-functioning human systems and then sending them back to the same settings. While it certainly is discouraging, it should not be surprising that successfully treated "cases" often return from these settings in six months, a year, or two years, with the same or more severe problems.

The Origin of Downstream Approaches to Meeting Human Needs

The demoralization of helpers raises a key question: how did the helping professions arrive at remedial (downstream) approaches as the preferred mode of responding to human needs? Two ways of thinking about people have helped to develop and entrench these approaches.

The medical model. First, as Szasz (1961) has noted, the assumptions of the medical model, which views many problems in social living as types of illness, lead to the conclusion that such problems need treatment.

Therefore, a person with problems in social living becomes a patient, and patients must have doctors or therapists. A patient, in the root sense of the word, is one who is helped by having things done for him or her. Indeed, once identified as patients, many people hand themselves over to be cured of problems in social living. Patienthood often means a loss of agency or assertiveness.

Overly individualistic psychology. A second and related source of current approaches to mental health is to be found, as Sarason (1974) has observed, in psychiatric and psychological theories and research on personality. Almost the entire tradition of North American psychology focuses on the individual. Sociocultural systems which have such a profound effect on the development of individuals, have, with few exceptions, been neglected in favor of a focus on individual behavior. A theoretical view giving primacy to the individual's thoughts, feelings, values, and behaviors while disregarding the sociocultural settings in which these emerge has led to highly individual-centered approaches to helping. Anyone who reviews typical curricula in programs that prepare people for the helping professions will quickly see that the emphasis is placed on the study of individuals rather than on the study of individuals in the context of the human systems in which they live out their lives. This overemphasis has led us to blame people for problems that originate primarily with society (Caplan & Nelson, 1973; Ryan, 1971). Blaming the victim prevents us from seeing the real causes of certain social problems.

Beyond Downstream Helping

Insensitivity to the *context* of human development has resulted in widespread failure on the part of the helping professions and those who are influenced by them to reflect in practice the distinction between "troubles" and "issues" suggested by Mills (1959). Troubles are the personal difficulties of particular individuals; issues are difficulties resulting from the social structures within which people live out their lives. A severe case of depression is a trouble, whereas chronic demoralization within a social group, such as working-class families (see Rubin, 1976), is an issue.

We have tended as helpers to respond to individual troubles at the expense of dealing with issues of human-system functioning. At the same time, many of us would readily acknowledge that perhaps the most fundamental realities affecting the quality of modern life—indeed, affecting our very potential for survival—are those realities that have to do with human organizations and the quality of their functioning. This becomes particularly apparent when we consider that the world of human systems ranges from microlevels, such as the family, to macrolevels, exemplified by international political systems. If the understanding of individual behavior can be extraordinarily complex and demanding, then confronting the bewildering complexity of the world of organizations, institutions, and communities may seem like an invitation to massive cognitive overload. Such a reaction probably accounts in large measure for our tendency to do what we know how to do, even in a world that seems to need much more.

Our belief is that our care-giving horizons must be expanded to include not only individuals but also their social settings. Although most of us accept as a given the profound effects of these settings on the development of people, we tend to do so in a way that suggests an essentially passive and perhaps pessimistic view of the situation ("you can't fight the system"). If organizations, institutions, and communities are powerful contexts for human development, they are so for weal or for woe. It is our suggestion that a social-environment perspective offers a key to an upstream approach for fostering the development of people and that the knowledge, skills, and commitment of helpers are desperately needed at this level. Our intent in the pages that follow is to offer a working model of people in systems that will suggest ways of moving upstream in a deliberate and systematic fashion. We begin this task with an overview of our model.

People in Systems: A Working Model

A model can be defined as a visual portrayal of how things actually work or how they should work under ideal conditions. A working model is one that enables the user to achieve behavioral goals effectively. It is a cognitive map with "delivery" potential. We have set two criteria for the models that we use: they must be complex enough to account for the reality they attempt to describe and portray, and they must be simple enough to use. A model that meets only the first criterion is likely to be of interest solely to theoreticians and researchers, whereas a model that meets only the second criterion would tend to be simplistic rather than simple and would therefore be useless as a working model. Lippitt (1973) suggests that models with applied utility need to be two-dimensional, linear, and basically nonmathematical. Three-dimensional, nonlinear, and highly mathematical models do not usually help the practitioner.

Our model is based on the familiar Lewinian equation

$$B = f (P \times E).$$

That is, behavior is a function of the interaction between person and environment. Adapted to our purposes, the equation reads:

$$HD = f[(P \longleftrightarrow S) \times (S \longleftrightarrow S)].$$

That is, human development is a function of the interaction between *people* (P) and *the human systems* (S) in which they are involved, and of the interaction of these systems with one another.

The Three Elements of the Model

The three basic elements of the equation are the three basic elements of the model: people, human systems, and the interaction between people and systems and between systems themselves.

People (P). This refers to individual human beings moving through the developmental stages of life, undertaking lifelong and stage-specific developmental tasks, and coping with lifelong and stage-specific developmental crises.

Human systems (S). This refers to the groups to which individuals belong, by which their lives are affected and in the context of which they move through life stages, undertake developmental tasks, and cope with developmental crises. Our model represents the world as hierarchical, with smaller human systems nested in more complex ones. The family, for example, is nested in and greatly affected by community, economic, and governmental systems of various types.

The interaction between people and systems and between systems themselves. Note that in our equation we use arrows that point in both directions to indicate that the interaction of people and the settings of their lives, and the interactions of these settings themselves, go in both directions. Groups, organizations, institutions, and communities affect people; people affect them; and systems affect one another in growthful and nongrowthful ways. These interactions can lead to development, stagnation, or debilitation of individuals as well as systems. This interactional picture can become quite complex; a student *(P)* interacting with a high school *(S)* might experience intellectual growth, physical stagnation, and social/emotional debilitation; whereas the student's high school is affected by its interaction with families, the neighborhood, and governmental agencies.

At any given moment individuals bring both resources and deficits to their interactions with any given human setting. For instance, a student who has learned practically no discipline at home can have an extremely debilitating effect on a classroom, whereas a student who has learned self-management skills and developed intellectual curiosity at home can have a very positive impact. In the same way, a system, such as a high school, or a subsystem, such as the counseling service of a high school, brings positive as well as negative forces to bear on the individual. A teacher, for example, unaware of the natural "kicking against systems" that goes on with many students in the process of identity formation, or a teacher lacking the ability to deal positively with such adolescent rebelliousness, might emphasize discipline or punishment to such an extent that potentially growthful oppositional tendencies and conflicts are suppressed.

The Quality of Interaction between People and Their Human Systems

The arrows in our basic equation $(HD = f\ [(P \longleftrightarrow S) \times (S \longleftrightarrow S)])$ represent interactions that can be analyzed from the standpoint of *quality*. These interactions may be unenlightened and unskilled and may therefore lead to negative developmental results. Positive interactions, on the other hand, are based on a combination of working knowledge and skills on the part of individuals and systems.

Working knowledge refers to information or understandings concerning self and the world that enable individuals to face both resourcefully. Working knowledge facilitates behavior. For instance, if someone tells you the combination of a safe, you have information that enables you *to do* something. Such knowledge enables you to apply skills or abilities that you already possess. We do not suggest that merely understanding something enables you to do it; however, understanding a problem increases the probability of solving it.

Skills refers to competencies that are necessary for effective living in the areas of self-management, involvement with others, and effective participation in communities and organizations. Working knowledge informs and enhances skills, and skills translate working knowledge into effective behavior. The individual needs both in order to become positively involved in groups and communities, which also need specific kinds of working knowledge and skills in order to become places where tasks are accomplished and development is fostered. Under ideal conditions, enlightened and skilled individuals and systems work synergistically, each contributing to the development of the other. The following is a short overview of the kinds of working knowledge and skills that are needed in order to accomplish this development.

Working Knowledge and Skills
Needed by Individuals

Individuals need a working knowledge of developmental processes, a working knowledge of the major systems that affect people's lives, and the skills of self-management, interpersonal communication, problem solving, goal setting, and program development.

A. Working knowledge of developmental processes. We suggest that an individual's ability to pursue tasks and face crises will be enhanced if he or she develops a working knowledge of these tasks and crises at each stage of the life span, as well as a working knowledge of the developmental processes operative in the lives of the significant others with whom the individual is involved. For instance, it would be very helpful for a 16-year-old boy to have some fundamental information about the tasks and crises of identity formation: not textbook information, but information that will help him face the personal tasks and crises of his particular developmental stage. He could also benefit from some kind of working knowledge of the developmental stage of his 43-year-old parents. It would also be extremely helpful if the parents possessed the same kinds of knowledge with respect to themselves and their son. This would, in our estimation, increase the probability that the members of the family would face their family-related tasks more resourcefully and that they would be more helpful in their interactions with one another. This type of deliberate social/psychological education can be accomplished without making little psychologists out of children and bigger psychologists out of adults.

B. Working knowledge of the major human systems that affect people's lives. Such knowledge would include the way in which systems such as families and schools work and how individuals are affected and influenced by the systems in which they are involved. It would include ways of contributing to the development of these systems and of coping with their oppressive elements. High school students, for instance, would learn how schools instill certain cultural values even though these values do not appear explicitly in the curriculum (Giroux & Penna, 1977). Students would learn how to identify the implicit values of the school by examining how the school works or operates. Our assumption is that, by developing an explicit working knowledge of the school and its values, students will be able to invest themselves more intelligently in its processes and learn how to identify the values of a system by examining its actual policies and behavior.

C. Skills. One of the definitions of the word *skill* suggested by *Webster's New Collegiate Dictionary* is "a learned power of doing something competently." White (1959) has pointed out how important it is for individuals to develop a sense of competence. A combination of working knowledge and life skills, acquired through systematic education and training, is extremely important in achieving a sense of competence. Individuals need a wide variety of skills to involve themselves competently with self, others, and systems. These skills include self-management skills, interpersonal-communication skills needed to undertake people-oriented developmental tasks such as intimacy formation, problem-solving skills needed to cope with personal and developmental crises, and goal-setting and program-development skills needed to achieve personal goals and to involve oneself competently in the human settings of life.

This model suggests that acquiring the working knowledge and the skills needed to achieve goals and to support and challenge self, others, and systems should not be left to chance, on the assumption that people pick up such knowledge and skills from experience. Rather, such knowledge and skills should be offered systematically through formal and informal educational training systems.

Other things being equal, spouses who have a solid foundation in interpersonal-communication skills are more likely to maintain a successful marriage than those who do not possess these skills. It is never surprising when couples tell a marriage counselor that they "don't communicate well" with each other. Where were they to learn the complex skills of high-level interpersonal communication? Those who claim that most people pick up enough of these skills from experience in order to "get by" may be underscoring one of the reasons so many of us suffer from the "psychopathology of the average" (Maslow, 1968) even in our closest relationships. Training in interpersonal skills increases the probability of relating competently to others, especially if it is begun early in life. Many adults are presently engaged in interpersonal-skills training programs; this is a step in the right direction, but it is unfortunate that such training could not have been available to these people earlier in their lives, for with adults it often has a remedial character.

Working Knowledge and Skills Needed by Human Systems

Leaders of systems need a working knowledge of what systems look like, how systems are affected by the environment, and what developmental needs members have. Leaders must be able to assess the needs of the system members, set goals, develop and evaluate programs, support the developmental processes of members, and provide services as effectively and humanely as possible.

A. *Working knowledge.* Those who exercise leadership in groups would profit from the knowledge of what systems look like. An effectively designed and operating system has clear, operational, behavioral goals that are adequate translations of the mission of the system. In education and ministry, fuzzy goals often lead to programs that generate little enthusiasm and are ineffective translations of the missions of such systems.

Once the leaders of a community or organization understand the requirements for effective design and functioning, they can use this knowledge to diagnose their own systems, discovering how effectively they are accomplishing their missions by achieving clear, behavioral goals.

Leaders of a system would also profit from the working knowledge of how the system is affected by the environment. A family could examine the pressures placed upon it because of what is happening in the neighborhood. If a family lives in a racially tense neighborhood, it is going to be affected by the tension. But if the members of a family can ask themselves what is happening to them individually, and as a family, because of the situation in the neighborhood, this kind of exploration can help the family members become proactive rather than reactive with respect to neighborhood problems.

Leaders of a system would profit from the working knowledge of the developmental needs of those for whom they provide products or services. For instance, since serious illness is a different reality at age 10 or 40 than it is at 70, it would be quite helpful if those involved in the delivery of health services had a working knowledge of the developmental stage, tasks, and crises of persons being treated and how these might interact with an individual's illness. Educators need to understand the developmental needs of students as they are now and not only as they will be in adult life. Spouses who understand the developmental events of mid-life can use this knowledge to understand and to relate to each other more effectively.

B. *Skills.* Those responsible for the effective functioning of a community or an organization need a variety of skills. First, they need the ability to assess the needs of those for whom the community provides services. An organization cannot function properly until it first assesses the needs of those receiving its products or services. For instance, to improve the quality of life in the neighborhood, a neighborhood community council must be able to determine what the people living in the neighborhood need and want.

Second, the leaders of an effective community must be able to set concrete and realistic goals. Once needs have been determined, then goal-setting skills are called for that enable members of communities and organizations to set clear, concrete, specific, behavioral, realistic, measurable, and adequate goals. If the members of the community council set goals that go beyond available resources, then they merely frustrate themselves as well as the people living in the neighborhood.

Third, those responsible for the effective functioning of a community must be able to develop efficient, goal-related programs. Goals are ends, and programs are the means to those ends. Good programs are clear, step-by-step processes related to achieving specific goals. For instance, three families who form a friendship group feel victimized by the high-cost rundown housing available in their neighborhood. They decide to buy one of the dilapidated buildings in the neighborhood and renovate it themselves. The goal is clear at this stage, but now it is a question of developing the program—that is, the steps needed to achieve this goal, including finding the right building, pooling financial resources, getting a mortgage, determining what kind of rehabilitation is needed, and pooling skills and abilities.

Fourth, community leaders must be able to determine whether they are actually achieving desired results. A community council that has established a practical education program on neighborhood real estate in order to make residents more conscious of local real-estate conditions and more active in monitoring the quality of local housing now needs evaluation skills to determine the success of the program. Success is not determined by the way that people feel about the program but by concrete behavioral events, such as an increase in the number of rehabilitation projects, a decrease in the number of housing-code violations, or an increase in the number of volunteers working with the council's building inspector.

Fifth, leaders must be able to support the developmental processes of the members of a system. One of the authors has had contact with a family of seven that has a family meeting twice a week. Fifteen minutes of each meeting are spent in developing interpersonal skills that help members in their interactions with one another and with people outside the family. In our estimation, good systems develop the skills that are needed to support and challenge their members.

Finally, skills are required in order to provide services as effectively and as humanely as possible. Helpers need not only technical skills but also human-relations skills in order to deliver services effectively and humanely. A doctor who listens and responds empathically to his or her patient will develop a better relationship with the patient and will be in a better position to deliver technical services than a doctor who lacks these skills.

The ideal, then, is the interaction of people who have appropriate working knowledge and skills needed to support and challenge the human systems of their lives with systems that accomplish their tasks *and* promote the development of their members. All of this is put together schematically in Figure 1-1.

The human development *(HD)* of people *(P)* and systems *(S)* is a function of the quality of their interactions with one another.

$$HD_{P+S} = f[(P \longleftrightarrow S) \times (S \longleftrightarrow S)]$$

$P \longleftarrow$ enlightened and skilled interactions $\longrightarrow S$

People	Working Knowledge and Skills for Effective Interaction	Human Systems
Life stages (the when of human development)	Physical-development skills	Immediate personal settings (family, school, workplace)
Key systems (the where of human development)	Intellectual-development skills	Network of personal settings (interaction of family, school, workplace)
Developmental tasks (how individuals are challenged by new social roles)	Self-management skills	Larger institutions (government, economy, media, organized religion)
Developmental resources (how individuals must be supported in coping with developmental events)	Value-clarification skills Interpersonal skills	Culture (language, mores, folkways)
	Small-group skills	
Developmental crises (the subjective experience of crucial developmental challenges)	Systems-involvement skills	

Figure 1-1.
Human Development in Human Systems.

Mutual Support and Challenge in the Systems of Our Lives

There will always be conflicts between the needs of individuals and the needs of organizations and communities; however, this does not mean that individuals cannot support and challenge the systems of their lives and expect the same in return. After all, the human community is made up of people and systems interrelating, and support and challenge are the hallmarks of effective communities (see Egan, 1976; Kanter, 1972; Sanford, 1967). Mutual challenge will always mean conflict, but conflict, if faced in a supportive climate, promotes rather than hinders growth. The environment, through key human systems, is constantly making demands on individuals. Indeed, one way of looking at developmental crises is to see them as events and tasks that require individuals to develop new resources, skills, and behaviors. Human systems can provide support by educating and training their members to meet new tasks successfully and by understanding the crises experienced by them. Individuals, as they develop personal resources, can support the systems of their lives and challenge them to contribute to society as a whole and to provide resources for individual growth.

In our model, then, *development* refers to *individuals (P) as well as human systems (S)*. Ideally, human systems help individuals to develop the working knowledge (education) and skills (training) they need in order to complete developmental tasks successfully and become supportive and challenging members of society. Systems, of course, are not machines; they are made up of people. The quality of a system's results is a function of the knowledge, skills, and values of its members.

A basic theme of this model is that any approach to meeting the developmental needs of people must keep individuals and the systems in which they live *in focus simultaneously*. Those who work at an applied level cannot afford the constraints of a one-sided perspective, whether it favors the individual or the system (see Dollard, 1935; Sarason, 1974). Development is an adaptive process; people and systems change in order to meet new demands that arise from the environment. People who are concerned with the development of human beings need also to be concerned about the quality of life in the human settings of those with whom they are involved.

Giving the Social Sciences Away: The Social Scientist as "Translator"

Some members of the helping professions have suggested alternatives to the previously discussed "downstream" approach to meeting human needs. (See Carkhuff & Berenson, 1976; Hassol & Cooper, 1970; Morrill, Oetting, & Hurst, 1974.) Miller's (1969) position that psychology (we would say, more generally, the social sciences) must be "given away"—that is, that the knowledge and skills of the social sciences should be shared freely with people—is a theme promoted by the model under discussion. We believe that Miller's injunction should be implemented vigorously.

There is a great deal of discussion today concerning the relationship between professionals who deliver human services and their clients. Bledstein (1976) calls professionals to task for not "giving away" more of their knowledge and skills to their clients. He stresses the autonomy of individuals and maintains that they should be no more dependent on profession-als than they have to be. Haskell (1977), while agreeing that the human-service professions, like the other institutions of society, can become self-serving and, therefore, "deserve unrelenting criticism and reform" (p. 33), respects both their accomplishments and their necessity:

> If modern man displays an alarming tendency to defer thoughtlessly to expert opinion, it is largely because alternative guides to conduct such as common sense and the customary ways of his local community have long since failed him in important areas of life. The Victorians treasured Emerson's advice to "trust thyself," but they could not live by it and neither can we. The condi-tions of modern society place a high premium on esoteric knowledge, espe-cially when it comes stamped with the special authority of an organized community who police each other's opinions and thereby create something approaching a consensus of the competent. . . . Their (the professions) claim to be mankind's best means of cultivating and preserving insight into the "nature of things" ought to be taken seriously [p. 33].

Both Bledstein and Haskell invite professionals to reexamine the issue of how best to serve people. We believe that this service should in-clude greater efforts to give the professions away in ways that do not di-minish their integrity. Professionals concerned with human welfare and development might move in this direction by dealing with their clients in ways that reflect trust in the client's own initiative, abilities, and values, rather than by prescribing solutions from a superior and often value-laden position. (See Rappaport, 1977.)

Parker (1974) suggests that professionals have not yet developed the technical capability they need to give the social sciences away. We believe that this capability is currently being developed and is already available in many forms to those entrusted with educational and training programs. Technologies for skills training have been developed in such areas as help-ing (Carkhuff, Pierce, et al., 1977; Egan, 1975; Gazda, 1975; Goldstein, 1973; Goldstein, Sprafkin, & Gershaw, 1976; Means & Roessler, 1976a, 1976b), education (Carkhuff, Berenson, & Pierce, 1977; Gazda, 1973), problem solv-ing and program development (Blechman, 1974; Blechman & Olson, 1975; Burglass & Duffy, 1974; Carkhuff, 1973, 1974; D'Zurilla & Goldfried, 1971; Goldfried & Goldfried, 1975; Spivack & Shure, 1974; Spivack, Platt, & Shure, 1977), self-management (Watson & Tharp, 1977; Williams & Long, 1975), interpersonal communication (Egan, 1976, 1977), values clarifica-tion (Kirschenbaum, 1977; Smith, 1977), and physical fitness (Collingwood & Carkhuff, 1976a, 1976b). In addition, the growing self-help movement (Gartner & Riessman, 1977) is not waiting for the institutions of society to develop technologies to give the arts and sciences of the professions away. Rather, these groups are seizing what they see as rightfully theirs. The model developed in these pages speaks to the needs of professionals, of the self-help movement, and of individuals committed to achieving as much mastery over their lives as possible.

The sluggishness of the human-services professions in responding more effectively to a broad range of social concerns is caused by an inability or a refusal to forge a working interface between theory and research on the one hand and practical delivery of services on the other. Sarason (1974) and others have noted the enormous gap between those who develop theory and do research and those who are involved with direct delivery of services to people. There is often a thinly disguised contempt on the part of practitioners for research, and on the part of theoreticians and researchers for "working with people." Practitioners have a right to question petty and inconsequential research, but they can also benefit substantially from meaningful and well-executed theory (model building) and research. Theoreticians and researchers might question premature or ill-advised practice, but the skilled transformation of good theory and research into effective practice is the ultimate social payoff. Effective practice is the point where human systems *(S)* meet the person *(P)*. We cannot afford the kind of elitism that keeps research and practice apart.

The translator. If practitioners are honest with themselves, they realize that there are times when they are not in touch with the theory and research that could make a difference in the delivery of human services. On the other hand, theoreticians and researchers often have little understanding of the complex realities faced by practitioners in the field. We suggest that there is a need for what we call *social-science translators*— people who are in touch with the best in theory and research, who can translate these into effective programs, and who can evaluate these programs. Translators are thus social scientists who have a commitment to theory-and-research-based action for people. Theoretically, those who graduate from programs in such fields as social work and clinical and counseling psychology are prepared to be translators. We fear, however, that there are far fewer effective translators than we might expect (see Azrin, 1977).

Working models. In our experience, one of the translator's most effective tools is the working model for intervention (Egan, 1975, 1976; Widick & Cowan, 1977). Working models (as opposed to models devised primarily to *understand* social phenomena) do the following:

- they provide vehicles for translating theory and research into visualizations of how things work;
- they constitute frameworks for action or intervention (delivery) by practitioners;
- they suggest programs and the technologies needed to implement these programs;
- they suggest areas of action-based research with "delivery" potential; and
- they remain open to modification and development as they are influenced by new theory, research, and ongoing practice.

Translators can use working models to devise, implement, and evaluate human-services delivery programs. When translators devise educational programs that give the social sciences away, they provide the kinds of working knowledge and skills needed by individuals and systems to collaborate in working for goals.

Applying the
$HD = f [(P \longleftrightarrow S) \times (S \longleftrightarrow S)]$
Model: A Preview

The implications and applications of a model that links human development to the world of systems are so numerous and far-reaching that they are almost unsettling. Ultimately, as we have noted, such a model needs to become embedded in both individuals and the social settings of life. It can be a working model only if individuals and systems use it once they have a working knowledge of it. In this section, we discuss several principles that can guide people who are working to implement this model.

It is important to develop a people-in-systems focus. Human systems have a potent effect on the growth of their members and are, therefore, logical targets for those who wish to enhance human development. A family, for example, that develops a people-in-systems perspective, instead of falling into the "identified patient" trap when one of its members experiences trouble, could examine itself as a system in order to see the operation of the system itself and how it contributes to the problems of any individual member. Or the minister who is concerned about a rash of adolescent "acting out" in his or her congregation may wish to consider establishing a family-support-and-training center located in and staffed by members of the community. The minister, if qualified, can become an educator/trainer of community members who will support, educate, and train families in crisis. Similarly, the high school administrator may decide to explore team-building and interpersonal-skills training for faculty members so that they might develop the capacity to function as a democratic community. This may prove a viable alternative to dealing individually with underinvolved and burned-out teachers.

Effective social living demands both working knowledge and skills. Development over the life span places demands on the individual to function competently in increasingly complex tasks (student-trainee-worker-supervisor-manager) and to manage multiple roles (mother-wife-executive-friend). Figure 1-2 represents what individuals need to know and do in order to meet such demands.

This diagram can serve as a preliminary assessment device, helping us to discover the sources of the problems in living that we address. For instance, it may be that parent/child, teacher/child, or teacher/administrator conflicts are basically due to a lack of interpersonal-communication skills. Or these same conflicts may occur because the parties involved feel caught in a web of human systems that they simply don't understand. The

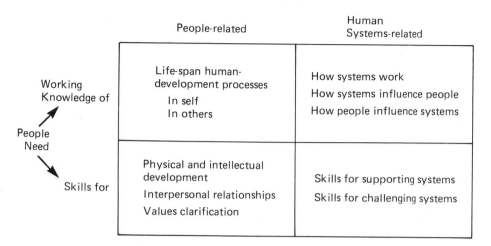

Figure 1-2

minister, teacher, or community leader who wishes to work "upstream" may define his or her task as the initiation of a social/psychological education or training process, based on the four areas outlined in Figure 1-2. This can be accomplished partially through educational materials and training programs that are currently available.

Effective agents for human development in an upstream approach are capable of giving away working knowledge and skills. We believe that helping persons tend to be overly committed to direct-delivery approaches and that this is a fundamental block to effective upstream work. The model outlined here emphasizes training, education, and support, which are essential to human development, rather than the direct delivery of human services. However, the adage "No one gives what he or she does not have" is pertinent here. Human-services delivery people must possess working knowledge and skills plus the education and training needed to impart them. We do not advocate the abandonment of direct services to people in crisis, but we do suggest that a substantial portion of our available resources should be invested in humanizing systems.

No system can afford to ignore the developmental needs of its members. Although this principle might seem to apply in a special way to systems that are involved in the delivery of human services, it applies to *all* systems. Argyris and Schön (1974; Argyris, 1976a, 1976b) attempt to show that what they call Model-1 systems, which are rigid and incapable of dealing with human feelings, are less efficient and effective than Model-2 systems, which are flexible and sensitive to human feelings. This difference in systems is not apparent to most people, they suggest, because Model-1 systems predominate in our world. In addition, the energy involved in transforming a system from Model 1 to Model 2 is considerable; therefore, it is easier to assume that we must live in a Model-1 world. Herzberg (1968), working with the problems of motivation in organizations, claims that motivation is related to human-development needs. Organizations that ignore these needs, he suggests, are less effective in meeting their goals than are organizations that take these needs into account. Some experts (see Trist, 1977) say that a more human collaboration between organizations and their members as well as among the larger institutions of society is needed for the very survival of society.

Support and challenge are needed by individuals and institutions. A great deal of this support and challenge must come from the interaction of individuals and the social institutions of their lives. Challenge without support is punitive and destructive; support without challenge is effete and unproductive. Individuals often resent the demands that come from organizations and communities, because they have not felt much support from these systems. The ability to support and challenge effectively is not learned automatically by individuals or institutions (see Egan, 1976), but it is essential if we are to move toward systems that foster development. Since social influence is a part of being human (King, 1975), our challenge is to humanize the influence process between:

$$\text{People} \longleftrightarrow \text{People}$$
$$\text{Systems} \longleftrightarrow \text{People}$$
$$\text{Systems} \longleftrightarrow \text{Systems}$$

Mutuality is the key to humanized social influence. Respect expressed behaviorally through mutual support, challenge, and affirmation can do much to humanize individuals and institutions. This theme is developed in greater detail in Chapter 11.

Conclusions and Implications

In the pages that follow, you will find our provisional attempt to flesh out the working model of people in systems that has been outlined in this chapter. This approach implies that, if the developmental events that occur throughout life—going to school for the first time, taking a job, entering into marriage, raising children, watching children leave home, dealing with retirement, and coping with old age and the prospect of death—call for growth toward greater competence on the part of individuals, then the society that provides individuals with the necessary resources for developing this competence supports the development of its people. The model also implies that if human systems are the contexts in which development is shaped, then a society that supports the renewal of its systems also supports the development of its people.

The fact that you are reading this book indicates that you have an interest in your own development and possibly a commitment to some form of service to others. It may even mean that you are interested in the

development of a new social order or a new world order. This book out-
lines the basic working knowledge and skills you need to pursue your own
development and to facilitate the development of others. It provides a
broad outline of some of the things you need to know about the organizations and communities that constitute the environment or context of development. Your task is to fill in this outline through further education and
experience. This book is not a training program in the skills you need to
deal effectively with people in systems, but it does outline the kinds of
skills you need to acquire.

As we have indicated earlier in this chapter, it would be a mistake to
equate an understanding of this model with the ability to apply it to any
given setting. A general understanding that does not take the form of par-
ticularized knowledge, skills, and experience is not to be mistaken for
power; however, it can be a significant beginning of power. As Shaull
notes:

> Every human being, no matter how "ignorant" or submerged in the
> "culture of silence" he may be, is capable of looking critically at his world in
> a dialogical encounter with others. Provided with the proper tools for such
> encounter, he can gradually perceive his personal and social reality as well as
> the contradictions in it, become conscious of his own perception of that real-
> ity, and deal critically with it. . . .
>
> When an illiterate peasant participates in this sort of educational ex-
> perience, he comes to a new awareness of self, has a new sense of dignity, and
> is stirred by a new hope. . . . And as those who have been completely mar-
> ginalized are so radically transformed, they are no longer willing to be mere
> objects, responding to changes occurring around them; they are more likely
> to decide to take upon themselves the struggle to change the structures of
> society which until now have served to oppress them [Shaull, 1970, pp. 13–
> 14].[3]

This model, then, is an educational tool based on humanistic and
democratic values. As Shaull (1970) has pointed out:

> There is no such thing as a *neutral* educational process. Education either
> functions as an instrument which is used to facilitate the integration of the
> younger generation into the logic of the present system and bring about con-
> formity to it, *or* it becomes "The practice of freedom," the means by which
> men and women deal critically and creatively with reality and discover how
> to participate in the transformation of their world. The development of an
> educational methodology that facilitates this process will inevitably lead to
> tension and conflict within our society. But it could also contribute to the
> formation of a new man and mark the beginning of a new era . . . [p. 15].

We offer this model as one instrument in the struggle to make education,
training, and social living more realistically "the practice of freedom."

[3]This and all other quotations from this source from the Foreword by R. Shaull to
Pedagogy of the Oppressed, by P. Freire. Copyright 1970 by The Seabury Press, Inc. Reprinted
by permission.

While we have made every effort to ground the model in current theory and research, we are fully aware that the ultimate impact of this or any model will not be found in its conceptual adequacy, but rather in the values and commitment of those who use it.

Chapter 1: Additional Resources

Frank, J. *Persuasion and healing* (Rev. ed.). Baltimore: The Johns Hopkins University Press, 1973. (See Chapters 2 and 12.)

Miller, G. A. Psychology as a means of promoting human welfare. *American Psychologist*, 1969, 24, 1063–1075.

Mills, C. W. *The sociological imagination*. London: Oxford University Press, 1959. (See Chapter 1.)

Nisbet, R. *The quest for community*. London: Oxford University Press, 1969. (See Preface and Chapters 1, 2, and 9–11.)

Sarason, S. *The psychological sense of community*. San Francisco: Jossey-Bass, 1974. (See Preface and Chapters 1 and 3.)

2

Human Development
through Life

We first meet Rachel at age 6 as she becomes a first-grader and moves with a mixture of excitement and apprehension into an important new world. She finds awaiting her there a bewildering array of new learning demands, a diverse group of people, and a set of rules and expectations that are different in many ways from those of her family. During the months that follow, Rachel learns and changes at a rate that startles her (and her family) at times. In both formal and informal ways she confronts questions about similarities and differences between girls and boys, conflicts between what she wants and the rules that apply to everyone, demands on her young mind to stretch and explore, and the joys and sorrows of playing and working with others like herself.

When we next meet Rachel, she is 15 and a student in junior high school, more sophisticated in many ways, and obviously at home in the school environment. But clearly these years hold another set of challenges for her. The physical changes that she is experiencing lead to new feelings and questions about herself and to new and often anxiety-provoking reactions on the part of others, particularly her male classmates. Rachel finds herself confronting academic demands that force her to reach beyond previous ways of thinking to a new level of abstraction. The pressure to belong is intense, and social status seems at times to be the central issue for herself, her classmates, and her friends. Being alone—left out—is frightening, and yet being included sometimes calls for behaviors and attitudes that somehow don't feel right to her. Rachel often feels caught, in a troubling way, between the expectations of her family, her peer group, and her school.

At age 23, Rachel deals with the excitement and stress of her new career and her recent marriage. Each holds demands for new behavior that sometimes take her by surprise, forcing her to reevaluate long-standing personal views and values about the issues of career and family life in light

21

of her current experience. Rachel finds, for example, that what she had taken to be a new acceptance of women in the corporate world is in reality less than wholehearted and that the tension arising from simultaneously maintaining her career and her marital commitments is very real indeed. The friendship group that had been her major source of interpersonal support during her college years has been largely dispersed, and she discovers that career and marriage do not lend themselves automatically to the formation of new relationships; if it is to happen, she realizes, she must act. But where is the time and energy to come from?

As Rachel approaches her 50th year, we find her engaged in thoughtful reflection on the course of her life thus far and her options for the future. Having managed a reasonable compromise between career and personal life, she finds that the recent departure of her youngest son for college has become a milestone of unexpected significance. The energy and commitments that are required of a parent are clearly no longer needed by Rachel. She and her husband find themselves facing each other alone again, and the result is both exciting and disturbing. The fundamental changes in her family life have provoked thought regarding her career, her friendships, and her general life-style as well. It is a time to examine and reevaluate the commitments of a lifetime.

As she approaches her 75th year, we find Rachel coping both with a reduction in her mobility and activity, and with the problem of filling the void in her life that was created by the deaths of her husband and two of her closest friends. While continuing to be vital, alive, and active in many ways, she finds in herself an increasing urge to think and talk about the experiences and commitments out of which she has woven the fabric of her life. A concern emerges in Rachel to articulate a pattern of meaning—to pull together the strands of her life into a meaningful whole. Rachel is in the process of saying "goodbye."

Rachel represents each of us, moving through life, encountering demands that provoke significant personal changes, and needing support of various kinds in coping with these demands. This blend of challenges and the availability of the resources needed to cope with them constitutes the basic mechanism that underlies human development through the life cycle (Sanford, 1967).

This chapter offers an overview of human development through the life cycle. It provides an introductory working knowledge of the psychology of being human, of the demands that human beings face throughout life and the supports they need to meet them, as well as of the ways in which individuals change as a result of this process of challenge and support. We call it working knowledge because it is the type of understanding that permits people to cope more effectively with their own developmental needs and to assist those with whom they are involved—their children, students, fellow workers—to do so as well. This assistance will often take the form of *basic empathy*—a willingness to understand other persons' experience from their frames of reference. Working knowledge of the process of human development through life can help the parent, teacher, friend, or helper to enter the frames of reference of others. It can also assist us to understand, and to cope more effectively with, the events of our own lives.

The experience of Rachel moving through life is one illustration of the interplay of similarity and change, of continuity and discontinuity that is characteristic of development through life.

Some examples of how a working knowledge of development can be of use in our own lives may be helpful at this point. Adolescents who question their beliefs concerning religious, moral, political, or social issues are more likely to resolve these questions in a mature way, rather than to retreat to earlier, absolutistic ways of thinking, if they understand that such questioning is a staple of healthy development and not a sign of moral laxity (Newman & Newman, 1975; Perry, 1970). Young adults who attain the career or family goals into which so much energy has been invested, only to find themselves plagued by feelings of incompleteness or limitation regarding their life situation, might avoid panic and impulsive action by understanding that such a crisis is normal and not an indication of immaturity or psychopathology (Levinson, 1978). Adults who experience the crisis of meaning often associated with mid-life (Neugarten, 1968; Peck, 1968) are better served if they are able to interpret this crisis as a part of continuing growth rather than as a symptom of personal failure or inadequacy.

A working knowledge of human development can also permit us to be supportive of others. Parents who understand that a satisfying and secure relationship between infant and care-givers is the basis upon which basic trust regarding the outside world develops in the infant (Erikson, 1963; Newman & Newman, 1975) can put the demands of caring for an infant into a perspective that adds meaning to their task. Parents and teachers who understand the coping styles and resources employed by children (Murphy & Moriarity, 1976) are in a position to encourage the development of autonomy and confidence in the children with whom they are involved. Parents and teachers who understand that a process of questioning authority is central to healthy adolescent development (Lefrancois, 1976; Newman & Newman, 1975) are less likely to personalize this response or attempt to use power to stifle it. Spouses who understand that the 30s tend to be a time of reevaluation and redecision concerning life commitments (Levinson, 1978) are less likely to interpret these changes as personal rejection and may be in a better position to allow their partners the psychological freedom they need to cope with this crisis of adult development. If the friends and family of an individual facing retirement understand the developmental significance of "saying goodbye" to a major aspect of one's life (Kimmel, 1974; Neugarten, 1968), then they will be better able to function as an effective support group for that individual.

In what follows, we look carefully at the words *human* and *development*. In our examination of the psychology of being human, we present a working model of the individual person in the here-and-now. In our examination of the psychology of human development and its sociocultural context, we develop a working model of what is to be encountered as the person moves through the life cycle in our culture. Finally, we will suggest an integration of *human* and *development* that incorporates the two models and outline a number of propositions regarding human development through life.

The Psychology of Being Human:
A View of the Person in the
Here-And-Now

The scientific study of individual behavior has produced a rich array of empirical data and theoretical models concerning particular psychological processes. We know a good deal about perception, attention, cognition, emotion, motivation, values, and various observable behaviors, but we know much less about the complex interrelationships among these aspects of being human. The elements that are analyzed and verified as valid and reliable dimensions of human psychology have yet to be adequately synthesized into an integrative model of the human being, although significant provisional attempts have been made (Mischel, 1973).

Although the attempt to put the person together is critical for the development of scientific psychology, it is no less critical for those concerned with the welfare and development of human beings. We would like to share with you one integrative model that has helped us greatly in interpreting theoretical/empirical psychology in ways that increase our ability to respond to individual human beings in real life situations.

We suggest that behavior occurs in four phases. In Phase 1, stimuli from the environment are taken in via the sense organs. In Phase 2, a portion of the sensory data is selected for attention; that is, figure emerges from background. In Phase 3, the individual transforms the salient stimulus so that it has a particular meaning. In Phase 4, the individual acts, based on the meaning of the situation as constructed in the third phase. A visual representation of the model is shown in Figure 2-1.

1   2   3   4

PERCEPTION → ATTENTION → TRANSFORMATION → ACTION

Figure 2-1.
The Cycle of Human Behavior.

As an example of the perception-attention-transformation-action cycle, imagine yourself walking down a busy city street at midday. As you turn a corner, you confront a variety of objects and events (Phase 1). You focus on two men dragging a third individual from the sidewalk into an alleyway (Phase 2). You judge that the individual is in need of help (Phase 3) and rush to assist him (Phase 4). If you had confronted the same scene (Phase 1) but had noted several large cameras focused on the struggle, a large truck with "Metro Motion Pictures" lettered on the side, and a rope to hold back a group of onlookers (Phase 2), would the meaning of the situation (Phase 3) have seemed different to you, leading to different action (Phase 4)?

It is important to note that the sensory, cognitive, motor, and cybernetic capacities of human beings are so highly developed and integrated that the entire cycle just described can occur virtually instantaneously (Woolridge, 1963). Human beings go through this process continually during their waking hours. Indeed, the perception-attention-transformation-action cycle provides one way of understanding what it means to be human.

> Increasingly as we ascend the scale of animal life, behavior is response not to a specific stimulus but to an "image" or knowledge structure or view of the environment as a whole. This image is of course determined ultimately by information received into the organism. . . . It is not a simple piling up or accumulation of information received . . . but a structuring of information into something essentially different from the information itself. . . . The difficulties in the prediction of the behavior of these systems arises largely because of this intervention of the image between the stimulus and the response. [Boulding, 1975, p. 28]

The key point is this: *as human beings we are unique because of the extent to which our behavior is mediated by an active construction of the meaning of an event; it cannot be explained by evoking a simple stimulus-response pairing* (Dewey, 1896; Mead, 1934). Those who wish to understand and deal with people effectively can benefit from a working awareness of the central role played by the active transformation of events by individuals. Any attempt to deal adequately with the psychology of being human must take into account the fact that persons' ways of construing their experience reach back to influence attention and reach forward to influence behavior. We need to understand the world *as seen and understood by the individual,* and to communicate that understanding, if we wish to teach, influence, or simply communicate with another in an effective way (Aspy & Roebuck, 1977; Rogers, 1951; Strupp, 1973).

How do people typically transform the events in their world in order to survive and to act in goal-directed ways? There are two primary modes of transforming what we perceive, and a third mode that represents a fusion of the two. Cognition or rational thinking represents one primary mode of transformation; affect or emotion represents the other primary mode of transformation. Values or attitudes, which may be thought of as cognitions with a feeling charge (Jones & Gerard, 1967), represent the third mode of transformation. Although these modes represent standard human capacities, people do not engage equally in all three. Marked preferences are often displayed for one or the other of the transformational modes because of genetic tempermental differences (Buss & Plomin, 1975) and particular sociocultural learning histories (Bandura, 1969, 1977). These differences are illustrated by the ways in which we label ourselves and others in this regard:

"He's highly emotional about things."

"She's like a computer; I never know what she feels."

"They're so preachy, always pushing their moral interpretation of things."

"I tried to be rational about it, but I couldn't control my revulsion."

Many images of human experience that are consistent with the one outlined here are to be found in classical theories of personality. Our model is, in fact, an attempt to synthesize these and other representations of human experience. Phenomenological theorists (Combs, Richards, & Richards, 1976; Rogers, 1951) stress the importance of understanding the world as perceived and organized by the person. Jerome Frank's classic work (1973) gives a key role in determining behavior to the "assumptive world" of the person. George Kelly's (1955) "psychology of personal constructs" deals with the guiding beliefs of persons about themselves in social interaction. Albert Ellis' (1962) rational-emotive therapy (RET) is based on the assumption that our feelings stem not from experience itself, but rather from what we say to ourselves about the experience.

Behavioral psychologists have also offered models that stress the individual's active transformation of experience. Bandura (1969), Rotter (1954), and others have identified the linkage role of expectancies in accounting for behavior. We all acquire many more behaviors than we typically use (Hilgard & Bower, 1975). What accounts for this well-documented difference between acquisition and performance? An important factor is the expected outcome of particular behaviors (Mischel, 1973). In a related vein, Meichenbaum (1977) and others have demonstrated the importance of "cognitive restructuring" of events in the process of behavioral change. A growing body of literature in social psychology, referred to as attribution theory, concerns itself with "the basic processes involved in perceiving the self, other persons, and the settings in which people function" (Jones, Kanouse, Kelley, Nisbett, Valins, & Weiner, 1972). There appear to be not only differences in attributional style but also attitudinal and behavioral differences linked to modes of attribution (Weiner & Kukla, 1970).

Linguists and psycholinguists (Bandler & Grinder, 1975) have long recognized the fact that our language filters our perception of the world and limits our ways of making sense of what we perceive. Bandler and Grinder emphasize the effects of the "reduction valve" function of the brain. The brain narrows the array of incoming stimuli to an acceptable range but in doing so necessarily limits our image of the world.

Gestalt psychologists (Koehler, 1947) actively concerned themselves with the figure-ground distinction in perception, questioning why selected stimuli become salient for us while others remain in the background. This work has continued in modern perceptual psychology and is basic to our understanding of perceptual processes (Barker, 1968; Combs, Richards, & Richards, 1976).

General-system theory as applied to human behavior (von Bertalanffy, 1968; Kuhn, 1974) suggests that there are three basic subsystems in the person-receptor, selector, and effector. According to this theory, the selector subsystem is viewed as channeling potential responses to selected stimuli into a discrete set of observed effector outputs.

Philosophers of science have come to stress the active role of the scientist in constructing testable models of reality from such fields as nuclear physics (Polanyi, 1958), the behavioral sciences (Royce, 1975), and inter-national-system relations (Laszlo, 1974). Such models both sharpen and limit what the scientist sees. As Kuhn (1970) has noted:

> Examining the record of past research from the vantage of contemporary his-toriography, the historian of science may be tempted to exclaim that when paradigms change, the world changes with them. . . . In so far as their only recourse to the world is through what they see and do, we may want to say that after a [paradigmatic] revolution scientists are responding to a different world [p. 111].

Similar images of humanity have emerged from philosophy (Cassirer, 1944; Heidegger, 1962; Kockelmans, 1967), sociology (Mead, 1934; Thomas, 1976), and theology (Luijpen, 1964). Other instances are, no doubt, familiar to you. In our view, these focus in a complementary way on a single, crucial image of *the person as builder of models*—models that allow us to transform experience and create psychological meaning (Au-subel, 1968) for the events of our lives. The meaning created and the action it leads to are generated in the perception-attention-transformation-action cycle we have described.

Given the important linkages among perception, attention, transfor-mation, and action, preferred ways of transforming experience in the indi-vidual will result in preferred ways of perceiving and doing in various situations (Mischel, 1973). One useful way of understanding "personality" is to see that an individual's unique transformational style leads to pre-ferred perceptual and behavioral styles that are, in turn, responsive to the social-environmental context. The proviso must be added that a person cannot engage in a particular behavioral style unless the behavior is either a part of his or her behavioral repertoire or the result of direct or observa-tional learning (Bandura, 1969, 1977).

In summary, the view of human psychology presented here suggests that an understanding of the capacity to transform events is crucial to any adequate developmental psychology of the person. There are complex in-terrelationships between perception, attention, and transformation on the one hand, and transformation and behavior on the other. In the words of Endler and Hunt (1969), human behavior appears to be "idiosyncratically organized in each individual" (p. 20). A psychology of human experience that ignores this uniqueness violates its subject matter in a fundamental way while flawing itself irrevocably in the process. The conception we offer here is, in Meehl's (1973) terms, behavior-relevant but not behavior-specific; it does not attempt to reduce the complexity of human beings to specific observable behaviors, but it is clearly relevant to actual behavior. The transformational process described here is a fundamentally internal and therefore unobservable event that has directly observable behavioral consequences. The perception-attention-transformation-action cycle offers us a model of the individual human being at a *particular moment*; this is crucial because we are always dealing with unique individuals at par-ticular points in their lives. It is also important, however, that we have a view of the unity of the person's experience *throughout the life cycle;* for this we now turn to the developmental perspective.

The Psychology of Human Development: A View of the Person through the Life Cycle

Having described how human beings tend to behave in the world at a particular moment in time, it remains for us to deal with an important fact concerning human behavior—the fact of development. There can be no doubt that, from birth onward, individuals tend to perceive, transform, and act in progressively complex ways (Kohlberg, 1969; Loevinger, 1976). The thinking of an infant, for example, differs markedly from that of a 7-year-old (Piaget, 1952). Although there is currently a controversy among developmentalists concerning whether or not intellectual decline characterizes adulthood (Baltes & Schaie, 1974; Horn & Donaldson, 1976, 1977), mounting evidence suggests that significant development of various kinds can continue throughout life (Kimmel, 1974; Levinson, 1978; Newman & Newman, 1975; Sze, 1975). During their lives, people change in important ways and yet retain a recognizable, continuing identity. We observe both differences and continuity in ourselves and others over a period of time.

What is *developmental* change? How can we come to recognize such change in ourselves and others with a view to providing conditions that are supportive of it? King (1977) has suggested that developmental change has four characteristics. First, it is *qualitative:* it involves the ability to perceive, transform, and act at new levels of complexity and integration, rather than simply to produce the currently available responses. As a college student, perhaps Rachel learned sophisticated philosophical arguments concerning "the good" or the concept of justice that gave her more information without helping her to engage in a qualitatively different way of perceiving, transforming, or acting morally in her personal world. By the time she moved beyond an ability to consider events and possibilities from multiple perspectives and began to make authentic personal commitments to career and marriage as a young adult, qualitative change had taken place (Perry, 1970; Widick, 1977).

Developmental change is also *cumulative.* As we move toward greater complexity and integration, we build on lower-level responses; thus, we progress from crawling to walking to running. The capacity to engage in lower-level responses remains, and such responses may be resorted to again. A concrete illustration of the cumulative nature of development is children's thinking (see Flavell, 1963; Gruber & Voneche, 1977; Piaget, 1954), which begins with direct sense impressions. At first, children understand only that which is physically experienced. This early capacity is referred to as *sensorimotor intelligence.* Children build on this capacity, developing the ability to deal with their world mentally, but they do so initially only in terms of events or situations that they have directly experienced or observed; they do not hypothesize about what might be. Such mental operations are known as *concrete operations.* Children then extend their ability to deal mentally with the world to include situations that they have not directly experienced or observed; they become capable of reasoning abstractly about hypothetical situations. This type of thinking is referred to as *formal operations*. These changes in patterns of thinking are cumulative, with each stage subsuming previous stages. Thus, as adults we retain the capacity to engage in simpler forms of thinking and often do so, particularly in situations that are new or threatening in some way (Parker, 1977).

Developmental change is also *systemic*. This means that, once a higher level of development has been reached in one area, it tends to spread out into other areas. (See the concept of "decalage": Flavell, 1963; Widick, 1977). As Rachel became capable of commitment to ethical values, she found that such thinking had an impact on the relationship and career issues of her life (Perry, 1970).

Finally, developmental change is *enduring*, rather than specific to particular situations; that is, development will tend to generalize to include situations beyond the one in which it first occurred. This is not to say that one's environment cannot impede or even destroy developmental gains, but these gains are not simply a function of the contingencies of the environment. Children who have developed a healthy sense of industry or competence (see Erikson, 1963; White, 1960) in the family and at school will take that sense of competence with them to new environments that will significantly affect their self-confidence.

What is the genesis of development as we have defined it? Is it possible to develop an overview of how this developmental process comes about? Our answer is yes, and we turn now to that task.

Basic Dimensions of Human Development through Life

In this section we examine human development in life's contexts. To organize this complex picture, we use five major dimensions: life stages, key human systems, and developmental tasks, resources, and crises.

Life stages refers to the fact that within particular societies important developmental events tend to occur with some predictability during specific age-related phases of an individual's life. The example of Rachel illustrates the concept of life stages in our culture. The task of coping with life beyond the family began in earnest for Rachel between the ages of 4 and 7. Issues relating to sexuality and sexual identity became critical for her between the ages of 12 and 17, and the challenge of initial commitments in the world of work and in family living tended to be predominant in her life between the ages of 18 and 30. Issues having to do with retirement and approaching death became salient for her during the last quarter of her life. In summary, life stages represent the "when" of human development through life.

Key human systems are those settings that are the focal locations of challenge and support during a particular life stage. The following is an illustration of the concept of key human systems in our culture. During the

first four years of her life, Rachel's nuclear family was of overriding importance in her development. From age 5 to age 18, the school system and
peer group took on central roles in her developmental process. The family,
the friendship group, and the workplace were key systems for Rachel during her adult years. In summary, the concept of key human systems represents the "where" of human development through life.

Developmental tasks are the challenges that confront individuals and
demand new patterns of behavior as they move through life. Examples of
developmental tasks that Rachel confronted in her culture included: learning to cope and learn in the classroom environment, learning to form relationships outside the family, developing independence from parents,
coping with initial career decisions, learning to manage intimate relationships, developing the ability to nurture others, and coping with the
deaths of significant people in her life and with her own death. In summary, the concept of developmental tasks represents the *challenge* aspect
of the "how" of human development through life.

Developmental resources are the supports that are necessary in order
to assist the individual in the mastery of developmental tasks. In our view,
these resources are of three varieties: basic human support, working
knowledge, and skills.

• *Basic human support* refers to the presence of other people who are
capable of understanding our experience from our own frame of reference.
Examples include members of the key systems of Rachel's life who are
capable of basic empathy (Egan, 1975, 1976). Parents, teachers, peers,
supervisors, spouses, and friends are examples of persons in a position to
offer such support.

• *Working knowledge* in this context refers to knowledge necessary
for coping effectively with current developmental challenges. Examples of
working knowledge that were helpful to Rachel in her development include basic information concerning the world during childhood, knowledge concerning dating and sexuality during adolescence, awareness of
the demands of marriage and other forms of personal commitment during her young adult years, and knowledge concerning wider involvement
with others in later adulthood.

• *Skills* in this context refers to the behavioral repertoire necessary
for coping effectively with current developmental challenges. A taxonomy
of life skills is presented in Chapter 3 of this book. In summary, the concept of developmental resources represents the *support* aspect of the "how"
of human development through life.

We have suggested that the "how" of human development through
life—those events that actually bring development about—can be understood as an ongoing process of *challenge*, in the form of developmental
tasks, and *support* in the form of developmental resources. In this respect
we follow Sanford's (1967) analysis of development as movement toward
increasing complexity that results when a person's current way of dealing
with the world is upset by new demands from the environment. As Rachel
moved through life, taking on the new and ever more complex tasks of
student, worker, and parent, she experienced a tension that motivated her
to incorporate new ways of perceiving, transforming, and acting. If there

are adequate resources available to assist us with such challenges, we become more complex and integrated as a result. There is no development without ongoing conditions of challenge and support in the human systems of our lives.

Developmental crises represent the process of developmental change as it is experienced by the individual. The word *crisis* (Erikson, 1963) is appropriate in this connection for two reasons. The Greek origin of the word *crisis* is *krino*, meaning "I divide." Developmental crises represent significant dividing points at which the individual's life is deeply affected for better or for worse. The second reason for the use of the word *crisis* has to do with the fact that these critical dividing points tend to be experienced as times of excitement, turmoil, and anxiety. Examples of developmental crises in Rachel's life include the basic trust or mistrust of the world developed during her infancy, the sense of belonging or of alienation during her early adolescent years, the sense of intimacy or isolation in her young adulthood, and the experience of meaning or of despair in her old age (see Erikson, 1963). In summary, the concept of developmental crises represents the phenomenology of development through life—the subjective experience of the process of development.

The Developmental Analysis of a Life Stage—Late Adolescence

In order to make the information presented here as concrete as possible, we present an analysis of the key human systems and the developmental tasks, resources, and crises of persons in one of the life stages—late adolescence.

The late-adolescent life stage typically covers the ages 18 through 22. The *key human systems* during this period are the peer or friendship group, the education or work setting, the family, and the surrounding community.

The peer group, including intimates, is likely to be the context within which the developmental tasks of independent living, internalized morality, and initial sustained intimacy are to be dealt with. The education or work setting provides challenges that are likely to provoke development in the areas of career choice and relativistic thinking. The family is crucial at this point, because offspring are typically beginning to live away from home for the first time—an event that may lead them into a variety of settings (Wilson, 1977). The surrounding community may be an important locus of development, because the late adolescent is either in transition toward, or in the midst of, independent living in precisely that context.

There are five *developmental tasks* that confront the late adolescent in the context of the systems described here:

- independent living,
- initial career decisions,
- initial experiences of sustained intimacy,
- internalized moral judgment, and
- the capacity to think relativistically.

Let us develop each of these briefly.

Independent living means that during this period the individual typically resides outside the nuclear family for the first time. This calls for two distinct types of tasks. *Maintenance* tasks are those involved in arranging for adequate food, clothing, and shelter for oneself. *Living-relationship tasks* are those necessary for negotiating and carrying out a workable routine with one's living and working partners, including the task of resolving the conflicts that inevitably arise.

Initial career decisions refers to the process whereby individuals take their first significant steps into the world of work. The assessment of potential, of opportunities, and of likes and dislikes, as well as the making and implementing of decisions, are all part of this career-development process.

Initial experiences of sustained intimacy are also encountered in late adolescence. Building relationships and handling intense feelings are part of this process. Adolescents must face the necessity of negotiating agreements with respect to sexual behavior and other forms of intimacy. Finally, decisions must be made regarding the necessary balance between career, desired life-style, and intimate commitments.

Internalized moral judgment refers to the fact that the individual must cope with personal ethical decisions and behavioral limit-setting with a degree of freedom far beyond that experienced while residing in the parental home. The locus of control (Rotter, 1954) must shift in the direction of greater internality if the individual is to successfully complete this developmental task.

Relativistic thinking (Perry, 1970) means that the individual begins to examine the "absolute truths" learned in the nuclear family and begins to consider alternative frames of reference for judgments and life decisions. Individuals at this stage are confronted with the reality that decisions concerning right and wrong, good and bad, and so forth should not be made for them by those in authority.

These are the kinds of demands that the human settings of our culture make on individuals during late adolescence. As people move through life, social roles become both more numerous and more complex. This increasing complexity of life can in itself be quite challenging.

What *developmental resources* are necessary if the individual is to successfully master the tasks of late adolescence? We suggest that, with the exception of the first four years of life, during which physical maturation and basic security dominate all other considerations, developmental resources have three basic aspects, *regardless of the life stage.* As we noted previously, in order to deal adequately with the demands that are experienced in late adolescence and throughout life, we all need basic human support, working knowledge, and skills for effective living.

Basic human support means that the significant others with whom we interact in the important systems of our world have the ability to enter empathically into what we are experiencing and to challenge us responsibly to develop our potential as human beings (Egan, 1976, 1977). In the case of the late adolescent, this combination of empathy and challenge will come, if it comes at all, from friends and those adults in the central roles of this life stage. An understanding of the developmental tasks of late adolescence gives the parent, friend, supervisor, teacher, or minister a crucial bit of working knowledge that will guide them in providing effective support.

Working knowledge has been defined here as information that helps us to understand *how* to act effectively in our own lives. In the case of the late adolescent, working knowledge in five areas relevant to the developmental tasks of this life stage—independent living, career decision-making, moral judgment, intimacy, and relativistic thinking—is a critical developmental resource.

Living skills are those behaviors that can be produced by the individual at will and in the appropriate context, in reponse to the demands of the environment (see Chapter 3). For persons in late adolescence, four sets of living skills constitute key developmental resources: self-management skills, interpersonal skills, decision-making skills, and values-clarification skills.

Whatever the demands of a particular life stage, the individual who is provided with the resources outlined here—basic human support, working knowledge, and living skills—will have a higher likelihood of positive development.

The *developmental crisis* experienced by those in late adolescence revolves around the emergence of an authentic sense of identity. Individuals tend to emerge from this stage of life either with a stable sense of who they are that has been confirmed by significant others or with varying degrees of confusion about who they really are (see Erikson, 1968). This sense of identity confusion can lead to the presentation of oneself in whatever way fits a particular situation and can increase the difficulty of dealing with the developmental tasks to come—particularly those that require authentic personal commitment, such as the establishment of intimacy in one's life.

A similar developmental analysis can be made for any individual or group of individuals with whom we are involved. Such an analysis can offer clues concerning the adequacy of developmental conditions in the systems that we influence and that influence us in our day-to-day living.

A Developmental Overview of the Life Cycle

Table 2-1 presents a developmental map of the life cycle. It is intended to provide an integrative framework for gaining a working understanding of developmental needs. This model is adapted from the work of Newman and Newman (1975), who draw their framework from Erikson's (1963) conception of developmental crises. We have also drawn on the work of Kohlberg (1969) on moral development, Perry (1970) on intellectual and ethical development, Loevinger (1976) on ego development, Havighurst (1972) and Chickering (1969) on developmental tasks, and Levinson (1978) and Kimmel (1974) on adult development.

Table 2-1.
A Developmental Map of the Life Cycle and Its Context in One Culture.

Life Stage	Key Systems	Developmental Tasks	Developmental Resources	Developmental Crises
Infancy (birth–2)	Family —nuclear —extended	Social attachment Sense of continued existence of non-self Sensorimotor intelligence and primitive causality Maturation of motor functions	Security Basic need fulfillment Stability	Basic trust or mistrust
Early childhood (2–4)	Family —nuclear —extended	Self-control Language development Fantasy and play Self-locomotion	Basic human support Human interaction Sensory stimulation Protected environment Limit setting	Independent sense of self or doubt and shame
Middle childhood (5–7)	Family Neighborhood School	Gender identity Early moral development Concrete mental operations Group play	Basic human support Appropriate models Explanation of rule setting Consistency in rule enforcement Peer-group interaction	Self as initiator or guilt concerning wishes
Late childhood (8–12)	Family Neighborhood School Peer group	Cooperative social relations Self-evaluation Skill learning Team membership	Basic human support Cooperative learning environment Cooperative recreational environment Effective skills teaching —learning to learn —basic interpersonal relationships Feedback on self and performance	Industry or inferiority

Stage (age)	Settings	Developmental tasks	Support needs	Outcomes
Early adolescence (13–17)	Family Peer group School	Physical maturation Formal mental operations Peer-group membership Initial sexual intimacy	Basic human support Physiological information Cognitive problem-solving and decision-making tasks Relationship-building skills Knowledge of sex roles and their cultural sources Opportunities for independent moral judgment	Belonging or social isolation
Late adolescence (18–22)	Peer group School or work setting Family Surrounding community	Independent living Initial career decisions Internalized morality Initial sustained intimacy Relativistic thinking	Basic human support Knowledge and skills for: —financial independence —self-exploration —making decisions —deepening relationships —dealing with pluralism Responsibility for choices and consequences	Individual identity or identity confusion
Early adulthood (23–30)	New family Work setting Friendship network Surrounding community	Family living Initial parenting Career development Life-style management Capacity for commitment	Basic human support Knowledge and skills for: —family financial planning and management —interpersonal negotiating and conflict resolution —parenting —role discrimination and integration	Social-living competence and intimacy or incompetence and alienation
Pre-middle-age transition (30–35)	Family Work setting Friendship network Surrounding community	Reevaluation of and rededication to commitments Parenting of older children Dealing with commitment reevaluation on the part of significant others	Basic human support Opportunity for evaluation and renewed decisions regarding: —relationships —career —life-style Knowledge and skills to form broadly based interpersonal support system	Renewal or resignation

Table 2-1 *(Continued)*

Life Stage	Key Systems	Developmental Tasks	Developmental Resources	Developmental Crises
Pre-middle age (36–50)	Friendship network Family Work setting Surrounding community	Mid-life evaluation of commitments Children leave home Changes in relationship with spouse Involvement beyond self and nuclear family	Basic human support Knowledge and skills for higher-order role taking Higher-order role differentiation and integration	Achievement and meaning in social living or incompetence and meaninglessness
Middle age (51–65)	Family Friendship network Work setting Surrounding community	Involvement beyond family Completion and winding down of career involvement Confrontation with personal mortality	Basic human support Knowledge and skills for: —involvement of self in community systems —teaching and advising Increased reliance on cognitive rather than physical skills	Lasting contribution through involvement with others or self-stagnation
Old age (65–death)	Family Friendship network Surrounding community	Increased dependence on others Evaluation of one's life Dealing with deaths of significant others Coping with one's own death	Basic human support Opportunity for meaningful involvement with others and in significant tasks Survival skills given diminished physical resources Capacity to say "good-bye" and grieve	Sense of meaning and worth or despair

Our task here is to offer an integrated and systematic overview of development through the life cycle that will offer some basic information concerning the tasks that people are likely to be dealing with at a particular point in their lives. The Additional Resources at the end of this chapter list sources of more detailed information on particular life stages.

In keeping with our intent to present a developmental view that will apply to actual situations, we offer the following set of "diagnostic" questions. They will help you to think in developmental terms about yourself and about those with whom you are personally or professionally involved.

- As you reflect on your life, what central concerns emerge? What concerns do you know or suspect to be most important to the lives of those with whom you are involved?
- Do certain systems seem crucial to your development and the development of those with whom you are involved? What are they?
- What are the concerns that emerged here regarding the developmental tasks with which you and others are faced?
- What developmental resources are available to you and others in coping with current life demands? What resources are unavailable? Basic human support? Working knowledge? Life skills?
- What are the "crises" (critical events) that are present or lying ahead in your own life? In the lives of those with whom you are concerned? Does the developmental perspective on these crises (see Table 2-1) seem to fit your current experience?
- Do the ages of those with whom you associate span a large segment of the life cycle?

Human and Development: An Integration of the Two Constructs

If you find the model of the person in the here-and-now (the perception-attention-transformation-action cycle) and the model of development through life to be useful tools in understanding the experiences of people, the question that emerges is "Can these two sets of constructs be integrated in such a way that they describe 'human development' meaningfully?" This question is absolutely central to our purposes, because all people are simultaneously human and developing.

A key to integrating these two models lies in the distinction between content and process—between *what* one is doing and *how* one is doing it. The perception-attention-transformation-action cycle is a *process* model of human psychology. Life stages and all that they imply may be thought of as representing a *content* model. The process model is concerned with *how* human beings behave, regardless of life stages, whereas the content model focuses on *what* human beings are likely to be confronting at a particular stage in life. Obviously, both *what* people are experiencing and *how* that experience occurs are crucial pieces of information for those who seek to foster human development.

What relevant working knowledge regarding human beings emerges from the fusion of these two models? Of what use is it to the parent, teacher, minister, spouse, or supervisor? One example may be helpful in answering these questions. In our own work on teaching and training design (Egan, 1975, 1976, 1977; Cowan, Egan, & Bacchi, 1978) we have begun to make use of what we call the "learning cycle." The learning cycle is illustrated in Figure 2-2.

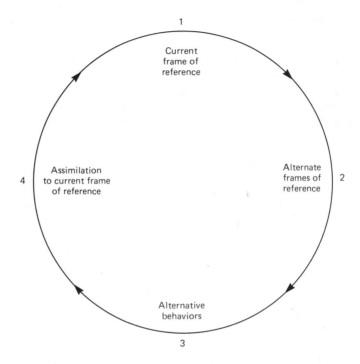

Figure 2-2.
The Learning Cycle.

In Phase 1 of the learning cycle, an individual reacts to a stimulus from the environment by simply taking it into his or her current frame of reference or by ignoring it if it doesn't "fit."

In Phase 2, an individual is presented with an alternate way of looking at the stimulus; this is accomplished by relating the new perspective to the current view held by an individual. Phase 2 is based on Phase 1.

In Phase 3, *new* action alternatives are generated by an individual because of the new frame of reference generated in Phase 2. Phase 3 is based on Phase 2.

In Phase 4, the new perspective and new behavioral alternatives become part of an individual's current frame of reference and behavioral repertoire.

Phases 1, 2, 3, and 4 are linked in an ongoing recycling process. Constant learning potentially characterizes the human condition. The perception-attention-transformation-action cycle is the psychological basis that underlies meaningful human learning.

If our task is integration, we must also link the learning cycle to the model of development through life. This linkage becomes possible when the distinction between process and content is kept in mind. *What* people are likely to be dealing with as we encounter them is partially a function of their developmental status (Widick & Cowan, 1977). For example, when we deal with young adults, developmental theory (see Table 2-1) suggests that the central issues that they are likely to be confronting include initial marital, familial, and career commitments, and we should be prepared to deal empathically and knowledgeably in those areas, helping them to use the learning cycle in the service of their own development.

In summary, when we wish to understand and support our own development or that of others, the p-a-t-a model helps us to understand *how* to facilitate learning, and the developmental model helps us to predict in *what* areas people may have particular learning needs.

We would like to submit a final word on the relationship between the process (p-a-t-a) and content (developmental) models presented here. One potentially useful way of understanding development is to view it as an ongoing series of changes in the ways in which people engage in the perception-attention-transformation-action cycle. Changes in the cycle that are consistent with King's (1977) criteria—qualitative, cumulative, systemic, and enduring—may be considered developmental in nature. The developing person, then, is one who:

- has progressively less need to filter out relevant dimensions of the world by means of selective attention,
- transforms what is perceived in a manner characterized by increasing complexity *and* integration,
- has an increasingly differentiated and flexible behavioral repertoire, permitting responses to a wide array of situations,
- finds that development in one area of life tends to generalize to include others, and
- experiences changes in personal identity and values that are enduring and do not occur simply because of new situations.

Some Propositions regarding Human Development through Life

Having presented an introductory working model of human development through life, we would like at this point to articulate several general propositions that we believe are important for those who would attempt to foster their own development or that of others.

• *Biological development assumes a critical role, particularly during certain life stages.* Biological changes are central during the early years of life and again as we reach old age.

• *Human development is age-related but not age-specific.* This proposition means that, although people in our culture *tend* to experience the stages, tasks, and crises described previously at the times suggested (see Table 2-1), significant individual differences can and do occur (Loevinger, 1976, 1977). A model of human development should not be applied in a rigidly prescriptive way but rather as a general framework for analysis and planning. Ultimately, one learns about the felt needs of particular people by listening empathically to them.

• *Human development is bound up in the human systems of our lives.* Development results from the quality of challenge and support available to us in our families, schools, workplaces, and communities. Persons wishing to affect human development cannot afford to ignore the systemic context of that development.

• *Working knowledge and skills for living are essential to human development through life.* Acquisition of the types of knowledge and skills discussed earlier and elaborated in the following chapter cannot be left to chance if our goal as a society is the development of people who are capable of effective and responsible social living. Human systems are the only available locus for the systematic provision of these important developmental resources.

• *Human support is a crucial resource for the developing person in any life stage.* Every person operates in a world that can only be understood and "connected with" if others are willing and able to enter the individual's frame of reference. The presence of people with the ability to enter one another's worlds sensitively *and* to challenge one another responsibly may be the best indicator of an environment's developmental potential (see Chapter 9).

• *The meaning of the word "development" varies with the cultural context.* The particular developmental map presented here is for one sociocultural context—contemporary American society. In many ways, it will not even fit the experience of many subgroups within that society. Development, in a very real sense, is what a particular culture or subculture says it is, and in our view this cultural relativity should be acknowledged and welcomed. The individual who wishes to foster development must have an appreciation of the cultural context within which that development is to occur.

In the following chapter we will look in detail at the skills of effective living that play a central role as resources for development through life.

Chapter 2: Additional Resources

Bandler, R., & Grinder, J. *The structure of magic* (Vol. 1). Palo Alto, Calif.: Science and Behavior Books, 1975.

Erikson, E. *Childhood and society* (2nd ed.). New York: Norton, 1963. (See Chapter 7.)

Levinson, D. *The seasons of a man's life.* New York: Knopf, 1978. (See Chapters 1–3 and 10.)

Newman, B., & Newman, P. *Development through life.* Homewood, Ill.: Dorsey Press, 1975.

Sanford, N. *Where colleges fail.* San Francisco: Jossey-Bass, 1967. (See Chapter 6.)

3

Life Skills:
The Basis of Competence

Introduction

The model we are proposing in this book is basically educational and developmental rather than traditionally therapeutic. We say "traditionally" therapeutic because we agree with people such as Anthony (1978) and Carkhuff and Berenson (1976), who maintain that training in various life skills and in the practical application of these skills to life problems constitutes, for many people, the most useful approach to therapy and psychological rehabilitation. In this chapter we present an overview of some core life skills from a developmental point of view.

Most people want to be competent and feel competent in the basic tasks of life, especially in the tasks related to interpersonal living. Toffler (1970) suggests that people need four basic kinds of skills in order to meet the challenges of life: the skills of coping, learning, choosing, and relating. One of the definitions of the term *skill* in *Webster's Collegiate Dictionary* is a "learned power of doing something competently." Education, in the sense of acquiring various kinds of working knowledge, is not enough to produce a feeling of competence in individuals, but through skills, this knowledge can be translated into behavior. People need increasingly complex skills in order to face increasingly complex developmental challenges resourcefully. Skills, then, are the basic instruments of competence. Although we emphasize skills over working knowledge in this chapter, it is impossible to talk about one without including or referring to the other.

Ideally, systems train individuals in the skills they need to fulfill new roles competently and responsibly. Drucker (1968) suggests that responsibility and authority are correlative terms; that is, if people are responsible for doing something, then they need the authority, or power, to carry out this responsibility. One important source of power is skill; therefore, if individuals are to assume increasingly complex roles with any degree of competence, then society must see to it that they acquire the skills they need to fulfill these roles.

People often undertake tasks and face crises for which they are unprepared. If they are not trained in basic problem-solving skills and do not learn how to take counsel with the significant people in their lives, they are likely to deal poorly with the inevitable crises of life. Some people seek out professional help, especially if the crisis is a devastating one, but most people muddle through as best they can, too often settling for less in life and sinking into the "psychopathology of the average." Increasing the number of professional helpers, which is a downstream approach, is not an answer to this problem, for training more helpers might underscore the assumption that people cannot handle significant problems in their lives by using their own resources. Also, as the number of professional helpers increases, so does the number of helpees (Schofield, 1964).

Of course, life does produce casualties, and helping, including professional helping, is necessary. However, if the helping process does not face up to the skills deficits of those who seek help, then the process becomes a part of the problem and not a part of the solution. As we have noted, helping that emphasizes training in the skills needed to undertake life tasks and cope with life crises (Carkhuff et al., 1977; Carkhuff & Berenson, 1976; Egan, 1975; Goldstein, 1973; Goldstein, Sprafkin, & Gershaw, 1976) is more useful than helping that merely encourages insight or provides human support (Schofield, 1964) or enables an individual to solve one particular problem. If helping is needed because individuals have not received training in the basic skills that would enable them to handle life crises, then training in these skills must lie at the core of helping.

The term *preventive mental health* is strongly rooted in the medical model and suffers the limitations of that model when applied to human development and human living. The notion of prevention, when applied to development and living, leaves something to be desired. After all, if prevention programs are successful, *nothing* happens! However, prevention programs (a better term would be *human development programs)* that impart the working knowledge and skills people need to be competent in life tasks offer tangible rewards. For instance, training upper-level primary school students in human-relations skills provides the stimulation of experiential learning as well as the competencies for developing peer relationships. Our hypothesis is that students so trained will be less prone to failure in interpersonal relationships in the future; that is, our hypothesis is that skills training is a good preventive program. If the training program helps individuals to apply skills to daily living, then these individuals can use newly won abilities and competencies immediately in real-life situations. Drucker (1968) complains that schools prepare students for life but never engage them in productive living. Skills-training programs, on the other hand, help students to demonstrate competence in the school system as well as in day-to-day living.

Although skills are essential, people need communities in which these skills can be developed and their use can be supported. In this chapter, however, the focus is on basic skills. The community, both as the social context of skills training and as a goal in itself, is discussed in a later chapter. In this chapter, we indicate groups or "packages" of skills people need to face developmental tasks and crises competently. We will review *basic* skills that can be put together in a variety of ways according to the demands of the situation in which they are used. What follows, then, is an initial list of these basic skills.

An Overview of Life Skills

Full human living means meeting the challenges of developing competence in relating to self, to other individuals, and to society and its institutions. The following is a preliminary outline of the basic skills needed to meet these challenges.

Skills have a developmental character; that is, as life becomes more complex, increasingly complex skills are needed. For example, the interpersonal skills learned in the second half of primary school provide a foundation for development in high school but are not sufficient to meet the more complicated interpersonal challenges of this later stage.

Six interdependent categories of basic skills are considered here:

- skills relating to physical development,
- skills relating to intellectual development,
- self-management skills,
- value-clarification skills,
- the skills of interpersonal involvement, and
- the skills of small-group involvement.

The skills individuals need in order to involve themselves creatively in systems are touched upon in this chapter and discussed more thoroughly in Chapter 8.

Skills Relating to Physical Development

The purpose of this set of skills is not merely to keep the body intact and free from disease, but also to make it a source of energy and to use it artfully. People with low energy are often those who have not learned the skills of making their bodies serve them. The following are included in this package of body-oriented skills: the skills of physical fitness, personal health care, athletics, esthetic use of the body, and grooming.

The skills of physical fitness. Many individuals discover the skills of physical fitness in middle age, embarking upon fitness programs that are largely remedial. The establishment of education and training programs in both family and school systems so that body-related skills, especially the skills of physical fitness, could be learned at appropriate developmental levels would benefit upcoming generations.

Eating a balanced diet is certainly related to physical fitness, and the working knowledge that leads to good eating habits can be learned early. Dieting skills include a knowledge of human nutrition, the ability to put together well-balanced meals, a working knowledge of the optimal relationship of weight to build and height, the ability to control weight in ways that respect the integrity of the body, and a knowledge of nutritional needs in different situations and at various stages of life.

Exercise is needed to develop and maintain physical flexibility, strength, and endurance. Other things being equal, a person who is physically fit has more energy for life tasks than the person who is not. In order to become physically fit, a person must learn and practice self-discipline, which can generalize to other areas of life. In therapy, for instance, it is sometimes good to start with a physical-fitness program rather than with the most difficult problems a client faces. Such programs are highly concrete and structured, progress is tangible and measurable, and the "spread" effect can be remarkable. Even modest success in an exercise program can be the beginning of an "I can do it" attitude toward life and its tasks. Moreover, a sense of accomplishment and competence with respect to the body can develop feelings of self-worth that were not previously experienced; the person is doing something, and it is something worthwhile. Therefore, the psychological benefits of exercise can be as powerful as the physical benefits. (See Collingwood and Carkhuff, 1976a, 1976b.)

The skills of personal health care. These skills include the ability to handle basic human maladies, such as a cold, to develop a practical hygiene such as daily dental care, and to learn what to do about particular symptoms in an emergency. Effective education and training for personal health care emphasizes that individuals are responsible for their own health and that even in sickness they can be agents of their own well-being rather than patients of a medical delivery system. For example, Israel Goldiamond (1978) has written a compelling account of how he took charge of his own convalescence after a serious accident. He applied to himself the principles of learning and behavioral change that he had long been teaching to others. The hospital staff were taken aback. Israel didn't have time to become depressed, because he was too actively involved in his own rehabilitation. He remained an agent, rather than becoming just a patient.

Athletic skills. Most cultures have developed games that require physical prowess, some of which are competitive; but even in noncompetitive games, individuals "compete" against themselves or against a standard of excellence. Athletes and athletics are highly prized in our culture, but many people prefer to watch rather than to participate, because they do not feel competent. Although we are not suggesting that we become a nation of athletes, we do maintain that if systematic training in athletics were offered through the family and the school systems, then more people would achieve a sense of basic athletic competence that would provide them with options for exercise.

Esthetic use of the body. Creative, systematic training in esthetics early in life opens individuals up to the joys of esthetic appreciation and expression in their later years. Training in esthetic bodily movement, such as dance, can provide people with a respect for their own bodies as instruments of expression. Also, training in some of the Eastern body-conditioning methodologies, in which body, esthetics, and spirit come together, leads to an esthetic use and appreciation of the body (Luchs, 1977).

Grooming. Physical attractiveness is highly prized in our society (Barocas & Karoly, 1972); in fact, most people agree that it is over-emphasized. Research indicates that physically attractive people often receive preferential treatment that they do not merit (Dion, 1972; Dion, Berscheid, & Walster, 1972). It would be useful to give people a working knowledge of the effects of physical attractiveness in order to de-mythologize it somewhat, thus eliminating its use as an instrument of manipulation. Everyone, moreover, by learning basic grooming skills at a relatively early age, could become less susceptible to the claims of the advertisers of beauty products.

Skills Relating to Intellectual Development: Learning How to Learn

Most schools, as they currently exist and operate, invest a great deal of their time and energy teaching skills that relate to intellectual development, usually to the neglect of other life skills. However, the fact that schools invest so much of their resources in the intellectual development of students doesn't necessarily mean that they perform this task well. There is a vast literature concerning all aspects of reading and the reasons why many young people do not learn to read properly, that speaks to us about our failure to teach in ways that instill an appreciation of reading. Colleges have become alarmed because students arrive at their doors without basic writing skills. It seems that the teaching of writing suffers from a lack of systematic approaches.

The ability to translate knowledge into working knowledge. In the first chapter of this book, we discussed the notion of *translator:* a person who is in touch with good theory and good research and who has the ability to translate these into effective programs. We believe that most people are capable of developing this skill to one degree or another. Although knowledge can be appreciated for its own sake, it is also beneficial to discover the various ways in which knowledge can be effectively used. In the study of history, for example, the principles of historical methodology and interpretation, learned experientially through simulations and the probing of personal and family history, could prove useful in training people to translate factual knowledge into working knowledge. (See Widick & Simpson, 1976.)

Learning how to learn. Since opportunities to learn continue throughout life, people should be trained in the skills of "learning how to learn" as early as possible. The *first major step* in learning how to learn is to become familiar with and be able to use the basic logic of problem-solving that has been with us formally since the time of Aristotle. Although this model is one of the basic instruments of effective living, our formal and informal educational systems normally do not introduce it to students in direct, systematic, and practical ways. Graduate students in science often learn this model under the rubric of "scientific methodology." But the logic of problem solving is for everyone and not just for the scientists among us. It is a process that relates both to solving intellectual puzzles and to handling problems in living. Students graduating from high school should be able to use the logic of problem solving with the same facility with which they perform basic mathematical functions.

There are four broad steps involved in the problem-solving process. (1) Explore the problem; that is, examine the facts involved. Diagnose the situation that calls for some kind of answer or solution. (2) Find a solution to the problem or to part of the problem; a solution that seems most likely to work. In order to come up with a solution or a variety of solutions from which to choose it is necessary to transform the data or facts that are being explored, to see them in a new light, and to discover new perspectives. (3) Implement the solution; take whatever steps are necessary to give the solution a fair trial. (4) See whether the solution works, either completely or partially. The solution may handle the problem completely, in which case the problem-solving process has achieved its goal and comes to an end. It often happens, however, that implementing a solution (action) solves the problem only partially, in which case the entire process is repeated in an effort to handle unfinished business. We have presented the basic problem-solving process here in its simplest form without delineating in any detail the skills needed to carry out each step of the process efficiently and effectively. Different situations and disciplines often require specialized skills to carry out each of these four steps, but the basic logic remains the same. The process and the fundamental skills that make it operative can be grasped fairly early in life.

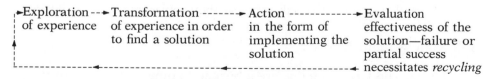

Figure 3-1.
The Basic Problem-Solving Process.

As you can see in Figure 3-1, the basic problem-solving process is directly related to the perception-attention-transformation-action model that was considered in Chapter 2.

As Argyris (1976a, 1976b) has pointed out, the second major step in learning how to learn is to apply the four basic problem-solving steps to each phase of the problem-solving process itself, thereby developing the skills and methodologies needed to implement each step of the process more efficiently and effectively.

To illustrate this procedure, the four steps could be applied to Step 1 (exploration) in the following way. (1) Explore how to go about the process of exploration—that is, how to attend to the situation and how to collect facts and data. Examine the skills and techniques that are used in exploration. (2) Try to come up with new and more effective ways of exploring. Examine and develop the exploration skills, techniques, and methods. (3) Acquire and try out new exploration skills, techniques, and methodologies. (4) Finally, determine whether these new skills, techniques, and methodologies of investigation work. If they do, then add them to your repertoire of skills and techniques. If they don't work, put them aside and look for better methods. Learning how to learn means applying this same method to each of the remaining three steps of the problem-solving process; that is, these same steps are used:

- to examine how to come up with solutions, to discover more effective ways of coming up with solutions, to try these new methods out, and to evaluate these new skills and methods.
- to examine how to go about implementing solutions, to find better ways of implementing solutions, to try these out, and to evaluate them.
- to examine evaluation skills and how to go about the evaluation process, to develop new evaluation procedures, to try them out, and to determine how useful they are.

This basic problem-solving and learning-how-to-learn process is important for two reasons: first, all of us are constantly learning and solving problems throughout our lives; and second, the ability to understand and use an expanded version of this model is critical for anyone who wishes to participate in the growth and development of society and its institutions. Later we will see an expanded version of this basic model when we consider the skills that people need to invest themselves creatively in society.

Self-Management Skills

People who lack discipline are a burden to others as well as to themselves. Self-management skills allow people to live spontaneously rather than haphazardly and provide the basis for the kind of discipline they need for investment in others and in systems. Outlined here are some of the key skills belonging to the "self-management package."

The ability to use a working theory of personality. All of us, usually without reflecting on it, construct "theories" that help us to understand, predict, and control the world around us. (See Wegner & Vallacher [1977] for a detailed account of this kind of implicit theory construction.) We develop implicit theories of motivation, personality, deviant behavior, social relations, and the self—theories that attempt to explain how we are put together and how we function as individuals.

These theories form the basis of our *working knowledge* of ourselves and of the world around us: they develop as we develop.

> As the child matures, his implicit theories become increasingly complex . . . differentiated and integrated. These changes reflect the person's accommodation to new experiences, and allow him to make judgments of these experiences with greater abstraction and less concentration [Wegner & Vallacher, 1977, p. 37].

One way of looking at working knowledge is to see it as the art of making implicit theories explicit, thereby increasing their validity. As Wegner and Vallacher note:

> Unfortunately, implicit theories about others and even about self can be mistaken. Unlike the scientist, who would most often correct or reject an erroneous theory, the layman may sometimes live with a mistaken view of people. This is because he builds his theories for pragmatic purposes; he must act on the basis of his conceptions [p. 37].

"Giving psychology away" means helping people to reflect upon, verify, and develop their implicit theories and equipping them with the skills they need to make these theories operative in understanding, predicting, and controlling behavior.

How a working theory of personality can be translated into a self-management skill is best demonstrated through an example. Transactional Analysis (Berne, 1973; James & Jongeward, 1971; Steiner, 1974) provides people—whether they are in therapy or merely seeking a fuller life—with a working theory of personality. The use of T.A. as a working model can be illustrated in three important areas: (1) the individual personality, (2) the personality in interaction with others, and (3) life patterns that result from styles of personality and relationship.

(1) T.A. theory suggests that every individual has three basic dimensions, or ego states: the Parent, the Adult, and the Child. These dimensions may be thought of as subselves (see Shapiro, 1969) or as different ways of being. The Parent ego state is that aspect of each person that evaluates and nurtures the self and others in ways that reflect how the person was "parented" in early life. The Adult ego state gathers information and makes decisions in the here-and-now. The Child ego state reacts to past and present experience with feelings. Transactional analysts encourage clients to understand their own personalities by analyzing the relative amounts of time and energy that each ego state is allowed in their lives and by seeing what situations lead to overuse or underuse of the various parts of the personality. For example, T.A. may help individuals to identify the source of

overcriticalness about themselves and the situations in which this critical-ness tends to occur and suggest some useful alternatives.

(2) T.A. theory also helps individuals to understand typical patterns in their style of relating to others. Individuals whose relationship style is characterized by evaluating or taking care of others relate on the basis of the Parent ego state. Those who relate to others primarily in a rational, objective, thoughtful way behave on the basis of the Adult ego state. Those who relate to people primarily on the basis of feelings activate the Child ego state in their relationships. Such analyses can lead to an awareness of those parts of the person that are typically neglected in relating to others; and this awareness can lead to improvement in the quality and range of interpersonal life.

(3) T.A. theorists have developed a means of analyzing recurrent pat-terns in life that is referred to as *life-script theory* (see Steiner, 1974). The basic concept of this theory is that early learning experiences in the family tend to set up expectations about how the world works and what can be expected from life. These expectations often go unchallenged and become the basis for self-fulfilling prophecies (Merton, 1968) that shape a person's life. Thus a person who was constantly criticized by parents for his or her behavior may come to expect such criticism and eventually learns to elicit it. Transactional analysis uses life-script theory to enable individuals to understand and confront self-limiting patterns in their behavior.

We do not suggest that transactional analysis should be adopted as the preferred working theory of personality. The point is that people who understand how they relate to themselves and how this relationship with self colors their relationships with others and with human systems are in a better position to understand, predict, and control their behavior. Frank (1973) intimates that people spontaneously develop a working theory of personality to help in facing themselves and their world. Individuals should be trained to identify, develop, and modify these eclectic working theories of personality in some systematic way so that these theories may become more finely honed instruments of understanding, prediction, and control.

The study of personality in psychology has produced vast amounts of theory and research, little of which filters down into educational systems as working knowledge. Helping individuals to develop integrated working theories of personality is one constructive way of giving this important branch of psychology away.

The ability to apply the basic principles of behavior to practical situa-tions. A second self-management skill that would greatly increase the per-sonal power of individuals is a working knowledge of the basic principles of human behavior and the ability to apply these principles to a wide vari-ety of life situations. Young people should be taught the concepts of rein-forcement, punishment, modeling, shaping, and aversive conditioning (Bandura, 1969). Many people, including professionals, are fearful of "be-havior modification" because of its potential for manipulation and misuse. One way of counteracting potential misuse is to see to it that *all* people possess a basic working knowledge of these principles so that one individual or group cannot use them to manipulate or control another. Instead of using these principles to control others, we can give this working knowledge and these skills away so that individuals can use them to control their own behavior.

Aversive conditioning is one of the principal mechanisms at work in the psychopathology of the average mentioned earlier. Aversive conditioning means that people are rewarded for not doing something or for avoiding something. For instance, Fred, a college student, slips off to a local haunt to have a few beers with his buddies instead of doing some necessary studying. Avoiding painful study is rewarding in itself (negative reinforcement), but the situation is made worse by the fact that a very pleasurable activity (positive reinforcement) is substituted for the unpleasant one. A working knowledge of aversive conditioning tells us that Fred is using the principles of human behavior to work against himself. A working knowledge of the principles of behavior, and the ability to use this knowledge, is a practical necessity for the person who wants to live fully.

Problem-solving and program-development skills. In considering intellectual skills, we outlined the basic logic of problem solving in the context of "learning how to learn." Problem solving, applied to the challenges of everyday life, is also a key to self-management skill. Let us briefly examine problem solving as a self-management methodology by outlining a somewhat expanded form of the basic process. What we present here is a version of a model used by Egan (1975) to present a systematic approach to helping and to the learning of helping skills. The model has four stages: exploration, goal setting, program development, and implementation and evaluation. Each stage has an expanding and a contracting phase.

(1) As we have seen, the first step in problem solving is to explore a situation—that is, to review the facts and come to understand the problem thoroughly enough to have intimations about possible solutions. In the expanding phase of exploration, the problem solver reviews the total *context* of the problem and reviews the related significant facts. Since it is impossible to focus on all problems or every dimension of each problem at once, the problem solver makes the process manageable by focusing on one or two critical issues that he or she is going to face immediately; this is the contracting, or focusing, phase of exploration.

(2) In the second stage of problem solving, a deeper understanding of the issues is gained so that something can be done about them. One way of gaining an understanding of oneself and one's problems is to try to see both from a more objective frame of reference. In the expanding phase of working toward goals, the problem solver tries to see himself or herself from other people's perspectives. As people begin to see themselves and their behavior more objectively and develop new perspectives on the consequences of their behavior, they begin to see alternate ways of acting; that is, they begin to establish behavioral goals that are related to the problem areas of their lives. This goal setting takes place in the contracting phase of working toward goals.

(3) Once behavioral goals have been established, it is necessary to consider and choose the means for achieving these goals. Usually there is more than one way to reach a goal. The first step in program development is to consider as many means as possible in order to establish a "pool" from which the most viable, efficient means, and the one with the highest probability for success, can be chosen. This consideration of possible means is the expanding phase of program development. In the contracting phase of program development, the problem solver chooses specific means by weighing both the cost and the potential effectiveness of each means or combination of means and committing himself or herself to a particular program.

(4) The final and most crucial stage is trying a program and seeing whether it works. In the expanding phase of this implementation/ evaluation stage, the problem solver tries the means he or she has selected. If the program is complicated, the problem solver ensures that it is a clear, step-by-step program and that each step is followed as outlined. Finally, in the contracting phase of implementation/evaluation, the problem solver assesses the effectiveness of the program. If it is successful, achieving the behavioral goals that were determined in the contracting phase of Stage 2, then the problem solver turns his or her attention to other issues. If the program is not successful or only partially so, it becomes necessary to re-cycle the problem-solving process.

Choosing specific behavioral goals (Stage 2) and the specific means needed to achieve these goals (Stage 3) involves the ability to make deci-sions. A decisive person is one who has been trained in the skills of choos-ing (Janis & Mann, 1977). Practical methodologies for learning problem-solving models and the skills needed to implement these models are now available. (See, for example, Carkhuff, 1973, 1974; Egan, 1975.) Spivack, Platt, and Shure (1977) relate problem-solving models and skills to social adjustment. They review research as well as training programs that relate skills of increasing complexity to different developmental stages.

Shure and Spivack have developed methodologies for teaching problem-solving skills to children at school (1974) and at home (1978).

Value-Clarification Skills

Attitudes and values, together with knowledge and skills, form what has been called the "curricular triumvirate." We do not live in a value-free world. Human systems deliver value orientations (as this book itself does) as well as services. This makes it important for people—those delivering services and, ideally, those receiving them—to know how to identify and clarify their own values and to discover how they are being affected by the value orientations of individuals and institutions.

Raths, Harmin, and Simon (1960) describe a value as something that a particular person prizes and cherishes, chooses freely from alternatives after considering the consequences of these alternatives, and acts on rather than merely thinks about. If reading is a value for a person, then he or she *reads*, finds time for reading, and doesn't merely think that it would be nice to read if there were time.

Values differ from opinions, interests, feelings, beliefs, and attitudes in that the latter do not necessarily lead to action. Values, then, govern behavior and life-style. A person's values are significant to identity, commitments, and self-image.

Curran (1968) suggests that many people experience social and emotional crises because of conflicting values. Since values underlie commitments to self, others, and systems, people should learn as early as possible in life how to clarify their values. Learning the skills of value clarification helps individuals to determine what values they would like to pursue and to identify the values embodied in the behavior of other individuals and in the behavior of organizations and social institutions. For instance, if a husband tells his wife that their family is the prime value in his life but still invests almost all of his time in projects that take him away from home, then it becomes clear that his values are exemplified by his behavior and not by his words.

Rokeach's research indicated that many people have a practical set of values that actually determine behavior as well as an idealized set of values. However, he has also discovered that, in many cases, when it is pointed out to people that they have opinions, interests, feelings, beliefs, and attitudes—notional values—that have not yet become real values, they often begin to translate these notional values into behavior. This kind of *values confrontation*, especially when it is self-confrontation, is an important self-management skill.

We have already stated how important decision making is in problem solving and program development; however, intelligent setting of goals and choosing of means is impossible without the ability to choose on the basis of clear-cut values. A number of educators have realized how important values are for a "self-managed life-style" (Williams & Long, 1975) and have introduced value-clarification programs into their curricula. Value-clarification seminars for teachers and other professionals are now relatively common, and the literature on training approaches to value clarification is growing (Harmin, Kirschenbaum, & Simon, 1973; Raths, Harmin, & Simon, 1966; Rokeach, 1973; Simon, 1974; Simon, Howe, & Kirschenbaum, 1972; Smith, 1977). People who know their interpersonal values are better prepared to relate to others effectively, directly, and with little confusion. Although training in interpersonal skills is important, it is not a substitute for clarification of interpersonal values.

The way in which developmental tasks outlined in Chapter 2 are pursued is greatly influenced by the values of the individual, of the significant others in the person's life, and of the organizations and institutions of society. For instance, the way in which Tim Garcia pursues career development, a task of early adulthood, depends, in part, on:

- his own values (he values creativity, freedom, and autonomy in work more than money),
- the values of his wife (she comes from a financially deprived

background and now wants the things that money can buy), and
· the values of the accounting firm for which Tim has begun to work
(this company expects its younger members to be ambitious and to
put in a 60-hour week).

Value-clarification skills don't provide magic solutions to the conflicts
that arise in life, but they do help individuals to clarify these conflicts and
to gather data that is essential for solving problems and making decisions.
(See Goodman [1976] for a review of some of the important value-
clarification literature.)

The Skills of Interpersonal Involvement

People's lives are defined, in significant ways, by their relationships.
However, many of us are not as effective as we could be in our communications with others. We learn how to relate to others by observing and
imitating adult models, but our learning often is haphazard and leads to
self-defeating patterns of relating. Schools have traditionally left the task
of learning how to relate to people to the family, peer systems, and the like.
But there is little evidence that these systems equip people with the skills
of high-level communicating and relating. The following is a brief overview of the skills that are needed in order to attain effective interpersonal
communication. (For an extensive treatment of these skills, see Egan, 1976,
1977.)

Self-presentation skills. Self-presentation skills include appropriate
self-disclosure and the expression of feelings and emotions in concrete
terms. The ability to talk about oneself is in no way equivalent to dropping
secrets. Appropriate self-disclosure is suitable to the setting, to the nature
of the relationship, and to the goals of the interchange. Many situations
require a degree of emotional distance between people. Intimate revela-
tions have no place, for example, in the typical business office unless the
people there are friends as well as co-workers. Communication in business
tends to be task- rather than relationship-oriented.

With intimates, on the other hand, indirectness, impersonality, and
emotional distance are clearly inappropriate. Love requires an intensity of
personal knowledge and trust that can only result from experiences of
shared intimate disclosure. If loving and being loved are what a person
wants, then the public virtues of objectivity and tact become private vices,
just as the private virtues of emotional and physical openness become
exhibitionistic in public. Self-presentation skills involve the ability to
judge the depth of self-disclosure that is possible or desirable in a given
situation and then to act accordingly. Knowing that different kinds of
self-disclosure are appropriate to different social situations is a part of social intelligence (Walker & Foley, 1973).

Responding skills. The skills of responding effectively include attending, listening, basic accurate empathy, and the behavioral communication

of respect and genuineness; these are the basic ingredients that go into the building of trust and, therefore, into the building of relationships. As Bullmer (1975) has pointed out, we tend to listen to one another evaluatively and to respond to one another with evaluative comments. However, listening for understanding and evaluative listening are qualitatively different. The former says "What is this person trying to say, and how does he or she feel about it?" The latter says "What is right or wrong with what this person is saying, and how does it affect me?" Many of us listen evaluatively instead of listening for understanding, even though effective evaluation logically follows understanding. If people began to respond to one another with accurate empathic understanding, then this significant response would constitute a veritable revolution in communication.

The effective use of responding skills promotes mutuality, relationship building and dialogue, and is at the very heart of support. It would be ideal if people were able to respond with accurate empathy—an understanding of what the other says from the other's frame of reference—just as instinctively as they respond with evaluative comments. In our view, respect and genuineness are not just moral qualities; they are *modes of communication*. It makes little difference if we feel genuineness and respect for one another unless in some way our behavior, both verbal and nonverbal, communicates both of these.

The skills of challenging others. Effective community living is built on both support and challenge. Continual support without challenge becomes effete and sterile, whereas challenge without support is harsh, punitive, and ultimately self-defeating. In dialogue, moderately intimate self-sharing and empathic responding provide support, whereas more intensely intimate self-sharing, confrontation, and immediacy provide challenge.

• *Confrontation* is perhaps an overused and misunderstood term. At its best, confrontation is an *invitation* to other people to examine their behavior socially—that is, with at least one other person. It is a form of intimacy and a way of getting closer to someone, not a punitive act of rejection. High-level communicators confront the strengths of others rather than their weaknesses (Berenson & Mitchell, 1974); that is, they focus on what others *can* do (even though they are not presently doing it), rather than on what they do poorly or fail to do altogether.

• *Immediacy* refers to the ability of two or more people to talk to each other about what is happening between them. There are two kinds of immediacy. *Relationship immediacy* refers to the ability to assess the quality of one's relationship with another. When a husband and wife sit down and ask themselves "Where do we stand in our relationship with each other?" they are involved in relationship immediacy. *Here-and-now immediacy* refers to the ability to discuss with another what is happening in a particular conversation. For instance, if I feel you are belittling me and controlling what I may or may not say to you, I exercise immediacy if I tell what I see happening in *this* conversation and invite you to discuss it. Immediacy is a difficult and complex skill; it includes the ability to disclose oneself appropriately, to share hunches about one's own and another's behavior, and to confront others.

Ideally, people learn how to challenge themselves, inviting others to help them in this task. Generally speaking, the people who contribute most to the support and challenge dimensions of a community are those who challenge themselves first, who ask others to help them in this process, and who challenge others only after taking the time to understand them. Mutuality is more likely to develop in a community if self-challenge, rather than the challenging of others, is normative.

Challenging is strong medicine. If challenging is not carried out skillfully, however, either community living will be impaired or a silent decision will be made to bar challenging from community interactions. In the latter case, the community might become peaceful, but it might become sterile as well.

Interpersonal skills are not ends in themselves, but rather they are used in building relationships and communities (Egan, 1976, 1977) and establishing effective organizational communication. In order to be effective communicators in communities and organizations, we need to know the goals and values we are pursuing through involvement with these systems. We can use communication skills to pursue a win-or-lose game in organizations, or we can use them to promote an open atmosphere, characterized by free and informed choice (Argyris, 1976a, 1976b). We can use communication skills to manipulate others or to promote the value of caring (Mayeroff, 1971). Interpersonal skills do not provide techniques that automatically improve the quality of living, nor do they constitute interpersonal values; but they do help us to go about the business of relating intelligently and effectively, and they can become the instruments of our interpersonal values.

Most of the developmental tasks of life involve relating to others; therefore, a solid repertoire of communication skills is a developmental necessity. It cannot be assumed that high levels of these skills will be acquired through experience or chance. Like the skills of problem solving, basic interpersonal communication can be taught to children both in the home (Shure & Spivack, 1978) and in school (Spivack & Shure, 1974).

Skills of Small-Group Involvement

Much of human relating takes place in small groups such as families, discussion groups, work teams, committees, peer groups, and the like. The three sets of skills discussed in the previous section, together with the ability to share needed information with others, are the building blocks of effective group participation; but the person who possesses these microskills is not *automatically* an effective communicator in a group. In order to contribute to a group, it is necessary to translate basic interpersonal or communication skills into effective group interaction. (See Reddy, 1975, and Reddy & Lippert, 1977, for a comprehensive bibliography of books and articles on small-group training.)

Groups constitute relatively complex situations with regard to communication. Even in a relatively small group of six members, each member must continually decide whether to speak to the whole group or to one of the other five members. This numerical complexity is a sign of the psychological and communicational complexity of the small group. When individuals participate in a small group, one-to-one skills need to be complemented by group skills. Some of the common small-group behaviors that we place under the rubric of group-specific skills are discussed in the following paragraphs.

Clarifying the goals of the group. A group, like any other system, works poorly if its goals aren't clear. Early in the brief history of the human-potential movement (Howard, 1970), "planned goallessness," in theory and in practice, characterized many small groups that were devoted to personal growth. This theory contradicted the research in social psychology that showed that small groups work more effectively if the members are clear about the group's goals and can agree on the general means to achieve these goals (Egan, 1970). In our opinion, the ability to help the members of any group to clarify both goals and means is a primary group-specific skill. In addition, since a group is a system with a purpose, it ordinarily functions best when the principles governing the design and operation of systems are observed. These principles are reviewed in Chapter 8.

Initiating in a group. The larger a group becomes, the easier it is to fall silent and "let George do it." People tend to feel self-conscious when they use individual communication skills in a group; therefore, we find it useful to train people to become assertive in groups, fulfilling their own needs while respecting the needs of others. To ensure the smooth running of a group, it is especially important to see to it that support is provided, in terms of listening and communicating empathic understanding. Group members often become lost in the group task and fail to provide the support needed to encourage self-sharing and to sustain challenge. On the other hand, low levels of initiation on the part of group members lead to a lack of challenge in the group. Small groups, like other social systems, thrive on a combination of support and challenge.

Using the resources of a group. Another group-specific skill is the ability to use the resources of the group. For instance, John uses the resources of the group if, when he confronts Mary, he checks out his perception of her with the other members. The use of resources will mean different things in groups with different tasks, but the underlying principle is the same. Groups, too, can suffer from the "psychopathology of the average" if they fail to tap their own resources.

Owning into group interaction. This skill is another form of assertiveness. When two people are talking to each other in a group, the tendency of others is to sit and watch them interact. Many people are afraid of interrupting others; but there is a difference between disrupting a conversation and contributing to it, though both might involve some form of interruption. If a third person has something to contribute to the interaction between two others, then that person's interruption is not a disruption but a resource. Obviously, what is said should be worthwhile, and timing is important. The counterpart of *owning* is the skill of *inviting*. The information and resources that are important for the work of the group will not be lost if those who adopt the role of observer are invited to share what they think and feel.

Although the ability to participate effectively in a small group requires more sophisticated skills than those required in one-to-one interactions, simple group-specific skills can and should be taught throughout the school years (Ball, 1974; Barnes & Todd, 1977; Berkovitz, 1975; Bessell, 1973; Newman, 1974; Schmuck & Schmuck, 1975). More sophisticated group-specific skills can be taught to young people as they acquire the developmental capacity to use them (Egan, 1970, 1976).

Small-group training can become an effective instrument of human development. Group approaches to such tasks as continuing education, problem solving, and social and emotional development are becoming more and more common. Corey and Corey (1977) not only outline the kinds of skills needed for effective group participation but also describe specific kinds of groups for different developmental stages from childhood to old age. Such groups can be included among the key systems associated with each stage of human development. The self-help movement (Caplan & Killilea, 1976; Gartner & Riessman, 1977) is not restricted to therapy groups; it includes associations that can help people face developmental tasks, including the transition from one role or status to another.

The skills of effective involvement in organizations and institutions are considered in Chapter 8.

Skills Training as Assertiveness Training

Interest in assertiveness training has grown rapidly in the past few years. (See Alberti & Emmons, 1974, 1975; Lange & Jakubowski, 1976; Lazarus & Fay, 1975; Liberman, King, DeRisi, & McCann, 1975.) In a sense, however, all skills-training programs can be considered as forms of assertiveness training. Most of the skills we discuss here have three components: (1) an awareness component, (2) a technology component, and (3) an assertiveness component.

(1) Most skills start with an awareness of self, another person, a social situation, or a need. For instance, in order to be empathetic, it is necessary to be aware of the other person's frame of reference. In order to develop a program, it is necessary to know what means are available to reach a goal. Awareness has two aspects: awareness of a situation and awareness of possible alternative responses.

(2) Next, it is necessary to be able to respond appropriately and competently to this awareness—to have the "know-how" or technology to de-

liver what is called for. For instance, if empathy is called for, one must not only be able to correctly identify the speaker's emotions and the experiences and behaviors that underlie these emotions, but also to translate understanding into effective communication. Awareness counts for little if it is not communicated.

(3) Finally, high-level awareness and excellent "know-how" are meaningless unless one has the initiative to use them when they are called for. People with good perceptive abilities and a solid grasp of the technology of a variety of skills often fail to use these resources when they are called for. Effective skills-training programs, therefore, use role-playing, rehearsal, homework, and other techniques to develop assertiveness in trainees.

In terms of the model in Chapter 2, perception-attention-transformation-action, *awareness* is an *input* (perception and attention), *technology* is the way in which the input is *transformed*, and *assertiveness* is an *output* (action).

For instance, Mathew's boss is yelling at him because he did not get an important document into the mail in time for next-day delivery. Mathew is aware (1) that his boss is venting her feelings, blaming him for her failure to draw up the document in time to get it typed, and that he is feeling mistreated. He is also aware (2) that he could lose his temper and yell back at her, or say nothing, swallow his feelings, and let the whole thing blow over, or confront her by describing her behavior, the impossibility of finishing the task in time, and his reaction to her emotional outburst. He may want to choose the third alternative but not have the communication skills or the courage (assertiveness) to do it well. Awareness plus skills plus action is the total assertiveness package.

The best assertiveness-training programs provide people with the skills they need in order to stand up for their rights without infringing on the rights of others. (See Kelley, 1977, for a review of the literature on assertiveness.)

Cautions and Criticisms

Acquiring and using the kinds of skills we have briefly described here requires a great deal of work. Using them well is a function of both interpersonal style and general life-style. Citing the fact that skills training works in some respects but not in others, Mahon and Altmann (1977) offer certain cautions and criticisms for those involved in skills-training programs. In the following paragraphs, we review some of these cautions and criticisms and comment on them.

Trainability. Problem: Not all individuals respond to skills training with the same degree of success.

Comment: This is true. The same can be said with regard to education and training generally. Neither education nor training works magic; in fact, they are harmful if done poorly. Like teaching, training is in constant need of improvement, especially in the case of those who do not respond well. Let us not make the same mistakes in developing and using these relatively new skills-training programs that have been made in our educational systems.

Difficulty and complexity of skills. Problem: Some skills are much more difficult to impart than others.

Comment: This, too, is true. For instance, among interpersonal-communication skills, the skill of attending is learned much more quickly than the skill of immediacy. The challenge is to reduce complex skills to simpler components and to teach these gradually through well-shaped programs. Also, opportunities should be offered to integrate these components and to practice and use each complex skill.

Effective and ineffective training programs. Problem: Not all skills-training approaches are consistently effective.

Comment: First of all, a program is only as good as those who use it. Moreover, the skills-training movement is in its infancy. Training programs offer a great deal of promise, but, in Mahon and Altmann's words, "The components for effective skills-training programs need to be more clearly identified and researched" (p. 48). Skills programs that make exaggerated claims should be discounted. We need well-validated training methodologies, and training programs are the laboratories in which effective methodologies must be elaborated and tested.

Transfer. Problem: Some research shows that trained skills do not necessarily transfer to nontraining settings.

Comment: Other research shows that they do. We might say that they transfer under certain conditions. We suggest that skills transfer to new situations when this transfer is taken into consideration in the training program. For instance, we found that learning the skill of accurate empathy in one-to-one practice sessions did not mean that this skill would automatically transfer to a small-group setting (Downs, 1973); however, it did transfer when we provided further training in the use of accurate empathy in a group setting. (See Egan, 1976, Chapter 12.)

Setting up analogs of life settings, using rehearsal techniques and homework, and following up skill development and use through practicum experiences (Egan, 1976 [Chapter 13]) all raise the probability that skills will transfer, but again there is no magic. Skills transfer if they become a part of the communication style of the person, who is free to put aside even well-learned skills for any number of reasons. A trainee once told us that she was not using the communication skills she was learning in her day-to-day life because she discovered that intensive interpersonal living was not a value for her. The cost was simply too high given her personal values.

Life is bigger than skills. Problem: Mahon and Altmann point out that there is more to life than skills. For instance, there is more to the communication process than just a package of microskills. Attitudes and values are important.

Comment: Mahon and Altmann are absolutely right. Skills are important instruments of effective living, but they need to be presented in a wide human context. Training programs should include the presentation of theory and offer integrating models. The people-in-systems model is elaborated in this book because we find that we need a broad integrative approach in order to do skills-training well. We also suggest that trainees would find this model useful in helping them to see the need for skills and how they are integrated into the various settings of their lives.

We agree with Calia (1974), who said that a good training program imparts more than microskills; it helps the trainees to transcend their training. Trainees need tools for expanding their view of the world, and a training program can help them acquire a wider vision only if it is built on solid theory and offers integrating models. The ideal program, Richardson and Island (1975) point out, is an integration of theory, skills, and transfer. We would add that all skills-training programs would benefit by integration into a wider human-development/human-systems model.

Poor research. Problem: Mahon and Altmann suggest that the research that demonstrates the benefits of skills-training programs is shoddy and is characterized by poor methodology and short-term studies.

Comment: The implied assumption that studies that demonstrate the value of skills training are shoddy whereas studies that disprove its effectiveness are well designed and well executed will probably not withstand deeper scrutiny. The point is that effective evaluation programs for skills-training methodologies, including follow-up studies, are needed. The same can be said of counseling and related disciplines. Long-term field research is difficult, but it is the direction in which we need to move. The publication of new journals such as *Evaluation and Program Planning* is a sign of a more general awakening to the importance of effective evaluation skills.

Person, not skills. Problem: It has been contended that skills-training programs place more importance on the skills than on the person using the skills.

Comment: Mahon and Altmann answer this objection themselves when they say "It is not the skills themselves which are all important, it is the *control* of their use, the intentions with which they are used, and their flexibility or changeability that is crucial" (p. 48). They go on to say that "personal qualities underlying and unifying 'skills' need as much or more emphasis as the skills themselves" (p. 49).

Skills-training programs need to be a part of full human-development programs. In our counselor-training programs, the primary focus is on the person of the counselor and his or her development (Egan, 1975, 1976). Skills are important, but the way in which the trainees integrate these skills into their interpersonal and helping style and into a broader framework of human development are far more important. We see counselors as consultants to the human-development process. Therefore, the training of counselors, including microskills training, must take place in a human-development context.

Temporary appendages. Problem: Mahon and Altmann claim that newly acquired skills are appendages rather than purposive behaviors, and that skills learned in training programs are not permanent.

Comment: We see the problem in a somewhat different way, however. People with newly won skills may well be awkward in the use of these skills. Naturalness and ease come with practice and with use in real-life situations, when the trainees integrate their new skills into their own individual styles. This requires time. Skills training with adults is often remedial. They are learning skills that should have been learned, developmentally, at a much earlier stage. They have often developed rigid communication patterns that a short-term training program cannot be expected to remedy. Skills training can be the beginning, but follow-up efforts are needed. With those who have developed highly rigid and defensive patterns of communication, skills training may be too little too late.

The issue of lack of permanence is related to the problem of transfer. Unused skills die away or remain unintegrated and awkward. If skills are used infrequently, then using them becomes a laborious and unrewarding task and the skills tend to be discarded. If the systems in which the skills are being used do not reward their use, then the skills will atrophy. When children learn basic communication skills in one class but get into trouble when they use them in other situations, these skills will no longer be used. Interpersonal skills such as confrontation and immediacy make sense only in the context of challenging working conditions and intensive interpersonal living. Our experience shows that skills persist in environments that support their use.

Mechanical use. Problem: People use newly won skills in a mechanical way and rigidly adhere to models that call for the use of these skills.

Comment: For many this is true only in the beginning. When people feel awkward, they rely on structure a great deal. The technology of skills and the steps or stages of a model provide such structure. Counselor trainees use accurate empathy constantly instead of when it is appropriate, and they lean on the techniques and methodologies of a particular helping model; however, this tendency eventually disappears. In the beginning, skills and models use the trainee, but with sufficient time for practice and application under supervision, the trainee begins to use the skills and models. The helping situation itself and the needs of the person being helped dictate how models and skills are to be used. However, the person who is equipped with a systematic helping model and the skills and methodologies needed to implement this model will offer more consistent high-level help than the person who moves into counseling practice equipped with highly cognitive models but not with skills training. We find that working models and skills eventually enrich the helper's spontaneity rather than stifle it.

No pre-assessment, no follow-up. Problem: According to Mahon and Altmann, the skill level of trainees entering programs is not assessed, nor is there any kind of follow-up to determine the effectiveness of the training program.

Comment: If, as we suggest in these pages, there were systematic life-skills training programs throughout life, then these objections would be answered. For instance, interpersonal-skills development could be monitored in the same way that reading development is now. We find that, with adults, making no assumptions about initial level of skills helps them to be less defensive. We point out that the training program can be used as a skills "check-up," as a way of renewing skills that have fallen into disuse, and as a way of developing new skills. Short, patchwork, limited training programs are neither instant nor universal remedies for the "psychopathology of the average."

Effective relating, not brief training in discrete skills. Problem: Mahon and Altmann maintain that the process of effectively relating to others cannot be accomplished by acquiring specific discrete skills.

Comment: This is true. Skills-training programs that offer nothing more than brief training in discrete skills are useless. Such short-term efforts are demonstrations of the possibilities of skills-training programs rather than programs themselves. Furthermore, good programs focus on people and their development rather than on discrete skills alone. While admitting the validity of this objection, we offer a related hypothesis: even though effective relating to others cannot be accomplished merely by acquiring specific skills, it cannot be accomplished *without* acquiring specific discrete skills.

Skills without impact. Problem: Mahon and Altmann maintain that skills do not have the intended effect on those with whom they are used.

Comment: We assert that skilled people, not skills in themselves, have impact on others. Those who use skills awkwardly or whose skills aren't used in the context of broader models, as well as those who, in terms of skills, are technically competent but are indifferent to others, will have negative rather than positive impact.

Mahon and Altmann's criticisms and cautions are extremely useful, because they provide important guidelines for designing and implementing skills-training programs and help us to realize the instrumental nature of skills and to keep in focus the human person developing in the context of human systems.

Not long ago, *sensitivity training* became a victim of the "law of the instrument" (Kaplan, 1964), which states that when people are given an instrument—a technique, a methodology—they tend to find as many uses as possible for it. The proponents of *sensitivity training* soon discovered that it was "needed" everywhere: in growth groups, in schools, and in businesses, to name a few. Failure to heed the criticisms reviewed here could mean that skills-training programs, which are becoming popular, could suffer the consequences of the "law of the instrument."

Skills training is important to human development, and it must be used wisely. Misuse of such programs, including the encouragement of unrealistic expectations, can only harm what is presently a good approach. The present danger is that presumptuous and poorly designed programs or good programs in the hands of inept trainers will crowd into the marketplace and cause people to identify this ineptness with skills training itself.

Skills-training programs or life-skills refresher courses for adults can provide settings for the concrete working out of unfinished developmental issues. In our counselor-training programs, trainees come from basically normal populations, but still they have unfinished developmental business to take care of as they prepare themselves to become helpers. Skills training, including training in interpersonal, problem-solving, and behavior-management skills, provides the format, while the developmental issues of the participants provide much of the content of the program. Since skill development is an action program that puts the trainees in close contact with one another, they do not merely discuss developmental issues but give behavioral expression to these issues in their relationships with one another. A working knowledge of human development, along with skills, enables them to develop satisfying patterns of behavior.

In this chapter, we have presented an overview of various groups of life skills that are important for carrying out developmental tasks and, together with the systems-involvement skills to be discussed in following chapters, for effective give-and-take with the key settings of life. We have made no attempt to explore the training methodologies that have been and are currently being developed to impart these skills; obviously, such an exploration is beyond the scope of this book. Information concerning specific skills-training programs can be obtained by consulting the references to these programs made throughout this chapter.

Chapter 3: Additional Resources

Argyris, C. Theories of action that inhibit individual learning. *American Psychologist*, 1976, *31*, 638–654.

Carkhuff, R. R. *The art of problem solving*. Amherst, Mass.: Human Resources Development Press, 1973.

Egan, G. *Interpersonal living*. Monterey, Calif.: Brooks/Cole, 1976.

Watson, D., & Tharp, R. *Self-directed behavior* (2nd ed.). Monterey, Calif.: Brooks/Cole, 1977.

White, R. W. *The enterprise of living* (2nd ed.). New York: Holt, Rinehart and Winston, 1976. (See Chapters 9, 13, & 17.)

4

The Social Context of Human Development— Level I: Personal Settings

Following the suggestion of John Dollard (1935), we are constructing a working model of human development that deals not only with developmental events of the life cycle but also with the context in which these events take place. While keeping in mind the developmental stages, tasks, and crises that are reviewed in Chapter 2, we shift our attention to the settings in which these take place.

Understanding Systems: An Introduction

In the view of certain scientists and philosophers of science (see Laszlo, 1972), the entire world can be thought of as a system:

> Contemporary science has become ... the "science of organized complexity." ... Equipped with the concepts and theories provided by the contemporary sciences, we can discern systems of organized complexity wherever we look. Man is one such system and so are his societies and his environment. Nature itself, as it manifests itself here on this earth, is a giant system maintaining itself. ... Setting our sights even higher in terms of size, we can see that the solar system and the galaxy of which it is a part are also systems, and so is the astronomical universe of which our galaxy is a component [p. 12].

We don't expect people to become philosophers of science, but we do hope that they can begin to acquire a working knowledge of systems that will help them to pursue their developmental tasks more creatively.

65

A deeper understanding of the term *system* is gained in the following elaboration of (1) *system*, (2) *human system*, and (3) *systems world*.

1. A *system* is a set of components that affect or influence one another. One component cannot be adequately understood unless the influences that affect all of the components are known. In this sense, the atom, the human body, and our galaxy are all systems.

2. A *human system* is one in which the components are people, including a people's history and culture as these affect the system in the present. Examples of human systems are families, schools, businesses, neighborhoods, governments, and voluntary associations.

3. *Systems world* refers to the fact that all of us participate in, influence, and are influenced by human systems that affect one another. Individuals are affected by their families and the places where they work, businesses are influenced by other businesses and by the economic system, and nations influence one another in the political world order.

It is impossible to understand human development merely by focusing on individuals or on what transpires inside them, because the ways in which individuals develop are influenced not only by other individuals but by society as well.

Individuals participate in a number of systems—the family, the school, the work setting, the neighborhood—that exert a profound influence on development and are themselves embedded in a complex and interdependent network of organizations and institutions, such as the economic system, that constantly influence them. (See Berger & Neuhaus, 1977; Brim, 1975; Bronfenbrenner, 1977b; Keniston, 1977; Turk, 1977.) Individuals are affected not only by the personal systems, such as family and neighborhood, in which they participate but also by the larger systems of society.

One thesis of this book is that educators, helpers, ministers, and social-policy makers should take a systems perspective when dealing with people and making decisions concerning them, since ignorance of the systems context of development can have destructive consequences (Berger & Neuhaus, 1977; Sarason, 1972, 1974). Moreover, all individuals can acquire a basic and practical working knowledge of the systems that envelop them from birth to death. This working knowledge will enable them to involve themselves in, cope with, and contribute to the development of these systems. We believe that individuals can become involved in even larger institutions of society without being reduced to the status of sociological data. If people develop a practical working knowledge of the important systems of their lives and acquire the kinds of skills that are needed to involve themselves creatively in them,—even if at times this means creative coping—they will be better able to survive as individuals in a complex world. Although people experience the groups, organizations, and institutions of their world on a daily basis, they learn little about them in any kind of formal way. The average person is taught very little, if anything, about the systems that influence his or her life so profoundly from day to day. Modern systems theory (Buckley, 1967, 1968; Kuhn, 1974; Ruben & Kim, 1975) provides us with a source of useful concepts to help us acquire the working knowledge we need.

One of the clearest examples of a systems context for development is the nuclear family. Andrews (1974) has provided us with an excellent illustration of the family as a system (see Figure 4-1):

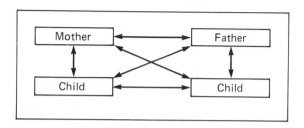

Figure 4-1

In a family of four ... there exist six dyadic, reciprocal relationship possibilities. These tie each member of the family to every other member directly and indirectly through another person to whom he is directly related. One might construct a physical model of this diagram by using paper clips to represent each family member and connecting rubber bands to represent the relationship vectors in the diagram. If the paper clips are each fastened down and the rubber bands drawn taut, the model will assume a stability that can be altered at any time. Plucking any of the rubber bands will reverberate the entire model. Similarly, any action or reaction pattern between any two family members will resonate throughout the entire family. Marital difficulties between parents will often manifest themselves in symptomatic behavior in one of the children. This "family resonance" phenomenon is the perpetuating mechanism of characteristic behavior within a family. Reinforcement of certain kinds of behavior is not unilateral or even bilateral but multilateral; thus, change can either be encouraged or resisted [p. 8].[1]

A Family in a Systems World

In order to make our discussion of systems as concrete as possible, we consider here some of the ways in which an actual family and its members were influenced by social systems. Tom Mason worked as a nurse practitioner in the mountains of Appalachia, providing services in several federally- and state-funded clinics, while his wife, Cindy, taught third grade in a local public school. Tom, who had always been interested in service to poor people, had worked as a volunteer in Africa during his college years. It was there that he decided to pursue a career in health care. Because the Masons had both grown up and received their education in large urban areas, they found it difficult to adjust to rural mountain culture and to find friends with educational backgrounds and interests that were similar to their own. Cindy found it especially hard to adjust to rural living, because having an active circle of friends was very important to her. Teaching in the local school also presented her with problems. She had taught middle-class children in a large midwestern city, but she found the children in Appalachia to be less developed than her former pupils. These rural students came from homes in which there was little intellectual stimulation, they were quite passive and unresponsive in the classroom, and at times their basic needs for food, clothing, and health care were not met.

Tom, on the other hand, enjoyed the freedom he had in the clinics. Since there were practically no doctors in the area, he played a major role in the delivery of medical services, and the doctors who made the rounds of the clinics relied on him heavily. As a result, his experiential learning was much greater in Appalachia than it would have been in a city, where much of the work would have been handled by interns and residents. At the same time, however, his work was endless and he spent long hours in the clinics, more often than not spending a large part of Saturday and even Sunday working. This schedule disrupted the Mason's family life, since it meant that Cindy had to tend to the needs of their preschool daughter and do household chores after teaching school during the day. When Tom was home, much of his time was spent working around the house and giving Cindy a reprieve from caring for their daughter. Tom was accustomed to working long hours, for he had done so in Africa; but he had been single then. Now that he was married, he felt guilty about subjecting his wife and daughter to certain hardships in order to pursue values that were important to him. Cindy didn't complain; she was adventurous, and she liked the fact that Tom was idealistic. But Cindy's attitude did not relieve the tensions they were experiencing.

Tom enjoyed the autonomy the doctors gave him, but he came to feel used when he did a great deal of extra work for little or no pay. Neither his nor Cindy's job paid very much, and they were constantly facing money problems that added to the tensions of family living. The situation worsened when Cindy became pregnant with their second child. Also, Tom came to realize that financial support for the clinics was not high on the priority list of either the state or the federal government. The clinics had been opened as part of an experimental program to provide health care for rural areas, but funding had begun to dry up and there was talk of closing some of the clinics.

In this brief scenario, we see a number of interactions between individuals and systems—between Tom and the clinics, and between Cindy and the school—and between systems themselves—between the Mason family and the economic system, between the Mason family and the local culture, and between the clinics and governmental agencies. These types of interactions have significant consequences for the development of both individuals and systems. Tom and Cindy were facing the common developmental tasks of young adulthood that were outlined in Chapter 2, including family living, parenting, career development, and life-style management. The systems that provide the context for these tasks are the family, the work settings, the friendship network, and the surrounding community. But in the Masons' case, there was little time for family life, Cindy felt frustrated at her job and Tom was beginning to feel used at his, their closest friends lived 60 miles away, and they felt like outsiders with respect to rural 'mountain culture.

Being basically intelligent and well-integrated people, the Masons faced their problems with a great deal of resourcefulness. They spent four full years in Appalachia, even though Tom had committed himself for only two. Later, however, when Cindy reviewed her experience in terms of the people-in-systems perspective, she had this to say:

> We feel that we did a pretty good job in Appalachia. We matured quite a bit, sometimes in spite of ourselves, it seems. We feel that we could have done a better job if we had had an understanding of the people-in-systems model and the kinds of practical working knowledge and skills it talks about. It's not that we were ignorant or unskilled, but we were rather naive and went about problem solving in a haphazard way. Of course, we never thought of ourselves as undertaking developmental tasks or of the family as a system. And we never examined in any kind of formal or explicit way the impact that the systems in which we were involved, like the school or the clinics, was having on us. We believe that it would have helped us to do so. It would have given us a kind of clarity that we did not have. We muddled through. Some would say that we muddled through quite well. But this model would have given us some of the tools we needed to face family, career, and life-style issues in a much more systematic way.
>
> When we look back on our own rearing and education, including professional education, we were not prepared for the world we met in Appalachia—and maybe much of the rest of the world. The values imparted to us now seem too narrow; some of them hindered us in dealing with the world as it really is. We think that an education that takes a broader perspective than the one we received both at home and in school is needed for our own children. Basing that education in part on the people-in-systems model makes sense to us.

The people-in-systems model is one way of achieving the kind of behavioral clarity that greatly helps the problem-solving process. The Masons did not suggest that knowledge of the model would have worked magic in their lives but rather that it would have enabled them to see more clearly the kinds of social influence that were affecting them and the kinds of resources they needed to meet developmental challenges more creatively.

If the notion of *system* is to help people understand the settings in which development takes place, then they need a deep understanding of the concept of "system."

The Social Structure of the Human-Systems World

The human-systems world is so complex that even its simpler subsystems escape complete understanding. For instance, economics is hard pressed to achieve the status of an exact, predictive science, because of the complexity of the systems and subsystems with which economists must deal. And yet economics is typically considered to be highly developed in its predictive abilities when compared with the other social sciences. (See Kuhn, 1974). Our purpose in Chapters 4, 5, 6, and 7 is to present a schema of the structure of the world of systems that will help to explain the various direct and indirect ways in which the groups, organizations, associations, and institutions of society affect life and development. We believe that when people begin to understand how they are being affected by the systems in their lives, they will be in a better position to cope with, cooperate with, and challenge these systems.

A Brief Overview of Levels of Systems

The following categorization of systems is adapted from Brim (1975) and Bronfenbrenner (1977b), who describe four categories, or levels, of systems: microsystems, the mesosystem, the exosystem, and the macrosystem. The following is a description of each of these categories. The microsystem is developed in detail in this chapter, while the other three categories are examined in Chapters 5, 6, and 7.

Microsystems, or personal settings. These are the small, immediate systems of our everyday lives. Examples of important personal settings are the family, friendship groups, immediate work settings, and classrooms. Each of these fulfills the definition of a human system; that is, they are groups of mutually interacting individuals organized into a whole.

Personal systems affect the lives of their members in many ways. A mother is affected by the policies of the payroll department where she works, the kinds of people in the office, and the ways in which they interact with one another. The fact that the members of the union provide a great deal of support for one another affects a father. Dissension on the basketball team over a hard-nosed coach who keeps driving the players affects a child.

The mesosystem, or network of personal settings. At this second level, we find the network of personal settings and the interactions among them. Not only does a personal system affect the individual member, but one personal system can directly or indirectly affect another. What happens to children in the classroom affects the family at home; in this way, the classroom affects the family. What happens at church can influence the way people act at home, at work, with friends, and in school.

You are a member of a number of different personal systems, and what happens to you in any one of these settings can affect your behavior in any of the others. For instance, Mark comes home angry from a party where he felt his friends were drinking too much and ruining the good time people were having. He kicks the dog, snubs his sister, and amazes his parents by cleaning up his room to work out his anger. What happened in

Mark's peer group affected his behavior in his family; that is, one personal system affected another.

The exosystem, or the larger institutions of society. The term *exosystem* refers to those larger institutions that do not directly and immediately envelop us but do influence us, our personal systems, and the network of our personal systems. Such institutions as governmental agencies, the economic system, the business world, and religious organizations have profound effects on individuals, families, and neighborhoods.

The city government is not an immediate setting; it is one of the large institutions that affects people both directly and indirectly. When the city council votes to raise property taxes in order to provide better garbage removal and sewerage services, the families and neighborhoods in the city are affected in a number of ways. The rise in property taxes will mean that the family will have less money to spend but it may also mean that they will no longer have to live with backed up sewer gases. The improved services may provide jobs for a number of people, and these jobs will be good news for their families. The vote for improved services may also mean that the streets of a neighborhood will be torn up for a while and that traffic and parking will be disrupted. In this example, the larger organization of city government has both direct and indirect effects on individuals and personal systems.

This level of systems also includes interactions among organizations —interactions that can have profound effects on individuals and the personal systems of their lives. For instance, governmental agencies affect the organizations of the business world, the economic community affects welfare agencies, and businesses affect one another by competing for similar markets.

The macrosystem, or culture. The macrosystem, the most pervasive level of systems, refers not to particular individuals, organizations, or institutions but rather to the culture that shapes them. Webster's dictionary defines *culture* as "the customary beliefs, social forms, and material traits of a racial, religious, or social group."

At first glance, it might seem strange to call culture a "system," and yet the "customary beliefs, social forms, and material traits" of a group of people are a set of components that mutually affect or influence one another. Moreover, culture influences all the systems of our lives, just as it influences each of us as individuals. American Peace Corps workers in Botswana soon discover that the ways of southern Africa are not the ways of Chicago or San Francisco and that the way they live and work is affected by the culture in which they find themselves. But it isn't necessary to leave one's country to be influenced by culture. Individuals are so immersed in their own culture that they ordinarily do not advert to the ways in which it affects them and the systems of their lives. The people-in-systems model suggests that it may profit individuals to discover some of the significant ways in which culture affects behavior.

Summary

We have, then, four levels of systems in society:

- personal settings, such as the family, which are the immediate contexts of life;
- the network of personal settings, or the various ways in which personal systems interact with and influence one another;
- the larger organizations and institutions of society and the ways in which they affect one another, individuals, and personal systems; and
- culture, which pervades and influences all levels of systems.

This is one schema that can help us to develop different kinds of working knowledge of the ways in which we participate in systems and are affected by them. In this chapter, we take a more detailed look at the first level, the personal settings of our lives. In Chapter 5 we consider the network of personal settings; in Chapter 6 we examine the larger institutions of society; and in Chapter 7 we examine the ways in which cultural influences pervade all systems.

The First Level—Personal Settings (Microsystems)

A personal system may be defined as the set of relationships between the developing person and the immediate social environment (Bronfenbrenner, 1977b, p. 514). The family and the workplace constitute immediate settings that give rise to a number of interactional possibilities. Other personal systems include voluntary associations (a ski club, the Elks, a senior citizens' club, a company bowling team), self-help groups (Alcoholics Anonymous and Recovery Incorporated), religious organizations (a parish prayer group, a bible study group, the teen club, the social-action committee, a "house church"), school organizations (the classroom, athletic teams, extracurricular activities), peer groups (the neighborhood gang, school chums, friends who party on weekends), and groups in work settings (teams, committees, typing pools). Some of these personal systems affect us more deeply than others. Our families and schools exercise a profound influence on us, and later in life our work settings become major influences in our development. Personal systems constitute the principal context for directly experienced developmental events. The following is a close look at some of these systems.

A Family

In simpler personal settings, such as the family and peer groups, the kinds of mutual influence that take place are easier to grasp than are those in larger systems. If parents are at odds with each other, then this affects the development of their children, who may come to assume that marriage and intimacy are distressing and destructive. Later on, as adolescents and young adults, these same children may eventually face the dilemma of wanting and yet fearing the security and comforts of intimacy.

System interactions have developmental consequences. A father's preference for the younger of two sons can cause rivalry between the boys, affect the relationship of each to the mother, strain the father's relationship with his wife, contribute to a climate of mistrust in the family, and lead to the formation of coalitions. All of this disrupts family living and the pursuit of developmental tasks by family members. For instance, one boy becomes very competitive and the other becomes very passive at a time when it is appropriate to establish cooperative social relations. This disruption can take place without a word being spoken among the members about what is happening to this system called "family."

Families often scapegoat one of their members as the "identified patient" when the family itself has become a problematic system. Over the past decade or two, however, the helping professions have become increasingly aware of the family as a system (Andrews, 1974; Haley, 1976; Satir, 1964; Satir et al., 1975, 1976) and have come to view the family itself, rather than any individual member, as the client. This treatment of the family is certainly an advance over treating individuals in isolation, but family members themselves should begin to see the family as a system. If individual members learn about the family as a highly personal human system, then the probability of their being able to handle family-related problems will increase. Children could come to understand that their actions affect parents and siblings and the way in which they relate to one another. We don't suggest that children should be turned into junior psychologists, but if they learn about the family as a system, they will be prepared to involve themselves in systems outside the home. Young people can both benefit by and suffer from participation in the various personal systems of their lives. It seems reasonable, therefore, to equip them with the ability to deal effectively with systems as early as possible in life.

We do not suggest that the only value in developing a working knowledge of systems is that it enables individuals to cope with the destructive influence systems can have on members; working knowledge of systems opens up creative possibilities beyond coping. Projects that might seem too much for any individual member of a system to accomplish become possible through cooperation with other members. For instance, the mother of a family wants to go back to school to lay the foundation for a career she would like to pursue now that her children are growing up, but she can't go back to school unless the household tasks are distributed, including the task of coordinating the work. Her four children, ranging from age 9 to 16, and her husband will all have to do their share. Sharing in the responsibility of running the household gives the children an opportunity to learn and practice cooperative social relations—one of their developmental tasks—in a work setting rather than just a play setting. If the members of the family see themselves as a unit or a system in which each member, including mother and father, has legitimate developmental needs and wants, they can cooperate in systematically using their resources in programs that can satisfy those needs and wants. On the other hand, each member of the family could attempt to pursue his or her own needs without considering what the others may need and what help they might need to achieve their goals. Some people see this type of excessive individualism and self-centeredness as endemic in our society and as a serious threat to the development of a sense of community.

A Network of Friends

All of us experience a need for affiliation (Schachter, 1959), and practically all of us meet this need in part by developing various sorts of friendships. Friendships are included under what sociologists, following Cooley's (1909) lead, call "primary groups." Primary groups are those in which:

- people react as whole persons rather than players of certain restricted roles;
- communication is relatively personal, deep, and extensive and includes the expression of feelings and the sharing of attitudes and beliefs; and
- personal satisfaction in terms of personal development, security, and well-being is of paramount importance.

Primary groups, such as friendships, are based upon and sustained by primary relations.

One way of looking at friendships is to see each of them as a unique relationship. Another possibility, however, is to consider the *patterning* of these relationships; that is, to see friendships as systems, or networks of friends. You may be involved with a group of people who do things together, in which case the term *system* would apply. However, even if you have friendships with people who do not interact with one another, you have a friendship network that can be one of the most important personal systems in your life.

We don't know how many people pause to take stock of their friendships or how many people try to determine whether their affiliative and social needs are being met. Our guess is that relatively few people evaluate their friendships in any systematic way. However, from early adulthood until the end of life, a person's friendship network is a key developmental system. The lack of close friends was one of the most critical problems to be faced by the Masons, whose life in Appalachia we reviewed briefly.

Leaving friendship to chance can lead to an oppressive loneliness that Gordon (1976) finds pervasive in American society in all age groups and social classes. Many people long for companionship and yet can't seem to find it. "The search for companionship becomes a competitive and desperate undertaking. Relationships have become scarce, like a precious commodity . . . " (p. 309).

Gordon suggests that many people end up lonely because they make the mistake of thinking that their needs can be satisfied by an intimate relationship with one other person; but, instead of becoming the answer, the relationship becomes the problem:

> Our experience with loneliness is that it tends to spiral. We believe the answer to it is an exclusive relationship, and so we give up community, friends, and family in the name of that alliance, only to find that in so doing we have harmed the very relationship we meant to fortify. And then we find that we have neither community nor family nor friends to support us should close relationships falter [p. 308].

The answer to this dilemma lies in learning how to establish a network of relationships of varying degrees of closeness.

Gordon cites the industry that has grown up to handle loneliness as evidence that this problem is not just a superficial phenomenon. "When scarcity occurs . . . there's usually somebody around to exploit it. Relationships have been turned into commodities by a service industry that covers its exploitative intentions with psychological jargon" (p. 309). She goes on to score what she calls the "loneliness business," which includes encounter groups, computer dating, singles bars, gurus, seductive and repressive religious sects, and the like.

Gordon's work is not a carefully designed sociological study; she is a journalist rather than a sociologist. However, she amasses enough data to make her readers stop and consider the role that a network of friends can play in their lives. Most of the research on friendship deals with the topic from a broad philosophical or a narrow psychological point of view. Perhaps it is time now to conduct research on friendship from a systems point of view.

The Workplace

The places where people work can be analyzed on a number of different levels from a systems point of view. The immediate workplace is often one among a number of subsystems in an organization—the accounting department of a large business, the shipping room or the customer service department of a large store. The organization itself may be one of the significant institutions of society, such as the government or a multinational corporation, but it may contain many subsystems that are immediate to individual workers. In this chapter, we consider the work setting as a personal system.

Large organizations affect workers in many indirect but profound ways, whereas the immediate work setting affects them directly every working day of their lives. For instance, a single person working in an office may experience most of his or her social contacts at work. If relationships that are mutually respectful and friendly can be established at work, then these relationships can provide a great deal of support. On the other hand, if friendliness is discouraged, then the workplace can become a human desert. Work settings have habits just as people do, and these habits and rules are so customary that they go unnoticed for the most part and yet may have an overwhelming effect on what members may become, as illustrated in this statement by a working-class man about his job:

> "A lot of times I hate to go down there. I'm cooped up and hemmed in. I feel like I'm enclosed in a building forty hours a week, sometimes more. It seems like all there is to life is to go down there and work, collect your paycheck, pay your bills, and get further in debt. It doesn't seem like the circle ever ends. Every day it's the same thing; every week it's the same thing; every month it's the same thing" [Rubin, 1976, p. 158].

Many people do not have careers; they have jobs. And even those who do have careers often come to see them as merely jobs. For many people, work is a grinding process that provides little, if any, satisfaction (Rubin, 1976; Terkel, 1974). Humanization of the workplace is becoming an issue in our society (Appley & Winder, 1977; Harman, 1977; Heisler & Houck, 1977; Morrow & Thayer, 1977; Trist, 1977), but work, for many, is still a chore that provides little satisfaction. Working as a coal miner is a grinding reality under the best of conditions. Still, miners can, because of their relationships with their coworkers, experience their work settings as beneficial personal systems. This experience does not eliminate the drudgery from their work, but it can be an important factor in its humanization. Of course, relationships with coworkers aren't substitutes for the organizational and institutional changes that will lead to a more radical humanization of the workplace, but these relationships are significant.

Since people spend so much of their lives in their place of work, they should develop the ability to assess the workplace as a personal system, including:

- how the job setting functions as a social system;
- what impact it has on their lives; and
- how the influences of the job interact with developmental stages and tasks.

To return to the example of the Masons, Cindy found that the rural school in which she was teaching offered her very little as a social system. The unresponsiveness of the children and the fact that she had a much wider range of interests than most of the other teachers were challenges she had to face. She had to learn a great deal about a new culture, and she was forced to be inventive in attempting to get through to the children, but she felt that she received relatively little in return. Her workplace provided a great deal of challenge, but it provided little support. Careerwise, she felt that she was at a dead end.

Tom, on the other hand, was invigorated by his work. His coworkers were likable and friendly, and the people for whom he provided health care came to appreciate him very much. He did not establish close friendships at work, but the relationships there did provide him with a great deal of support. This support, coupled with the fact that he was learning a great deal, meant that he found his workplace, especially during the first two years of his stay, to be a challenging personal system. It was not the workplace as a personal system that eventually made Tom reconsider his commitment but rather the politics of medical-care delivery in the state.

Tom Mason was fortunate in that his job was valued and interesting. However, for many people, work consists of a small number of tasks performed over and over again. The developmental impact of a repetitive task differs from person to person and depends upon a host of interacting variables. If individuals have the knowledge and skills that are needed to assess the impact that work systems have on their lives, then they will be in a better position to affect their work settings or to cope with them when nothing can be done immediately to change them. If we want to gain greater control over our lives, then we need to know what forces are shaping them. A knowledge of the workplace is an important part of the total working knowledge of the systems that affect our lives.

Voluntary Associations

Berger and Neuhaus (1977) define a voluntary association as "a body of people who have voluntarily organized themselves in pursuit of particular goals" (p. 34). They exclude business corporations and other primarily economic organizations. A voluntary association is a "free association of people for some collective purpose" (p. 34). Included in this definition are stamp clubs, community councils, orchestras, local chapters of Alcoholics Anonymous, athletic teams, yoga groups, and the like.

Some people satisfy many of their affiliative and social needs through membership in voluntary associations. In *The Consul's File*, a group of short stories about life in a Malaysian provincial town as seen through the eyes of the American consul, Paul Theroux (1977) describes voluntary associations almost taking over the social life of the town:

> Ayer Hitam was full of clubs—Chinese clan associations, secret societies, communist cells, Indian sports clubs, the South Malaysia Pineapple Growers' Association, the Legion of Mary, the Methodist Ramblers; and I was in one myself. No one lived in the town, really; people just went to club meetings there [p. 123].

Voluntary associations serve many purposes. One of the obvious advantages of belonging to voluntary associations is that within them you can find people with whom you would like to develop closer friendships. Berger and Neuhaus suggest that voluntary organizations perform a political function by schooling their members in democratic procedures:

At least since de Tocqueville, the importance of voluntary associations in American democracy has been widely recognized. Voluntarism has flourished in America more than in any other Western society and it is reasonable to believe this may have something to do with American political institutions. Associations create statutes, elect officers, debate, vote courses of action, and otherwise serve as schools for democracy. However trivial, wrongheaded, or bizarre we may think the purpose of some associations to be, they nonetheless perform this vital function [p. 34].

Voluntary associations affect the lives and the development of their members. It may be that people are more open to the influence of associations that they have joined freely than they are at work or in the family. Churches and the great variety of clubs, committees, councils, task forces, and other groupings they contain are examples of important voluntary associations.

Conclusion

One way in which individuals can take stock of their involvement in personal settings is to consider the roles that arise as a result of membership in systems. Some of the roles that emerge as a result of participation in personal systems are mother, father, daughter, son, friend, neighbor, volunteer, administrator, teacher, student, and worker. The term *role* refers to a set of expectations concerning the behavior of someone in a given position and to the actual behavior of the person occupying the position. As social theorists suggest, people's roles within a social network account for much of their behavior. When someone assumes a certain role because of membership in a system, the members of that system apply social pressure on that person to engage in the behavior specified by that role.

Satisfaction or dissatisfaction with roles that arise from membership in personal systems are indications of the kind of influences that these systems have on their members. If individuals feel role "overload"—that is, if one of their roles consumes too much of their time and energy—or if they feel role dissatisfaction, then they should examine what is happening between themselves and the particular personal system in which they assume this role. Finally, if the members of a system begin to complain about an individual's behavior, then that individual should examine the member-system relationship. For instance, if patients begin to complain about the behavior of a volunteer in a hospital, then the supervisor of volunteers and that individual need to examine what is happening from the viewpoint of the members of that system.

We have considered the family, friendships, the work setting, and voluntary associations as examples of personal systems that envelop individuals and directly and immediately affect their lives and their development. Each of these personal systems interacts with and is affected by the other systems of an individual's life; this network of interacting and mutually influencing systems comprises the mesosystem, which is examined in Chapter 5.

Chapter 4: Additional Resources

Andrews, E. *The emotionally disturbed family and some gratifying alternatives.* New York: Aronson, 1974. (See Introduction, Chapters 1–4, Section V introduction, Chapters 18–21.)

Bronfenbrenner, U. Toward an experimental ecology of human development. *American Psychologist*, 1977b, 513–531.

Giroux, H., & Penna, A. Social relations in the classroom: The dialectic of the hidden curriculum. *Edcentric*, 1977, *40–41*, 39–46.

Satir, V. *Peoplemaking.* Palo Alto, Calif.: Science and Behavior Books, 1972.

5

The Social Context of Human Development— Level II: The Network of Personal Settings

In each person's life there is a *network* of interacting personal systems that Bronfenbrenner (1977b) calls the *mesosystem*. This network stands between personal systems and larger institutions and organizations. Figure 5-1 is a portrayal of a network of personal systems.

As can be seen in Figure 5-2, the world becomes more complex as we move from interactions *within* personal systems to interactions *between* and *among* such systems. Although Figure 5-2 is incomplete, it helps us to visualize the complexity that arises from the interactions among a variety of personal systems. There are 15 possible two-way interactions illustrated in the figure, and if more than two systems interact at the same time, the number of interactional possibilities rises sharply.

If we take the family as an example, we can ask in what ways it is influenced by the friendships that each of its members develops, by the schools the children attend, by the different church organizations in which family members are involved, by participation in a variety of other voluntary associations such as clubs and gangs and teams, and by the variety of people and systems that make up the neighborhood. For instance, if the teenage children participate in a street gang, it can be expected that what they learn on the streets will affect the way in which they participate in the life of the family. We can also examine the ways in which the family affects the systems to which its members belong. The following examples

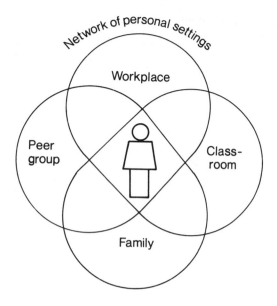

Figure 5-1.
The Developing Person in Context
Level II: The Network of Personal Settings.

will give you a clearer picture of interactions between systems and their importance for both individual and system development.

Some Examples of System/System Interaction: Personal Settings

In the following examples, we consider system/system interactions from the point of view of their impact on human development. These examples include the interactions that take place between marriage and work, family and school, self-help group and family, and halfway house and neighborhood.

Marriage/Work

At home and at work, the Greys are not merely individuals; they are members of systems that influence one another. A faltering or troubled marriage can cause the quality of their work to suffer, whereas an engaging and productive family life affects attitudes toward work, as well as performance, in a positive way. The workplace affects their personal life as well. Lessor (1971) illustrates the demands that are made of a working

	Peer group	Classroom	Church group	Teenage club	Neighborhood
Family	1.	2.	3.	4.	5.
	Peer group	6.		7.	8.	9.
		Classroom	10.	11.	12.
			Church group	13.	14.
				Teenage club	15.

Figure 5-2.
An Interaction Matrix of Personal Settings.

individual in the course of a day and the effects that these demands have on the individual's marriage.

> When we wake up in the morning and are fresh, we must go immediately to work. Then when the employer has wrung every bit of usefulness out of us, we are pushed onto a crowded bus or thrown onto a tangled expressway and told to fight our way home. Once there, at the low point of our energy, we pick up with our marriage [p. 8].

Investigations have shown that people can face boring jobs serenely and do them competently if some of the other systems of life are rewarding (see Blauner, 1964). For instance, if John Smith has an engaging family life and feels productive in his involvements in his church, he can put up with a dull job.

Family/School

The Johnsons have two boys in primary school who have learned little about discipline or self-management at home. They are loud, noisy, and disruptive in their respective classrooms, not even realizing the impact of their behavior. The Johnson family, then, has a negative impact on the classroom. The problem is not simply an individual problem; it is a problem that involves systems.

The following example illustrates how a school system can directly affect a family system. After learning assertive communication at school, Sally Brown begins to speak up for her rights without infringing on the rights of others. She does quite well in the classroom situation; however, when she begins to talk assertively at home, her father reacts with displays of anger and pouting withdrawal. Mrs. Brown, though at first startled by Sally's assertiveness, appreciates and reinforces it. She, too, becomes less compliant. Through Sally, the classroom has had positive as well as negative impact on the Brown family as a system.

Peer Self-Help Group/Family

In the following example, we consider the peer self-help group as a personal system that affects and is affected by the events in other personal systems.

Mrs. Montini is an alcoholic, but she refuses to admit it or to do anything about it. Her husband and children stay away from home as much as possible, because it is such a dismal place. A minister suggests that Mr. Montini and the children attend sessions for the families of alcoholics. They go to the meetings, grow closer together in mutual support, and learn how to avoid reinforcing Mrs. Montini's disruptive behavior without punishing her. Mrs. Montini eventually softens, admits her problem, attends the meetings with the rest of her family, and begins to talk about the frustrations of her life. This and other successful outcomes encourage the volunteer staff members who organize the meetings to continue and expand their program. The family system, then, has had a positive effect on the self-help group, while the self-help group has literally saved the Montini family as a system.

Experts are currently debating whether the family as a social system is losing ground (Bronfenbrenner, 1977a) or holding its own and reconsolidating itself (Bane, 1976) in the face of rapid social change. Both points of view agree that families are undergoing changes in structure that affect the functioning of the family system. Both points of view also agree that families are being bombarded by influences from other systems in society and cannot help but be molded by these influences. We suggest that the family that is aware of these influences is in a better position to cope with them. In this chapter, we are considering influences from other personal systems. In Chapter 6, we consider the influence that larger systems and the culture itself have on families and other personal systems.

Halfway House/Neighborhood

The members of a city mental-health agency, who wish to establish a halfway house for parolees, fear that their proposal will be rejected by people who are living in the neighborhood and so establish the halfway house without consulting the residents. Those who live in the neighborhood resent the fact that the members of the agency did not discuss their project with them before moving ahead with it. As a result, the staff and residents find themselves being extremely cautious in their behavior in the neighborhood. They feel unwelcome and restricted. The persisting uneasiness continues to haunt both halfway house and neighborhood.

In this case, a good idea goes awry because those promoting the halfway house fail to handle intersystem realities effectively. It would probably have been better to work with representatives of the neighborhood in establishing the house, even if this meant choosing a different neighborhood where the house would at least be tolerated, if not openly accepted and promoted. Failure to assess mutual influence among personal systems can lead to unfortunate consequences.

Development as a Result of Membership in Systems

Human beings are studied extensively in a variety of environments, but there are very few studies in which development is examined as a function of membership in different systems.

> In the traditional research model, behavior and development are investigated in one setting at a time without regard to possible interdependencies between settings. An ecological approach invites consideration of the joint impact of two or more settings or their elements. This is the requirement, whenever possible, of analyzing *interaction between settings* [Bronfenbrenner, 1977b, p. 523].

Admittedly, the effects of the interactions between systems on development are much more difficult to study, but they are potential sources of significant learning. For example, a group of investigators from the department of pediatrics at Case Western Reserve University set out to explore mother/child contact immediately after birth (Hales, 1977; Kennell et al., 1974; Klaus, Kennell, Plumb, & Zeuhlke, 1970; Klaus et al., 1972; Ringler, Kennell, Jarvella, Navojosky, & Klaus, 1975). They modified established hospital procedures in order to permit mothers to have their naked infants with them for about an hour shortly after delivery and for several hours daily after that. In the control group, mothers and infants experienced regular hospital procedure: "a glance at their baby shortly after birth, a short visit six to twelve hours after birth for identification purposes, and then twenty to thirty-minute visits for feeding every four hours during the day" Kennell et al., 1974, p. 173). Bronfenbrenner (1977b) summarizes the results of these experiments.

> The reported results of these experiments strain the credulity of the reader. One month after the brief extended contact at birth, the mothers in the experimental group were more attentive and affectionate toward their babies

and more solicitous about their welfare (Klaus and others, 1972). Not only were these differences still in evidence at the end of the first year, but two years later, the mothers, in speaking to their children, used significantly more questions, adjectives . . . and fewer commands and content words than did the control mothers [p. 519].

Hales (1977) replicated the study with a larger sample in a different cultural context (Guatemala). He modified the experiment by having one group of mothers make physical contact for 45 minutes with the newly born immediately after delivery and by delaying this contact for twelve hours in the case of a second group of mothers. Only mothers in the immediate contact group were affected.

In this experiment, we see that altered behavior within a personal system (mother/child) has positive developmental consequences. Moreover, the hospital as a system changed its behavior toward the mother/child dyad and the changed interaction between these two personal systems led to positive developmental results. This demonstrates positive developmental outcomes from altered interactions between systems. This study wasn't set up as an ecological experiment—that is, an experiment across rather than within systems—but it does demonstrate the potential for such investigations. This kind of experimentation will increase in frequency when researchers begin to think more consistently in terms of systems and interaction between systems. The possibilities for such ecological investigations across the entire life span are endless.

Roles in the Network of Personal Settings

As we saw in Chapter 4, membership in personal systems leads to certain roles and role expectations. At times, interactions among personal systems lead to *role collision* (Hare, 1962). For instance, Mrs. Clark begins to feel pulled apart by her roles as mother, as wife, and as chairperson of the social-action committee at her church. She now experiences role collision because she has allowed herself to become the victim of role transition. The social-action committee began as a discussion group and required relatively little of her time; it has evolved, however, into an action group with a variety of programs. As Mrs. Clark spends more and more of her time coordinating the activities of the social-action committee at her church, her roles as wife and mother begin to collide with her role as volunteer worker. Tensions arise in her family as well as in her church group, and, since these tensions affect her behavior in both systems, they also affect the systems themselves. Mrs. Clark would benefit from an ability to analyze her behavior and her tensions in relation to the roles she has assumed. This analysis won't solve her problems, but it will enable her to clarify them, and such clarification is the first step in the problem-solving process.

In a more positive vein, consider the case of Ted Parker, who benefits from role compatibility. He teaches organizational theory and practice at an urban university and is involved with his local church. From talks with the pastor and other church members, he comes to realize that his expertise is useful for the church. He becomes a consultant in the reorganization of the parish and watches organizational theory at work in the church setting. His role as volunteer and his role as teacher complement each other, and both his classroom and the church system develop as a result of this role compatibility. His wife, as a church member, becomes involved with him in new ways and this adds to the fullness of their marriage.

Examining the roles played in personal systems is one way of developing a working knowledge of the network of personal systems. In Chapter 10, we suggest a roles-assessment exercise you can use to develop a working knowledge of how your personal systems interact and how you are affected by this interaction.

Ecological Transitions

Life abounds with what Bronfenbrenner (1977b) calls *ecological transitions*. Examples of such transitions are: moving away from home, graduating from school, starting a career, changing careers, getting married, becoming a family with the advent of a first child, the entrance of a child into school, moving to a new town, divorce, and retirement. Since such transitions often involve relationships between systems, we suggest that people might make these transitions more smoothly by acquiring a working knowledge of the new system together with its role expectations and of some of the principal ways in which the new system might interact with the old. For instance, when two people get married, they both come trailing remnants of influence from their respective families. These norms, values, and ways of acting necessarily influence their relationship. Similarly, later on, when they visit their families, they can bring new ideas, norms, values, and ways of acting that are peculiar to their own marriage. These can affect their families in a variety of ways. If wife and husband have learned to think contextually in terms of the mutual influence of systems, they will be better prepared to handle both their relationship to each other and their relationships with their families. According to Bronfenbrenner (1977b), developmental research is impoverished because of this lack of contextual focus:

> The almost exclusive focus of past research (particularly in developmental psychology) on the properties of the individual with little reference to context has generated a curiously broken trajectory of knowledge that has a brave beginning, a sad ending, and an empty middle [p. 525].

What Bronfenbrenner says about ecological research also applies to the social/psychological education and life-skills training advocated in this book; they, too, need a contextual or systems focus.

Linkage between Personal Settings

The idealization of independent individual action is fictional if it ignores system/system interaction. Murrell (1973), who sees individuals as "linking pins" between systems, believes that people should think about themselves as members of systems as an antidote to an individual-oriented conception of the world.

> It is not easy to "get into" the idea that as individuals we are as we are partly because of the forces in our social systems. Our culture constantly emphasizes the individual dominating his environment. Our television heroes conquer all through direct (often violent) independent action. . . . We boast of our frontier forebears who "conquered" the wilderness. . . . We have "conquered" space by going to the moon. . . .
>
> This cultural emphasis on the individual is good to the degree that we value each and every person. . . . The idealization of independent individual action is fictional if it ignores individual–system *interaction* [p. 25].[1]

If the two systems being linked are opposed in any way, their opposition puts the individual under pressure. On the other hand, if the two systems are well suited to each other, the individual can experience great rewards. Murrell cites opposition, enriching accommodation, and compatibility as three conditions that may exist between systems and illustrates them in the following examples.

First, an example of opposition:

> If, for example, the classroom demands strict conformity, quietness, neatness, and a restriction of opinion, and rewards these behaviors; yet the child's family encourages and rewards loud and unconventional expression, independence of opinion, and messes . . . that child is in a bind [p. 63].

Next, an example of cooperation:

> If a classroom expects and rewards good reading ability, high verbal comprehension, and strong motivation for abstract reinforcements (grades); and if the child's family is one in which reading is a frequent and high status activity, where vocabulary level of the parents is high, and where they reward the grades with large amounts of interpersonal attention and praise . . . that child is in good shape [pp. 63–64].

Finally, an example of mere compatibility:

> If the classroom makes no demands and has no expectations regarding religious beliefs, and if the child's family maintains strong and conventional religious beliefs and engages in conventional religious behaviors, there is no effect on the child [p. 65].

---

[1]This and all other quotations and material from this source are from *Community Psychology and Social Systems*, by S. Murrell. Copyright 1973 by Human Sciences Press. Reprinted by permission.

"Linking pins" are not merely people who are affected because of multiple membership in various systems; they are agents of influence and change in these systems. Children in the classroom, for example, represent the values and desires of their parents and, therefore, tend to modify the educational approach of the faculty of a school.

The link between the school and the family is usually the child, but it need not be only the child. Schools would probably respond more to family needs if the family members involved themselves more directly in the school through discussion with the school's principal or school-board members. A well organized and effectively functioning PTA could be the vehicle of this kind of intervention. Parents would need both interpersonal (Chapter 3) and systems-involvement skills (Chapter 8) in order to involve themselves effectively with the school system.

Substantive involvement in systems on the part of "linking pins" increases the probability that the systems will affect one another. For example, a parochial school in an inner-city area accepted students without regard to religious affiliation on the condition that the parents of the students actively participate in the school. The parents were asked to volunteer a certain amount of time each month, involving themselves in one or more of the school's programs. The contributed services of the parents helped the school financially; in fact, it is doubtful whether the school could have kept its doors open without their help. But, more importantly, as a result of the interaction between the school and the students' families, the school became a personal system for the parents as well as their children.

Building linkages between personal systems is one way of assuring us that we are living our lives in a *community* of systems rather than in a series of disparate subsystems. Families can become involved in schools, homes can be the meeting places of neighborhood committees, volunteer associations can offer services to schools, churches, and families and recruit volunteers through these systems. We do not envision a utopia where all personal systems are linked in harmony, but we do maintain that people need skills to construct necessary linkages among the systems of their lives.

The School as an Example of a Network of Personal Settings

It is helpful to see the school as a mesosystem itself; that is, as a network of personal settings in which relationships and the sources of influence on individuals are more complex than those of a personal system such as the family. Figure 5-3 is an illustration of some of the possible interactions that take place in a school. However, this diagram only begins to illustrate the complexity of possible interactions; it doesn't indicate the possibility of one administrator influencing another, one teacher influencing another, and so forth. Figure 5-4 begins to take this complexity into consideration.

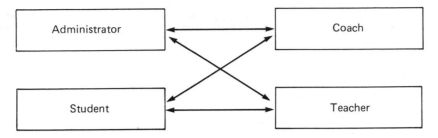

Figure 5-3

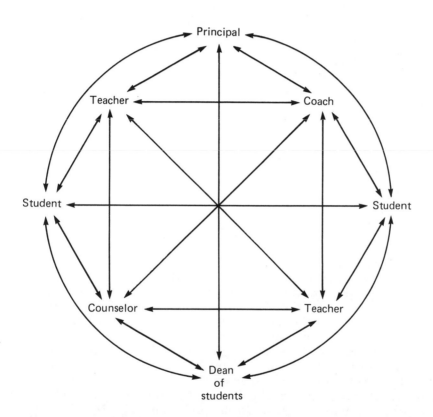

Figure 5-4

As complex as Figure 5-4 is, it is still incomplete. It is possible for each person portrayed in the diagram to interact with seven others in the diagram, but only five of these possibilities are illustrated. Furthermore, the groups in a school setting interact with one another and influence one another. This interaction among groups is illustrated in Figure 5-5.

We have not included all possible subsystems in Figure 5-5. We could add each classroom, the math club, various parents' clubs, and the like.

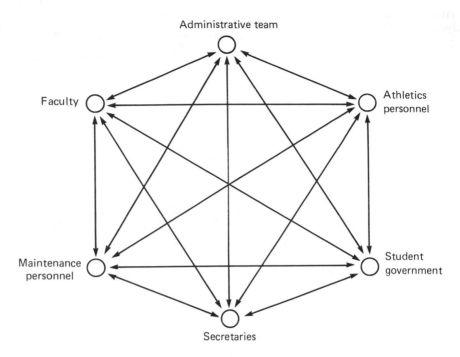

Figure 5-5

These groups can constitute systems in their own right, and individuals are affected by the interactions taking place among the groups or systems to which they belong. Students usually feel the impact of the classroom in more direct and immediate ways than they feel the impact of the administrative team, but the influence of the latter is profound.

Even though students principally experience a school through the subgroupings in which they participate, such as classrooms, teams, and clubs, we believe that they would benefit by the acquisition of a working knowledge of the school system itself. This knowledge could help them to develop their view of the world beyond the smaller personal systems of their lives and help them to think of the wider environment in systems terms. How ready are schools to expose themselves as systems to students so that students can use the school as a laboratory in which to learn about and experiment with systems? Giroux and Penna (1977) feel that too few schools are ready for such innovation in education.

If we take into consideration all possible individual and group mutual-influence possibilities in the school, the total array is bewildering. However, no one individual is expected to have a full and complete understanding of any system in all its detail. Students and coaches interact on a daily basis, but the administrative team does not have to know the details of these day-to-day interactions. However, we believe that all the members of a complex system could develop a working knowledge of that system that would enable them to pursue their goals more effectively, integrate what they do with what other members of the system do, cope with the dysfunctions within the system, contribute to the growth of the system through support and challenge, and help the system change in ways that benefit all the members. For example, the kind of working knowledge an administrator needs differs from the kind of working knowledge a student needs. But we believe that a working knowledge of the school as a system, however it might differ for the two, could benefit both administrator and student alike. In Chapter 6, we offer some suggestions on how to develop a working knowledge of relatively complex systems.

The Neighborhood as a Network of Personal Settings

Berger and Neuhaus (1977) suggest that the neighborhood is a personal system, and they include it in their consideration of the "mediating structures" that help people to cope with larger organizations and institutions. In their view, the neighborhood has a "private face" (the resident feels at home in his or her neighborhood) and a "public face" (it is a mediating structure between the individual and the larger city). However, since the neighborhood often includes families, work settings, schools, peer groups, and other personal systems, it has a "mesosystem" quality; that is, it is itself a network of personal systems.

For most people, there is something very personal about a neighborhood; however, this does not mean that every neighborhood must have a small-town or village flavor in order to be a good neighborhood. Berger and Neuhaus explain the functions of various kinds of neighborhoods in the following way:

> It is not necessarily true that a vital neighborhood is one that supplies a strong sense of social cohesion or reinforces personal identity with the group. In fact, many people want neighborhoods where free choice in association and even anonymity are cherished. That kind of neighborhood, usually urban, is no less a neighborhood for its lack of social cohesion. Cohesion exacts its price in loss of personal freedom; freedom may be paid for in the coin of alienation and loneliness. One pays the price for the neighborhood of one's choice. . . . It is not possible to create the benefits of each kind of neighborhood in every neighborhood. One cannot devise a compromise between the cohesion of a New England small town and the anonymity of the East Village without destroying both options [Berger & Neuhaus, 1977, pp. 9–10].[2]

The implication here is that it can be quite useful to understand the kind of neighborhood in which one lives or into which one intends to move. As a help to this, Warren and Warren (1977) have devised a taxonomy for understanding different kinds of neighborhoods and the degrees of cohesion that characterize each. For example, a woman who as-

[2]This and all other quotations from this source are from *To Empower People: The Role of Mediating Structures in Public Policy*, by P. L. Berger and R. H. Neuhaus. Copyright © 1977 by the American Enterprise Institute for Public Policy Research.

sumed it would be easy to make friends in a very large city moved to Chicago and chose to live in a neighborhood in which, unknown to her, anonymity, rather than social cohesion, was normative. Her loneliness became intolerable. There were people everywhere, and yet she failed to find friends. This woman did not have a working knowledge of the neighborhood into which she moved, and this lack of knowledge led to her loneliness. The neighborhood did have immediate settings, such as the church and university groups and classrooms, but she did not think of the neighborhood as a network of personal systems and did not know how to plug into them. We suggest that a working knowledge of systems makes them less mysterious and impenetrable and therefore increases our ability to make them work for us instead of against us. It was unfortunate that this woman could not make the neighborhood work for her. As Berger and Neuhaus note: "In a large city almost everyone is an outsider by definition. To put it another way, in the world of urban emigrés there are enough little worlds so that everyone can be an insider somewhere" (p. 10). This woman left Chicago without finding a niche for herself. Even though she did not discover it, there is something personal even about a neighborhood where anonymity is cherished.

A neighborhood acts as a buffer between its particular network of personal systems and the large impersonal city. In this regard, the neighborhood is being rediscovered in many cities. Local councils are being formed to ensure that neighborhoods are safe, clean places to live and that decent housing and city services are made available to the residents. The neighborhood, at its best, envelops its personal subsystems benignly; it is a community rather than an organization. However, neighborhoods can also be destructive environments. Hope lies in the fact that society is able to help neighborhoods to become constructive networks of immediate settings and to help the individuals of the neighborhood to cope more effectively with the larger units of society.

If the people of a neighborhood are to organize themselves successfully, they need to develop a working knowledge of the neighborhood as a system and acquire the skills and tools of organizing (Warren & Warren, 1977). Morris and Hess (1975) see many, if not most, neighborhoods as similar to "underdeveloped" nations: "They now suffer from aspects of imperialism similar to those of the third-world countries: outside intervention in local affairs" (p. 14). The answer is not to make neighborhoods bastions of political power, but to empower them to do what they do best—"making life livable and resolving problems which have remained untouched by the movement toward huge, dehumanized scale in social organization" (Morris & Hess, 1975, p. 5).

Personal Settings as Mediating Structures

A consideration of personal systems and networks of personal systems as mediating structures (Berger & Neuhaus, 1977) can prepare us to move from this second level to the third level of systems—that is, to the larger organizations and institutions of life. Berger and Neuhaus define *mediating structures* as "those institutions standing between the individual in his private life and the large institutions of public life" (p. 2). According to Berger and Neuhaus, these larger institutions include the modern state itself, "the large economic conglomerates of capitalist enterprise, big labor, and the growing bureaucracies that administer wide sectors of the society, such as education and the organized professions" (p. 2).

Berger and Neuhaus prize personal systems and maintain that they serve as buffers between public life, including the demands of large institutions such as government, and private life, which they see as "a curious preserve left over by the large institutions and in which individuals carry on a bewildering variety of activities with only fragile institutional support" (p. 2). People view many of the demands of large institutions as malignant, and they need personal systems to act as buffers. According to Berger and Neuhaus, personal systems "have a private face, giving private life a measure of stability, and they have a public face, transferring meaning and value" to large institutions and organizations. They maintain that, if personal systems were given more recognition and support in public policy, then individuals would be more at home in society and the political order itself would benefit. Berger and Neuhaus want personal systems to remain the value-generating and value-maintaining agencies of society. If these functions relating to values are abdicated by personal systems, then they will be taken over by large institutions, especially the state. A democratic society sees personal systems as essential to its democratic purposes, protects and fosters the development of personal systems, and uses these systems whenever possible for the realization of social purposes.

We can do more than consider our networks of personal systems as buffers between ourselves and potentially destructive influences from the larger institutions and organizations of society. The immediate settings of life are the places where we experience developmental events and processes most forcefully. Since these personal systems serve the developmental needs of individuals most directly, it is ultimately to the advantage of society to do whatever it can to promote the development and welfare of personal systems as well as networks of personal systems.

Conclusion

We have been considering personal systems mainly from a personal point of view. Berger and Neuhaus, on the other hand, consider these systems mainly from a *social* point of view. They briefly examine the social anatomy of these systems, showing how large institutions of society impinge on them, and they suggest ways in which personal systems might be supported so that they can make a contribution both to the human development of individuals and to the common good.

According to our thesis, once people develop a working knowledge of the personal systems of their lives and the skills needed to participate actively in them, they will be ready to develop a working knowledge of the network of these systems and the higher-order skills they need to participate actively in this network. This means, among other things, coming to terms with their roles as "linking pins" and discovering and understanding the ways in which one personal system touches and influences another. This education and training should relate to actual systems rather than to hypothetical cases.

Ideally, all the major personal systems of peoples' lives would be involved in this education/training process. For instance, the notion of "linking pin" would be discussed at home, at church, and at school. And all of these systems would provide training in the kinds of systems-involvement skills that would enable people as "linking pins" to take an active stance toward the settings that shape their lives. We do not want to give the impression that this task is an easy one, but we do claim that many opportunities to implement such education and training programs already exist. Mere awareness of the system realities of life won't change individuals or institutions, but awareness is an important first step. Nor do we want to underestimate the power that institutions of society have over individuals, personal systems, and the various networks of personal systems. In Chapter 6, then, we turn our attention to the network of the larger organizations and institutions of society.

Chapter 5: Additional Resources

Berger, P., & Neuhaus, R. *To empower people: The role of mediating structures in public policy*. Washington, D. C.: American Enterprise Institute for Public Policy Research, 1977.

Keniston, K. *All our children: The American family under pressure*. New York: Harcourt, Brace, Jovanovich, 1977. (See Introduction and Chapters 1–5 and 10.)

Litwak, D., & Meyer, M. *School, family, and neighborhood*. New York: Columbia University Press, 1974.

Murrell, S. *Community psychology and social systems*. New York: Behavioral Publications, 1973. (See Chapters 2, 3 [pp. 51–68], and 5.)

Ryan, C. *The open partnership: Equality in running the schools*. New York: McGraw-Hill, 1976.

6

The Social Context
of Human Development—
Level III:
The Larger Institutions
of Society

Life in modern industrialized societies is not as simple as might be indicated by the analysis of systems we have made thus far. We and the personal systems to which we belong are influenced every day in many different ways by the larger institutions of our society, including the media, government, the economic system, organized professions, and the like. A complete picture of our lives has to take these larger institutions into consideration. Turk (1977) describes the pervasive influence of these institutions.

> Human life has become organizational life. The fortunes, both good and ill, of modern populations depend on schools, churches, gangs, fire departments, governments, labor unions, courts, cartels, consulates, armies, hotels, political parties, television networks, football teams, insurgent groups, airlines, and countless other associations. The actions and interactions of organizations such as these form the affairs of cities, nations, and still larger social units—and even constitute their identities.
>
> Interorganizational relations are everywhere in evidence. Corporations forge ties with banks, supply houses, and law firms; banks are linked to one another by clearing houses; armies establish liaison with one another; professional societies grant or withhold support of educational enterprises; revolutionary groups form alliances; and federal agencies concur with or oppose organizations from society's several institutional sectors. Moreover, organiza-

tions band into coalitions, federations, councils, congresses, and chambers. Indeed, granted the prevalent belief among social scientists that associations are the ubiquitous form of urban industrial or postindustrial society, the attempt seems warranted to view such a society or any one of its major subdivisions as a patterned aggregate of organizations [pp. 1–2].[1]

Because of the complexity of the interactions among large organizations, it is impossible for individuals to understand them completely. A more practical approach is to ask ourselves how we as individuals can acquire a working knowledge of large systems that fulfills the requirements for useful working models—complex enough to be real, yet simple enough to be useful. This working knowledge is akin to what the scientist is looking for: "The simplest system of thought which will bind together the observed facts" (Einstein, 1932, p. 138).

The Larger Institutions of Society

Bronfenbrenner (1977b) calls the larger social systems of life the *exosystem*; this includes systems that have a great impact on us but do not enfold us the way our personal settings do. The Greek word *exo* means *outside*, as in the word *exotic*, which refers to what is outside our normal experience. The structures of the exosystem "do not themselves contain the developing person but impinge upon or encompass the immediate settings in which that person is found, and thereby influence, delimit, or even determine what goes on there. These structures include the major institutions of the society . . . as they operate at a concrete local level" (p. 515). For example, the report of a Carnegie commission that deals with child development in the United States suggests that the fundamental factor affecting the stability of a family is not a psychological but an economic, or exosystemic, one—namely, stable employment opportunities for family heads. (See Keniston, 1977.) Figure 6-1 depicts the larger institutions as they impinge upon and affect an individual and the personal settings of his or her life.

The institutional world is complex and confusing, with criss-crossing lines of influence that are difficult to discover and to trace. Bronfenbrenner gives us a brief picture of the institutions and events that make up this confusion, and then suggests that investigation is needed concerning the relationship between this confusing world and human development. "Research on the ecology of human development requires investigations that go beyond the immediate settings containing the person to examine the larger contexts, both formal and informal, that affect events within the immediate setting" (p. 527).

While Bronfenbrenner places emphasis on research, our stress is on

[1]This and all other quotations from this source are from *Organizations in Modern Life*, by H. Turk. Copyright 1977 by Jossey-Bass, Inc., Publishers. Reprinted by permission.

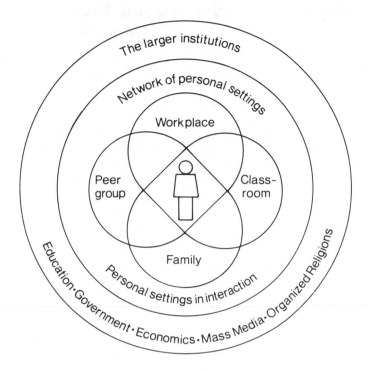

Figure 6-1.
The Developing Person in Context
Level III: The Larger Institutions

working knowledge. In order to acquire a full working knowledge of the ecology of human development, it is necessary to look beyond our immediate personal settings and even beyond the interactions between these settings. Instilling a working knowledge of systems includes alerting members of personal systems to aspects of the larger environment that may have critical effects on human beings and personal systems. Because of the complexity of these institutions, we suggest that people begin to acquire a working knowledge of them early in life, that they acquire this knowledge systematically and gradually, and that they use actual experiences of the exosystemic world as the starting point of such learning.

The difference between knowledge for understanding and working knowledge is illustrated by the comment of a Russian psychologist on the difference between U.S. and Russian research in child development: "It seems to me that American researchers are constantly seeking to explain how the child came to be what he is; we in the USSR are striving to discover . . . how he can become what he not yet is" (Bronfenbrenner, 1977b, p. 528). Working knowledge helps people to understand their lives; but more than that, it helps them to control and give direction to their lives.

The Larger Social-Systems Context of Our Lives—an Example

We can use what we have learned about systems thus far to analyze the larger systems context of our lives, thereby developing a working knowledge of these systems. In Chapter 5 we analyzed a school setting; we will now analyze a work setting and its context.

John Jencius works at Acme Farm Machinery, Inc., a company that manufactures and sells farm machinery both here and abroad. He works in the customer-service department of one of the branch offices located next to one of the manufacturing plants. His department is a personal setting where some of his social needs are met. What happens at home, with his friends, and at church (other personal settings) affects his mode of participation at work. That is, the kind of mutual influence that characterizes the network of personal settings is part and parcel of John's life in his immediate work setting.

The company for which John works contains in miniature a network of personal settings and the mutual influence that characterizes this type of network. Acme Farm has a number of departments that interact and influence one another in many ways. In fact, John, as a member of the customer-service department, has a front-row seat for some of these interactions. When a customer calls to check on delivery of a product that has been ordered, John deals with both sales and production and at times mediates the interactions between the two. All the corporate events, the economic condition of the company, and the acts of management are part of the network of subsettings within the corporation; and all of these systems, directly or indirectly, affect both customer service and John Jencius.

Finally, Acme Farm deals with the institutions and organizations that enfold it, and these organizations affect company ideology and company values. If Acme Farm is trying to capture a large share of the national and international market, then the government's taxation and trade policies have a direct impact on its success. Educational and economic opportunities in the surrounding community have an impact on Acme personnel. The religious institutions of the community may have very significant effects on the attitudes and behavior of Acme customers and personnel. The mass media affect the business practices of the company as well as the employees and their families. Notice that all three levels of systems and systems interaction discussed thus far are present in John's life as an Acme employee, and this portrayal of interaction gives us an idea of the influences that both limit and support his development as a person.

An analysis similar to the one we have just made of John Jencius and his occupational setting can be made of any of the larger systems to which people belong or in which one of their personal systems is embedded. For instance, local chapters of Alcoholics Anonymous are influenced by the larger organization, which is influenced by the peer self-help movement, the helping professions, governmental agencies doing research on alcoholism, and alcoholic-treatment units of hospitals. Any particular school is a likely candidate for this kind of analysis—from student and teacher interactions in individual classrooms to the impact of Supreme Court decisions on local integration policies and the impact of dwindling numbers of applicants on university entrance policies.

The Process of Developing a Working Knowledge of Institutional Systems and Their Effects

We can make our consideration of the process of developing a working knowledge of systems a bit more concrete by briefly considering particular systems and their impact. Many people see themselves as lay psychologists because they have developed a working knowledge of psychology and can use it in their day-to-day living. This working knowledge helps them to understand themselves and others, and hopefully such understanding will lead to more effective behavior. The probability of effective behavior increases as people develop behavioral skills in such areas as self-management and interpersonal communication.

One way of looking at the question of systems is to see ourselves developing a working sociology and anthropology. We are more accustomed to think of applying psychology to our lives than sociology and anthropology, but what social scientists tell us about social-systems structure and its impact can be translated into more effective behavior. This behavior includes developing a working knowledge of systems and acquiring systems-involvement skills. We will review these skills in Chapter 8.

Awareness of the larger institutions of society and how they affect individual lives can be enhanced by developing the following kinds of working knowledge:

1. what the larger institutions of society are like and how they work,
2. how some of the larger institutions of society affect us directly,
3. how specific subgroupings of people are affected systematically by the larger institutions of society,
4. how a society, through the workings of its larger institutions and organizations, generates specific societal problems, and
5. how specific systems, such as hospitals and the courts, affect people deeply at certain times of their lives.

We will consider an example of each of these categories.

1. What One of the Larger Institutions of Society Is Like and How It Works: The Police

Police departments are important organizations of the exosystem. Most information about the police comes to people through the media: reports of scandals in the police department, heroic acts by individual police officers, police demands for contracts and pay raises, drug and prostitution raids, and the like. Many people, as Hacker points out, use the police department as an all-purpose agency. Most people, however, don't get directly involved with the police, and, as a result, few people know much about the police department as a system and how it relates to the other important systems of their lives. However, as Hacker notes, "More has been said, written, and muttered about the police than any other group of public servants. This emphasis is understandable. Schoolteachers and social workers provide services. We look to the police for protection" (p. 3).[2]

Hacker (1977), in reviewing some of the recent books on the police, gives us some insight into the workings of this system (Alex, 1976; Brooks, 1975; Muir, 1977; Radzinowicz & King, 1976; Wilson, 1975). Many people assume that an increase in the number of police would lead to increased felony arrests or to increased safety; however, short of establishing a totalitarian state, it would be impossible to create a police presence pervasive enough to deter potential criminals. Police presence is only one of the factors related to crime rates; many institutions and events in the exosystem and macrosystem are related to the incidence of crime. Plato suggested in *The Laws* that the force of a law does not lie in the ability of a state to enforce it but in the willingness of the people to obey it. Crime, therefore, is not just police business; it is the business of the entire society.

Wilson (1975) cites a year-long experiment in police presence in Kansas City in which three comparable precincts were studied. In the first precinct, no changes in police patrolling were made. In the second, police cars were withdrawn completely, responding only to calls for help. In the third precinct, police patrolled two to three times as much as they did in the other two. There were no significant changes in criminal activity, amount of crime reported, rate of victimization, level of citizen fear, or degree of citizen satisfaction with the police as a result of this experiment. Wilson concludes that he cannot think of police-related innovations that are likely to reduce the incidence of crime. What is the answer, then, to increasing crime rates? Wilson suggests that, in order to reverse this trend, it will be necessary to improve the quality of community life rather than increase the police force in the community.

City size may be an important factor in shaping police attitudes and behavior. Alex (1976), who spent two years in New York interviewing police on the beat, found that they didn't feel much loyalty to the city that employed them or affinity with those they policed. Moreover, many of them lived in neighborhoods distant from those in which they worked. On the other hand, Muir (1977), who spent one year living with various officers in a small city, found that they were concerned for the dignity of the people they served and looked for signs of hope even in desperate situations. They lived closer to the neighborhoods they patrolled and would often see people they knew on the street. In these cases, city size was more

[2]This and all other quotations from this source are from "Safety Last," by A. Hacker. Reprinted with permission from *The New York Review of Books*. Copyright © 1977 Nyrev, Inc.

than a bit of sociological data; it had a significant impact on a major institution of society and, therefore, on the experience of individuals touched by that institution. The information gathered by Alex and Muir highlights *interactional* effects—in this case, city size and the feelings of police about the manageability of problems—among the larger institutions of society. The exosystem includes both these larger systems and their interactions with one another.

The books cited here provide a great deal of insight into the workings of a police department; they also point out unmistakably that the police department is a system embedded in a complex exosystem. We cannot understand police limitations until we understand the limitations of the community being policed. These books also point out that police reform without concomitant efforts at community reform will most likely be fruitless.

It is impossible to give an adequate working knowledge of one of the important institutions of the exosystem in a few short paragraphs. On the other hand, it isn't necessary to read all the available books that deal with the police to develop this kind of working knowledge. Hacker (1977) acts as a "translator"; that is, he tries to present theory and research on police in a form that is understandable without being oversimplified. He presents sociological data and different views of police and policing that challenge some of our myths and preconceptions. Inventive social-science teachers at all educational levels can act as "translators," not only by enabling their students to develop a basic working knowledge of some of the important institutions of the exosystem through facts and theory, but also by using techniques such as role-playing and simulations. Those who teach disciplines that deal with the institutions of society—civics, community psychology, anthropology, economics, environmental studies, history, political science, social psychology, sociology, and urban studies—can help students to see how their development is being affected by these institutions.

2. How Some of the Larger Institutions of Society Affect Us Directly: The Mass Media

The mass media constitute a major institution of the exosystem that affects most people daily (see Adler, 1975; Blumler & Katz, 1974; Gerbner, 1977; Wright, 1975). If people were to acquire a working knowledge of the media early in life, then they would be able to use the mass media for their own benefit.

The mass media are so pervasive and people are so accustomed to them that they scarcely notice how much of their lives are influenced by them. Radio, television, newspapers, periodicals, and magazines surround individuals and provide them with the following:

- *news*—local, national, and international, as well as commentaries on the news,

- *education*—articles on solar energy, book reviews, documentaries, and college courses on television,
- *advertising*—publications that contain nothing but advertising are now big business,
- *entertainment*—the comics, gossip, short stories, movies, situation comedies, talk shows, and
- *values*—through content, advertising, and implicit as well as explicit editorializing, the media constantly tell people what their culture is like and subtly or blatantly suggest what values they should adopt and pursue. In other words, the media (institutions of the exosystem) are extremely influential channels of the culture (the macrosystem). The media are both creators and purveyors of culture.

Since the major news media are supported by advertising, they compete for advertising money. In order to draw readers, listeners, or viewers, the media must entertain, and at times this need to entertain conflicts with the need to inform. As a result, news that captures the imagination of the public—terrorism, violence, human interest stories and the like—receives more attention because its entertainment value is high. Newspapers and magazines also must entertain. For instance, a newspaper or magazine might feature an article on unmarried couples living together rather than a story that demonstrates the changed character and relative stability of traditional family life (for example, Bane, 1976), because the latter lacks drama and entertainment value.

Powers (1977) criticizes TV newscasting for excessive showmanship and contrasts newspapers and television.

> The American newspaper, augmented by the rise of the suburban press and even by "alternative" weeklies, remains a voice of its environment: idiosyncratic, steeped in the complex history of local controversies and concerns, familiar with the performance patterns of civic leaders. Its faults are several and familiar. It is too responsible to "official" versions of controversial events, slow to accept social change as its host community is slow to accept social change, boosterish, encrusted with its own anachronistic biases. But through it all, the daily paper often manages to be a benign intervener, a flawed but reliable curator of the ongoing processes of a city's life.
>
> The television news department, by contrast, has seldom been able to escape a colonial persona. It is an emissary to a community, not an indigenous product of it. Its reference point is time present; unlike the newspapers, the TV stations seldom bother to accumulate a reference library in which reporters can check the past coverage of an ongoing issue. Often (as is the case with the 15 network-owned stations and the dozens of other "group" stations) the TV news staff responds to the pure marketing priorities of absentee ownership. The on-air men and women look and sound less like their fellow citizens than like some idealized product of genetic breeding. This may be good for viewers' sexual fantasies; it does not do much for a station's credibility. The anchor-gods and goddesses seldom remain long in a given "mar-

ket"; they are nomads on the move, their aspirations fixed on New York
whence their loyalty often derives [p. 237].[3]

For our purposes, the issue is not whether Powers is right or wrong in his
criticisms; the issue is how we can learn to evaluate television and other
forms of mass media critically.

Given the tension in the media between the need to entertain in order
to sell products and the responsibility of informing the public, it is difficult
for us to get a balanced view of what is happening in our world. The explo-
sion of mass media, which has turned our world into a "global village"
(McLuhan, 1964), has increased the amount of information we receive but
hasn't necessarily improved its quality. We believe that, as early as possible in life, people should acquire a basic working knowledge of the mass
media and learn where to go to get accurate information and reliable
news. Acquiring a basic working knowledge of the mass media includes
learning how to judge the quality of news, learning where to find quality
entertainment in the media, learning how to use the media judiciously,
learning how to separate editorials from the news, and learning how to
respond intelligently to advertising.

Neill (1968) has suggested that the radio and record industries are the
most potent emotional educators of younger people. The moods, melodies,
rhythms, and lyrics of popular songs lodge themselves in the minds of the
young (and perhaps the not-so-young). The messages are principally emotional, dealing with feelings about self, others, the world, love, caring, lust,
depression, and despair. And the messages are delivered continuously from
morning until night. Where do the values that are expressed in the
rhythms and lyrics come from? We are beginning to get an idea of how the
young are influenced by the violence that appears on television, but do we
have any idea of the short- or long-term impact of such emotional flood-
ing? We suggest that time spent acquiring a working knowledge of the
principal concrete ways in which the mass media are both transmitters
and shapers of our lives would be time well spent.

These, then, are a few examples of how large institutions and organizations affect us directly. The extent to which such systems influence and
in many ways control our lives can be frightening. How free are we even in
a supposedly free society?

3. How Specific Groups in Society Are Affected Systematically by the Larger Institutions of Society

Another way to understand the world of larger systems is to see how
these systems affect certain subgroups within a society. Students, the elderly, the poor, various ethnic groups, women, blue-collar workers, and

[3]From *The Newscaster: The News Business as Show Business*, by R. Powers. Copyright 1977 by St. Martin's Press, Inc. Reprinted by permission.

Blacks are examples of specific groups that are affected systematically by large institutions. We will now take a brief look at some working-class families in the United States and how they are affected by the larger institutions of society.

Rubin (1976) interviewed 50 White working-class couples in 12 communities in the San Francisco Bay area. Although many people maintain that the nuclear family is vanishing and that new arrangements called alternative life-styles are taking its place, Rubin, like Bane (1976), found that the nuclear family is more or less intact in the working class. She believes that the life of working-class families is crippled by their position in the class structure. Working-class men receive relatively poor wages, and even if they have jobs that pay well, the duration of these jobs is often uncertain. The jobs they work at have little dignity in the eyes of employers, of other members of society, and of the workers themselves. These men demand positions of absolute dominance in their families in compensation for their sense of powerlessness and abasement at work. They resist efforts on the part of their wives to achieve equal status in the home. No one in the family sees much of a future; their lives are filled with conflict and tension. Of the 100 men and women interviewed by Rubin, 46 came from families afflicted with problems such as alcoholism, divorce, or desertion.

Rubin's summary of what she discovered through her interviews is rather grim. She found not only troubled marriages, uncommunicative sex lives, unfulfilling work, and expensive leisure pursuits but also people locked into such a life by the structure of society itself.

> Consequently, we proliferate "people changing" programs—programs with which we hope to change the manners, the mores, and the lifeways of the poor and the working class. Then, we tell ourselves and them, they will be able to move into the more privileged sectors of society. A comforting illusion! But one that avoids facing the structured reality that there's no room at the top and little room in the middle; that no matter what changes people or groups make in themselves, this industrial society requires a large work force to produce the goods and services it needs—a work force that generation after generation comes from working-class families. These families reproduce themselves not because they are somehow deficient or their culture aberrant, but because there are no alternatives for most of their children. Indeed, it may be the singular triumph of this industrial society—perhaps of any social order—that not only do we socialize people to their appropriate roles and station, but that the process by which this occurs is so subtle that it is internalized and passes from parents to children by adults who honestly believe they are acting out of choices they have made in their own lifetime [p. 211].[4]

As Giroux and Penna (1977) have noted, the educational system further reinforces values such as a respect for authority, punctuality, cleanliness, docility, and conformity that prepare the children of the poor and of the working class to be "good" industrial workers. The educational system be-

[4]From *Worlds of Pain: Life in the Working-Class Family*, by Lillian Breslow Rubin, pp. 5, 210–211. © 1976 by Lillian Breslow Rubin, Basic Books, Inc., Publishers, New York. Reprinted by permission.

comes an instrument of the economic system, and the members of the working-class become victims of both.

Rubin's treatment of working-class families is of special importance for us because she takes a developmental perspective. She follows children of working-class families through childhood, marriage, and the early and middle years of married and family life, and she finds a disturbing degree of social determinism in the development of working-class people. Handel (1977) challenges this determinism in part:

> A working-class youth may not plan his work life, but that does not mean that it just happens. It happens somehow. And unless we adopt the assumption that some kind of choice is involved (based on some configuration of information, awareness, emotion, and preference), we have implicitly dehumanized working-class people and rendered them zombies. Rubin may feel that the issue is superfluous because the range of choice is not great enough to be meaningful, but such a judgment would be premature [p. 83].

Handel seems to indicate that a working knowledge of the economic system and the career possibilities it holds might make a difference for some working-class youths. In order for youths to acquire this knowledge, however, schools will have to provide better career-counseling and life-planning services than they do now.

The point we are trying to make is that the structure and interactions between the larger institutions of society often set limits on the development of certain subgroupings of people within society. If people acquire a working knowledge of the kinds of social determinism under which they live, then, perhaps, they will be able to develop enlightened coping strategies. Without such working knowledge, people have limited alternatives to feeling powerless and demoralized. We do not suggest that giving people a working knowledge of the structure of society and how it affects them will provide simple solutions to hitherto intractable social problems, but such knowledge is a starting point and is part of the solution.

4. How a Society, through the Workings of Its Larger Institutions and Organizations, Generates Specific Societal Problems

Our society, like others, is beset by problems that do not go away when they are ignored. Delinquency and vandalism in our cities, dwindling supplies of energy, chronic unemployment, and environmental pollution are examples of these problems that affect the development of both people and systems.

Many people tend to see societal problems as things in themselves, divorced from the situations that create them; as a result, they try to solve the problems without substantially altering the systems underlying them. Often, their "solutions" are mere palliatives that work temporarily. For instance, in attempting to solve the problem of juvenile delinquency, people often focus on delinquents—placing them in jail or trying to educate or entertain them—without concomitantly trying to do something about the socioeconomic and family conditions that spawn them. When people don't learn to conceptualize problems in systems terms, they over-simplify the problems and their potential solutions. Problems such as those listed previously are signs that the *system* is not working. When the members of a society realize that systems need to be changed, they apply political pressure to change them.

We suggest, therefore, that people learn to develop a working knowledge of social problems from a systems perspective. Commoner's book, *The Poverty of Power: Energy and the Economic Crisis*, is instructive because he takes a systems approach to the analysis and solution of problems and stresses the *relationships* among systems. He considers environmental pollution, the energy crisis, and the economic crisis, including inflation and unemployment, and maintains that we can see each of these problems separately and try to treat them separately: "environmental degradation by pollution controls; the energy crisis by finding new sources of energy and new ways of conserving it; the economic crisis by manipulating prices, taxes, and interest rates" (p. 1).[5] These, however, are further examples of attempts to treat problems without dealing with the systems that underlie them. The whole picture is complicated by the fact that solutions to one problem seem to aggravate some other problem:

> Pollution control reduces energy supplies; energy conservation costs jobs. Inevitably, proponents of one solution become opponents of the others. Policy stagnates and remedial action is paralyzed, adding to the confusion and gloom that beset the country [p. 1].

Commoner maintains that environmental degradation, the energy crisis, and the economic crisis are caused by the economic system, which he defines as the "recipient of the real wealth created by the production system"—that is, the system that "transforms that wealth into earnings, profit, credit, savings, investment, taxes; and governs how that wealth is distributed, and what is done with it" (p. 2). Logically, the economic system should conform to the requirements of the production system, and the production system should conform to the requirements of the ecosystem; in practice, however, the opposite happens.

> The environmental crisis tells us that the ecosystem has been disastrously affected by the design of the modern production system, which has been developed with almost no regard for compatibility with the environment or for efficient use of energy. . . . In turn, the faulty design of the production system has been imposed upon it by the economic system, which invests in factories that promise increased profits rather than environmental compatibility or efficient use of resources. The relationships among the great systems on which society depends are upside down [pp. 2–3].

[5]This and all other quotations from this source are from *The Poverty of Power: Energy and the Economic Crisis*, by B. Commoner. Copyright © 1976 by Alfred A. Knopf. Reprinted by permission of Random House, Inc.

After elaborating his argument, he intimates that the faults of our capitalistic economic system (an exosystemic reality) are based on culture and cultural values (see Chapter 7).

The point is that nations as well as individuals suffer if they do not take a systems view of life. A good citizen is often defined as one who obeys the laws of the country, but this definition needs a great deal of expansion. Good citizens are people who can challenge the society in which they live because they have developed a working knowledge of the society as a system and can see its major problems in nonsimplistic, interdependent terms.

5. Specific Systems, Such as Hospitals and the Courts, That Affect People Deeply at Certain Times of Their Lives

The larger institutions of society affect individuals in both direct and indirect ways in their daily lives. There are also significant institutions that directly affect people only at particular times in their lives. This doesn't mean that these systems are less significant than the systems we have been considering; the institutions that enter people's lives at particular times often do so in times of crisis. If people sue or are sued, they meet the legal profession and possibly the courts. If they are arrested and sent to jail, even for a brief time, they meet the police, the courts, and the prison system. When people become sick, the medical industry, including doctors, clinics, nurses, and hospitals, enters their lives.

The professions and professional associations have a great impact on individuals, their personal settings, and the larger institutions of society. Haskell (1977) claims that the complexity of modern life makes professionals indispensable:

> It must be recalled that modern society involves the individual in relationships both with other human beings and with physical nature that are vastly more complex than his ancestors before the nineteenth century ever had to contend with. If modern man displays an alarming tendency to defer thoughtlessly to expert opinion, it is largely because alternative guides to conduct such as common sense and the customary ways of his local community have long since failed him in important areas of life. The Victorians treasured Emerson's advice to "trust thyself," but they could not live by it and neither can we. The conditions of modern society place a high premium on esoteric knowledge, especially when it comes stamped with the special authority of an organized community of practitioners who police each other's opinions and thereby create something approaching a consensus of the competent.

Bledstein (1976) asks how society can make professional behavior accountable to the public without curtailing the independence needed for creativity and imagination. It is indeed a question our society is continually struggling with. One possible solution to this dilemma involves giving individuals a working knowledge of the professional systems that enter their lives. An informed public—that is, individuals with a working knowledge of professional systems—is an essential part of regulation and reform.

Practically all of us have had or will have experience as a patient in a hospital. Most of us are unprepared for this experience; that is, we lack an adequate working knowledge of the medical profession and of the hospital as a system.

The larger institutions of society will continue to exert unwarrantable power in individual lives until the members of society acquire the working knowledge and skills needed to change these institutions to live up to their social responsibilities. Moreover, this same knowledge and these same skills enable people to participate in and contribute to the development of large institutions.

Berger and Neuhaus (1977) maintain that government and other large institutions endanger the autonomy of the personal settings of life.

> In his classic study of suicide, Emile Durkheim describes the "tempest" of modernization sweeping away the "little aggregations" in which people formerly found community, leaving only the state on the one hand and a mass of individuals, "like so many liquid molecules," on the other. Although using different terminologies, others in the sociological tradition—Ferdinand Toennies, Max Weber, Georg Simmel, Charles Cooley, Thorstein Veblen—have analyzed aspects of the same dilemma. Today Robert Nisbet has most persuasively argued that the loss of community [which is experienced through "mediating structures"] threatens the future of American democracy [p. 4].

According to Berger and Neuhaus, large institutions aren't evil or bereft of good intentions, but the very size of these institutions robs them of the kind of versatility that would benefit particular individuals.

> The management mindset of the megastructure—whether of HEW, Sears Roebuck, or the AFL-CIO—is biased toward the unitary solution. The neat and comprehensive answer is impatient of "irrational" particularities and can only be forced to yield to greater nuance when it encounters resistance, whether from the economic market of consumer wants or from the political market of organized special interest groups [p. 41].

Larger institutions tend to promote centralization; and if the individual is to be fully respected and fully protected, the smaller settings of life—the "mediating structures" of society—will have to provide this respect and protection. Individuals may need to organize themselves into consumer groups or organizations such as Common Cause to challenge the larger structures of society. In other words, social systems can help to protect us from the adverse influence of other systems. In a world as complex as ours, it is extremely important that individuals and smaller systems understand how they are affected by the larger systems of society and realize their ability to organize themselves into groups that can effectively challenge the depersonalizing effects of larger systems. Systems influence systems, and people may influence systems best through other systems.

Our freedom lies partially in our ability to act through the systems that are closest to us and have the deepest regard for us as individuals—that is, through our network of personal settings.

Acquiring a working knowledge of systems, then, is not a luxury in contemporary life, it is one of the conditions of freedom. We suggest that people begin to learn about the larger social systems gradually but steadily as early as possible in life. A number of disciplines deal with these systems: economics, human ecology, political science, sociology, and urban affairs, among others. It is through disciplines such as these, "translated" and presented in practical ways, that people acquire the kinds of working knowledge they need.

Beyond a working knowledge of the systems of their lives, individuals need an understanding of culture and its permeation of social structures and individual lives. We examine culture in Chapter 7.

Chapter 6: Additional Resources

Kuhn, A. *Social organization.* In D. Ruben & J. Kim (Eds.), *General systems theory and human communication.* Rochelle Park, N.J.: Hayden, 1975, 114–127.

Nickson, J. *Economics and social choice* (2nd ed.). New York: McGraw-Hill, 1974. (See Preface and Chapters 1, 2, 10, and 11.)

Rubin, L. B. *Worlds of pain.* New York: Basic Books, 1976.

Turk, H. *Organizations in modern life.* San Francisco: Jossey-Bass, 1977. (See Chapters 1, 2, 5, and 6.)

7

The Social Context of Human Development— Level IV: Cultural Values and Their Impact

We have considered the development of individuals in the context of personal settings, the network of personal settings, and the larger institutions of society and the network they form. The fourth and final level of systems that we will consider is the culture in which individuals and systems are immersed. It might seem odd to consider culture as a system, but culture has profound systematic effects on both individuals and social structures (Parsons & Shils, 1951). Therefore, this fourth level of systems, which Bronfenbrenner (1977b) calls the "macrosystem," refers not to particular individuals, organizations, or institutions, but rather to the culture that shapes them. *Macro* is a Greek word meaning *large*, and culture is the largest of systems, enveloping and pervading all individuals and organizations.

As Bronfenbrenner points out, culture includes:

general prototypes, existing in the culture or subculture, that set the pattern for the structures and activities occurring at the concrete level. Thus, within a given society, one school classroom looks and functions much like another. The same holds true for other settings and institutions, both formal and informal. It is as if they were all constructed from the same blueprints. These "blueprints" are the macrosystem. Some actually exist in explicit form as recorded laws, regulations, and rules. But most macrosystems are informal and implicit—carried, often unwittingly, in the minds of the society's members as ideology made manifest through custom and practice in everyday life [p. 515].

These "blueprints" are exemplified by the fact that a classroom in the Soviet Union might look quite different from a classroom in the United States, but classrooms in Connecticut and California look pretty much alike. A burial ceremony in India differs from a burial ceremony in America in striking ways, but burial ceremonies in Florida and Oregon typically do not differ much from each other. The macrosystem, therefore, refers to the "overarching institutional patterns of the culture or subculture" (p. 515) as these concretely affect the development of individuals in the context of their personal and institutional systems.

Culture in its systematic effects is included in our model because so much of the day-to-day operation of organizations and communities is shaped by it. Unfortunately, the pervasive influence of culture can go unnoticed by those who attempt to assist individuals, communities, and organizations in their development. As John Dollard (1935) observed:

Before any individual appears, his society has had a specific social life organized and systematized, and the existence of this life will exercise a tyrannical compulsion on him. . . . One of the marks of an effective grasping of this point is the stated or implied "in our culture" whenever one makes any point in connection with individual behavior; it is a good thing to get into the habit, for example, of saying, "men are more able than women to exhibit aggressive behavior *in our culture*" [pp. 16–17].

Anthropologist Edwin Hall (1977) underscores Dollard's point by indicating one of the primary functions of culture:

One of the functions of culture is to provide a highly selective screen between man and the outside world. In its many forms, culture therefore designates what we pay attention to and what we ignore. This screening function provides structure for the world . . . [p. 85].

Cultural influences can go unnoticed precisely because they are so pervasive. Individuals are continuously wrapped in their culture to such an extent that they are rarely aware of the cultural assumptions around which so much of their lives are structured (Dollard, 1935; Sarason, 1974). That is why direct exposure to different cultures through travel can be such a jolting experience.

A Working Anthropology

Since anthropology is in some sense the science of human culture, we suggest that individuals develop a "working anthropology"—that is, a working knowledge of the ways in which culture affects their lives. This knowledge could refer, for example, to the effects a culture has on an entire nation or a particular school system. Harris (1977), in exploring the workings of cultures, raises the question of cultural determinism and its relationship to human freedom.

> As a cultural determinist, I have sometimes been accused of reducing human values to a mechanical reflex and of portraying individuals as mere puppets. These are doctrines that are alien to my understanding of cultural processes. I insist simply that the thought and behavior of individuals are always channeled by cultural and ecological restraints and opportunities [p. 194].[1]

Throughout his book, Harris claims that, in order to maintain a high degree of freedom, people must develop a practical knowledge of the ways in which culture affects them.

> In the birth of a science of culture, others profess to see the death of moral initiative. For my part, I cannot see how a lack of intelligence concerning the lawful processes that have operated so far can be the platform on which to rear a civilized future. And so in the birth of a science of culture I find the beginning, not the end, of moral initiative [p. 195].

He maintains that those interested in changing social systems for the better cannot do so unless they understand the mechanics of culture.

> To change social life for the better, one must begin with the knowledge of why it usually changes for the worse. That is why I consider ignorance of the causal factors in cultural evolution and disregard of the odds against a desired outcome to be forms of moral duplicity [p. xii].

We believe that individuals can gradually acquire a working anthropology, becoming aware of how social contexts are carriers of values, as well as "blueprints" for action consistent with those values. This working knowledge can help people to cope with cultural determinism and enable them to appreciate cultures foreign to their own.

The Impact of Cultural Values on Human Development: An Illustration

If we were to ask people what high schools teach, they would probably answer by listing such things as writing, English literature, history, science, mathematics, and foreign languages; but such a listing is radically incomplete. For example, Carole Bryer, a junior at Central High, experiences her homeroom as a personal setting; she feels at home there with her friends and has a good relationship with her teacher. But she is learning

[1]This and all other quotations from this source are taken from *Cannibals and Kings: The Origins of Cultures*, by M. Harris. Copyright © 1977 by Random House, Inc. Reprinted by permission.

more than the subjects that are taught in the classroom. Even though the word *values* does not appear in the curriculum, she is being exposed to, learning, and assimilating values; that is, there is in the classroom what Giroux and Penna, following Vallence (1973–4), call "the hidden curriculum."

> What students learn in school is governed as much, if not more, by what they learn from the "hidden curriculum." The hidden curriculum as used in this article refers to those unstated norms, values, and beliefs that are transmitted to students through the underlying structure of classroom as opposed to the formally recognized and sanctioned dimensions of classroom experience. More specifically, the hidden curriculum is based on a set of structural properties that promote social relations of education that are strongly hierarchical and authoritarian in nature [p. 40].

In other words, the macrosystem reaches down into the school and, through the personal systems of the school, affects Carole Bryer.

Bowles and Gintis (1976) describe the way in which schools produce a consciousness that legitimates the development and training of students for a stratified labor force. In their opinion, the demands of society—here, the demands of the economic system—determine some of the values that are to be inculcated through the school and its classrooms. They believe that the school, in a sense, becomes the instrument of economics and business and is not the freeing experience we would like to believe it is.

Education is never value-free, in content or the way in which that content is taught. Typically, education facilitates the integration of the younger generation into the logic of the present system and helps them to conform to it. Berger and Neuhaus (1977) contend that teachers and administrators, as well as the educational system itself, are carriers of specific values.

> By birth or social mobility, the personnel of the education establishment are upper middle class, and this is reflected in the norms, the procedures, and the very cultural climate of that establishment. This means the child who is not of an upper-middle-class family is confronted by an alien milieu from his or her first day at school. In part this may be inevitable. The modern world is bourgeois and to succeed in a bourgeois world means acquiring bourgeois skills and behavior patterns. We do not suggest, as some do, that the lower-class child is being culturally raped when taught correct English, but there are many other, sometimes unconscious, ways in which the education establishment systematically disparages ways of life other than those of the upper middle class. Yet these disparaged ways of life are precisely the ways in which parents of millions of American children live. Thus, schools teach contempt for the parents and, ultimately, self-contempt [pp. 21–22].

Culture—in this case, middle-class culture—reaches into the school and affects students through their participation in both classroom and extracurricular activities. According to Berger and Neuhaus, parents should be able to seek out alternative forms of education for their children. "We trust the ability of low-income parents to make educational decisions more

wisely than do the professionals who now control their children's education. To deny this ability is the worst bias of all, and in many instances it is
racism as well" (p. 22).

Jackson (1968) suggests that the "hidden curriculum," through which
the learning of ideology, norms, values, and attitudes takes place, is related
to three concepts: crowds, power, and praise. First, the school is unlike the
home in that there are more people at school—a crowd. Students learn
how to wait to use resources, how to postpone or give up desires, how to be
quiet in a crowd, how to be isolated in a crowd, how to be patient, and
how to suffer in silence. They learn that the teacher is in charge of the
crowd, or has power over it, and that the teacher grants privileges, allo-
cates resources, divides up space and time, and determines how they are
to be used. Finally, students are rewarded for exhibiting discipline, for
remaining subordinate, for producing intellectually- rather than emotion-
ally-oriented behavior, and for engaging in hard work that is independent
of intrinsic task motivation.

The most commonly held notion about education is that politics has
no place in the school and that political indoctrination of any kind is an-
tithetical to the educational values of Western democracies (Miliband,
1969). Although deliberate political indoctrination is ordinarily avoided in
schools in the United States, the kind of indirect political socialization
being discussed here is normative.

> In fact, schools in every society cannot avoid . . . socializing youth into the
> prevailing culture. Schools, along with the family, church, trade unions, and
> other institutions, constitute the ideological apparatuses that pass on the
> dominant prevailing belief and value systems of a given society to each suc-
> cessive generation. In accordance with the content, structure, and organiza-
> tion of schools, the pyramidal configuration of the entire society is repro-
> duced [Giroux & Penna, 1977, p. 41].[2]

We believe that, although it is impossible for education to be value-
free, schools should make their hidden curriculum public; that is, they
should be aware of their role as instruments of enculturation and make
students, parents, and the public at large aware of this role. Making the
hidden curriculum public involves more than teaching students the skills
of clarifying personal values; it means that the school itself, through its
teachers and administrators, must clarify its own values publicly and
teach its students the skills of clarifying and identifying the values that
institutions, including the school itself, enshrine and promote. The school,
then, would become a forum in which cultural influences in society would
be examined and critiqued, and students would be encouraged to take a
proactive stance toward cultural influences instead of surrendering pas-
sively to the many forms of enculturation promoted by the various institutions of society.

---

[2]From Giroux, H., & Penna, A., "Social Relations in the Classroom" *Edcentric Magazine*, Issue No. 40–41, 1977. P.O. Box 10085, Eugene, OR 97440. Reprinted by permission.

Giroux and Penna hope that by "blowing the cultural cover" of schools and school systems, people can begin to do the following:

> identify a new set of values and structural properties that are to be used in developing an "unalienating" pedagogical methodology; unalienating both in its attempt to link up theory and action, and to restore to students and teachers an awareness of the social and personal importance of active participation and critical thinking [p. 43].

Once the hidden curriculum is made public, a curriculum will be set up to promote alternate values such as critical thinking rather than passive acceptance and a combination of divergent and convergent thinking rather than convergent thinking alone; however, these values will be out in the open.

> The values and conditions which should provide the basis for the structural properties in such a course will include developing in students a respect for community and cooperation, in addition to an acknowledgement of the importance of a balanced healthy individualism. Every effort should be made to give students an awareness of the importance of developing choices on their own, and to act on those choices with an awareness of the situational constraints they have to face [pp. 43–44].

We do not assume that school administrators will jump at the chance to expose and examine their "hidden curricula," even though education is one of the most self-critical of the professions. There is a vast literature dealing with what is wrong with education, the schools, administrators, and teachers, but little of this information seems to seep down into the average classroom to effect changes in that system. As Drucker (1968) points out, all organizations are conservative; they do not easily change, especially when change involves the surrender of some of their power. Some hold no hope of school administrators becoming champions of the kind of education and training suggested here (Illich, 1971). However, they do see hope in establishing alternate schools and in sharing the responsibility of education and training with other systems, such as the family. We would like to see the upgrading of schools as they exist now and the establishment of alternate schools that can become models for schools trying to change.

As more and more students, teachers, and administrators take a systems view of education and schools and develop a basic working knowledge of systems involvement, there will be a greater possibility for change that has substance and direction. Moreover, those who develop this kind of working knowledge and skills have a better chance of coping with social systems that refuse to change and of seeking out more flexible social structures in which to involve themselves. Ideally, education can become the means whereby women and men deal critically and creatively with social reality and discover the possibilities for participation in the transformation of their world.

Social Stratification in
Human Systems

Figure 7-1 illustrates a systems view of the social world (Laszlo, 1972; Kuhn, 1974) and adds culture as a system to give us one picture of how the complex world of human systems fits together. This figure demonstrates that social living is *de facto* interdependent living.

- The individual shapes and is shaped by events in each of the personal settings of his or her own life.
- Personal systems such as the family, the immediate work setting, and the classroom shape and are shaped by events in the network of personal settings.

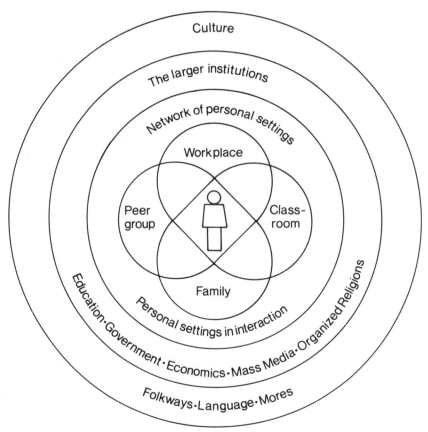

Figure 7-1.
The Developing Person in Context
Level IV: Culture

- Individuals and their entire constellation of personal settings shape and are shaped by the larger institutions of life such as government, economics, the professions, and the mass media.
- Finally, the basic social institutions of society shape and are shaped by the culture itself.

The repetition of the phrase *shape and are shaped by* underscores the interdependence of the human-systems world. The influence that exists between systems and individuals may be more powerful in one direction than another at times, but it is in fact unilateral. All of this can be summarized in a full equation of the people-in-systems model:

$$D_p + D_s = f\ (P \longleftrightarrow PS \longleftrightarrow PS\ NETWORK \longleftrightarrow LI \longleftrightarrow C);$$

that is, the development (*D*) of both people (*P*) and systems (*S*) is a function (*f*) of the interaction ($\longleftrightarrow$) between people and personal settings (*PS*), among personal settings *(PS NETWORK)*, between personal settings and the larger institutions of life *(LI)*, and between all the systems levels and the pervading culture (*C*).

A social scientist examining the systems model of concentric circles that we offer our readers as an introduction to the social context of human development will no doubt protest that we have ignored socioeconomic stratification—an aspect of society that major theorists view as fundamental to an adequate understanding of the social world (Bendix, 1976; Marx, 1909; Weber, 1946). Broom and Selznick illustrate the importance that social scientists typically attribute to socioeconomic stratification:

> Social inequality and social ranking are ... among the most pervasive aspects of human society. For this reason, stratification is the sociologist's favorite independent variable, and he can usually trace a connection between stratification and almost any other social phenomenon: child training, voting, social conflict, nutrition, accent, or marriage. The growing popular sensitivity to inequality and concern about the persistence of poverty in rich countries spur the sociologist's interest in stratification as an intransigent, compelling, and universal social issue [Broom & Selznick, 1973, p. 162].

We have omitted the critical social variable of socioeconomic stratification in favor of building a straightforward introductory concept of social structure for the reader who tends to think primarily in psychological, or individual, terms.

Events in the immediate settings, the network of immediate settings, the institutions, and the culture in which we live out our lives all *vary as a function of social stratification*. In other words, there are observable differences among the personal, institutional, and cultural experiences of individuals of differing socioeconomic status (Blumberg, 1972). For example, concrete differences have been observed in the child-rearing practices, career patterns, education, and family roles of individuals of differing status (Broom & Selznick, 1973).

Those who have an active concern for fostering human development will do well to learn about the effects of socioeconomic stratification. Issues of social justice, access to educational and economic resources, and political power clearly emerge in an analysis of stratification and its effects. As we noted earlier, human development is what a particular sociocultural group says it is; therefore, agents of development ignore questions concerning politics and societal values at great risk.

Although we do not undertake to examine them here, there are other major variables that affect the development of individuals. Specifically, we refer here to race, sex, ethnicity, and religion, which are often associated with a lifetime of stereotyped responses from others and eventually within oneself that can become major obstacles to the development of individuals. On the other hand, the concrete results of the civil rights and women's movements are an indication of the effectiveness of people who have decided to take collective action in challenging cultural stereotypes.

Conclusion

Our examples in this chapter have been necessarily brief. It has not been our intention to offer simplistic solutions to oversimplified sociocultural problems. Nor do we contend that training people from an early age to think of the world and smaller segments of it in social-systems terms and giving them practice in problem solving from a systems perspective will lead automatically to the solution of intractable social problems. Finally, we do not necessarily endorse the solutions to social problems suggested by the authors we have cited. We have cited these authors because they do think of social problems and social possibilities in terms of systems; that is, they provide us with *alternate perspectives*. A number of authors help us challenge commonly held myths about the institutions of the exosystem and about the relationships of individuals to these institutions. For instance, Illich invites us to take another look at schools and schooling (1971) and at health-services delivery systems (1976), Berger (1977) offers a different view of the Supreme Court, Chaliand (1977) presents a new perspective of the Third World, Jackson (1977) and Mitford (1973) reexamine the penal system, and Harrington (1977) explores poverty in the world. These people do not offer definitive solutions to the problems they treat, but they do help people to see the larger systems of society in new ways and to challenge some of the cultural myths concerning these systems. As we will see in the next chapter, developing alternate perspectives is important in problem solving and goal setting.

Our main point in this chapter is that people should be taught to think and act with an awareness of their cultural roots as a precondition to the management and perhaps the solution of many social problems. The challenge that faces both formal and informal educators is how to equip people with the working knowledge of social systems they need to promote their own development as individuals who live out their lives in the context of such systems. In Chapter 8, we examine the models and skills necessary for effective involvement in social systems.

Chapter 7: Additional Resources

Cole, M., Gay, J., Glick, J., & Sharp, D. *The cultural context of learning and thinking.* New York: Basic Books, 1971.

Frank, L. Cultural organization. In B. Ruben & J. Kim (Eds.), *General systems theory and human communication.* Rochelle Park, N.J.: Hayden, 1975, 128–135.

Geertz, C. *The interpretation of cultures.* New York: Basic Books, 1973.

Hall, E. *Beyond culture.* Garden City, N. J.: Anchor Press, 1977.

Sarason, S. *The psychological sense of community.* San Francisco: Jossey-Bass, 1974. (See Chapter 5.)

8

Models and Skills for Effective Involvement within the Social Systems of Our Lives

At the end of Chapter 3, we said that we would defer consideration of the package of skills we have called "system-involvement" skills to this chapter. The kind of working knowledge of systems that has been discussed in the last four chapters provides us with a context for considering these skills. The skills individuals need to invest themselves creatively in systems and institutions are similar to the skills needed by those who manage these systems and who are responsible for their design and functioning; that is, the models and skills of effective system functioning belong to managers and members alike.

If a system is in some ways oppressive, system-involvement skills provide members with the resources they need to cope with and change it. Once systems have been established (and this requires good design skills), they need to be renewed constantly in order to meet the changing realities of the environment and the changing needs of their members. In an organization in which there is concern for both the accomplishment of certain tasks and the development of members, there is always some kind of constructive, ongoing tension. Models of change and the skills and techniques needed to implement these models are required in order to manage the environments of a system. We will now review the two basic models that we use to portray organizational development and the basic skills required by those who want to contribute to the effective design and functioning of an organization or institution.

Model A, the logic underlying system design, is a prescriptive model that provides a systematic answer to the question: on what logic is an effectively designed and functioning system based? Model *A* helps us understand the complexities of the structure and function of any given system; it can be used to help design a new system or to diagnose a system that is already in existence. *Model B, a model for system change,* answers the question: how do those responsible for the functioning of a system change the system, or parts of it, so that it conforms to the logic of Model *A*? Model *A* presents the logic of a well-designed and functioning system, while Model *B* provides the logic of a step-by-step process of system change.

In this chapter, we will consider these two models and refer indirectly to the methods and skills needed to make them operative. We will not attempt to present system-related skills in any great detail or train the reader in these skills; these are tasks far beyond the scope of this book.

Applications of Model A
and Model B

Competent managers are not only expert in the comprehension and application of models *A* and *B*, but they also have the ability to help people appreciate the need to embed these models in systems; they have the ability to "give these models away."

Someone might say: "What you're presenting here refers to organizations with specific tasks. What about community-living systems such as families, peer groups, and neighborhoods? Do these models apply to immediate systems, which are extremely important for human development?" We believe the answer is yes, with some qualifications. Insofar as community-living systems are organized to accomplish certain tasks, the principles presented here do apply, since they are the principles of good organization. However, since the goals of community systems such as families are the establishment of effective relationships, mutuality, the interchange of services, the pursuit of mutual values, and the like, the principles of effective system design and functioning are applied differently from the way they are applied to a manufacturing concern. In what follows, we will apply these principles both to organizations (task or work systems such as businesses, mental-health clinics, governmental agencies, and hospitals) and to the family (a community-living system) in order to discover similarities and differences in application. We realize that it is unusual and perhaps a bit jarring (and certainly not very romantic) to apply system principles to community-living units such as families and peer groups. Some might balk at this overly rational approach to systems that are not always completely rational. We take this rational approach in order to determine whether these principles can make community-living systems more effective contributors to the development of their members.

Model A—The Logic Underlying an Effectively Designed and Functioning System

Every system produces either *products*, such as automobiles, houses, and food, or *services*, such as education, counseling, and surgery. While *organizations* produce products and services for others, *communities*, such as families and neighborhoods, produce services for their own members. Both organizations and communities are producers, although the producers of services in communities are also members of the community and therefore receive these services. For instance, whoever cooks the meal for the family also eats the meal.

The following is a list of the essential elements of Model *A*.

1. *Principles of behavior:* the ability to use the principles of behavior.
2. *Assessment of needs:* the ability to assess the needs of the receiving system.
3. *Mission:* the ability to establish clear mission statements.
4. *Goals:* the ability to set clear, behavioral goals.
5. *Programs:* the ability to draw up and execute well shaped programs that achieve established goals.
6. *Education and training:* working knowledge and skills needed for program implementation.
7. *Other resources:* the availability of resources other than information and skills.
8. *Structure:* division of work that serves program execution.
9. *Relationships:* structure leads to relationships.
10. *Communication:* effective communication, including the ability to share needed information and to give evaluative feedback.
11. *Climate:* the quality of a system's internal environment.
12. *The external environment:* the ability to manage the relationships between the system and the external environment.

The Ability to Use the Principles of Behavior

The ability to use the principles of behavior is first on the list of the elements of Model *A*, because the use or abuse of these principles affects every other phase of the model. In a well designed and functioning system, the basic principles that affect the maintenance and change of behavior *are thoroughly known, are respected, and are used.* Without a working knowledge of such principles of behavior as reinforcement, punishment and its effects, shaping, modeling, and aversive conditioning, system members are bound to make mistakes in both the design and the running of their system. Although common sense dictates that these principles be learned and practiced early in life, the reality is that these principles are not learned in any explicit way through ordinary educational channels; therefore, we have cases of otherwise intelligent people reinforcing, both in themselves and in others, behaviors they are trying to eliminate.

A working knowledge of the principles of behavior has high priority, because these principles remain operative whether they are known and explicitly used or not and because they affect every aspect of the working of a system. One reason for the "psychopathology of the average" is that people have not learned to use these principles of behavior for themselves or for the systems of their lives; as a result, the principles work against them. For instance, if the basic needs for sustenance, security, and belonging are being met, the most effective reinforcers in work systems are usually a sense of achievement, recognition, the work itself, responsibility together with authority, advancement, and personal growth (see Herzberg, 1968). Managers who try to motivate workers merely through good company policy, high-quality supervision, good working conditions, and increasing salary and fringe benefits might wonder why their efforts meet with relatively little success. They have overlooked the fact that reinforcements or rewards must be experienced as such *by the system members themselves*. If a reward isn't experienced subjectively, it does not function as motivation. (See Luthans & Kreitner, 1975, and Miller, 1974, 1978 for a treatment of these principles in organization.)

In Chapter 3, we pointed out that developing a working knowledge of the basic principles of behavior and the ability to apply them to day-to-day living are essential components of the self-management skills package. We believe that individuals should experience and learn the basic principles of behavior management in the family, because these principles are learned most naturally in the context of family living; this doesn't mean that parents should learn to use these principles to manipulate one another or their children. The use of the principles does not turn a family into an organization. Rather, families whose members are aware of and capable of using reinforcement, punishment, modeling, aversive conditioning, and behavior contracting may well pursue the goals of community living, intimacy, and mutuality more effectively than families without such working knowledge and skills.

The Ability to Assess Needs and Wants

A well designed and functioning system, whether it is an organization, a community, or a hybrid, meets specific needs and wants of the members of the receiving system. General Motors produces automobiles that satisfy a number of the needs and wants of consumers, including the basic need for transportation. A hospital provides for the health needs of the members of a community. A family provides for the needs of its members for care, intimacy, feelings of belonging, and security. A well designed and functioning system is *sensitive* to human needs and wants and channels its resources to meet them.

A system that ignores the needs and wants of people might well produce products or services that are not in demand, in which case the system will fail unless it can *create* a demand for these products or services. Human-service delivery systems, such as governments, church groups, schools, and the helping professions, frequently do a poor job in meeting the legitimate needs and wants of their members, and yet these systems stay in existence because their members don't realize that their needs are being met poorly and because the services provided by these systems, even when they are poor, are deemed essential for living. For instance, parents send their children to schools that do an inadequate job of educating and training them, either because they don't realize the schools are failing or because they feel they have no alternatives. A system that doesn't have accurate information about the needs of the members of the receiving system can be ineffective or even destructive.

The family is a human system, and yet few families ask themselves questions such as these: "What are the needs of family members? Why are we living together? What is the mission and the behavioral goal of families?" We believe the consideration of such questions will benefit all family members. Ideally, the family meets the needs of its members for safety, sustenance, companionship and intimacy, support in crisis, education and training, and the like. Since a family that knows its needs clearly and concretely is in a better position to meet them, the ability to clarify the needs of family members is an important family-living skill. The assumption that families should develop "naturally" without reflecting on what they need in order to function effectively or humanly as a community-living system is unwarranted. A working knowledge of developmental processes includes a working knowledge of developmental needs. Parents can ask themselves what their children need and what they themselves need in order to carry out developmental tasks effectively. Maslow's (1968) need hierarchy is a useful instrument in assessing developmental needs. Figure 8-1 is an illustration of the relationship between the producing system and the receiving system.

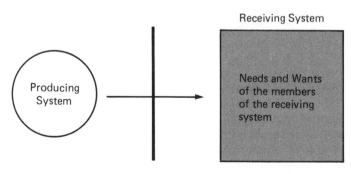

Figure 8-1

Mission—What the System Is About

The members of an effectively designed and functioning system know in an explicit way what their system is about: they know why it is in business. Mission statements are statements of the general purpose and the wide-ranging goals of a system. Very often, mission statements include the philosophy and the values of a system; they indicate in what spirit and under what conditions products and services are to be delivered. Such general statements are meaningful only to the degree that they are related to real needs and wants. We believe that mission statements should be written out and communicated to the members of both the producing and receiving systems. For instance, one of the mission statements of a hospital might be "We want to provide comprehensive, high quality medical care that meets the most stringent ethical standards at a reasonable cost to all the members of the community who wish to avail themselves of our services." Complex systems may have to formulate a number of mission statements. A hospital staff might formulate statements that relate to the general purpose and goals of the hospital, while members of each department could formulate more specific statements related to the needs of patients involved in these subsystems. Mission statements give a system concrete focus.

The members of a family can ask themselves what their purpose is as a family; since mission is related to needs, the general answer is "Our mission is to help one another satisfy our individual and collective needs —our needs for safety, intimacy, and support." Although this kind of reflexive thinking about family as a system, as we have said, is not usual, we do not see it as a mechanization of the family. Model A merely provides a family with a way of looking at itself critically. Figure 8-2 is an illustration of the importance of mission statements in the relationship between producing systems and receiving systems.

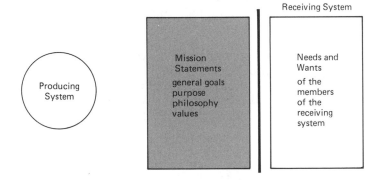

Figure 8-2

Goals—The Ability to Set Clear,
Behavioral Goals

Goals are behavioral translations of more general mission statements. When goals are achieved, the system performs well; that is, mission statements are translated into behavior, and the needs and wants of the members of the receiving system are actually met. Although mission statements can be general and philosophical, goals must be specific and behavioral. A well designed and functioning system, then, has goals that are:

- *behavioral*, clear, concrete, specific, operational;
- *measurable*, or in some way at least verifiable—it is clear when they have been accomplished;
- *realistic*, not set too high, capable of being accomplished with available resources;
- *worthwhile*, not set too low, not petty or meaningless; and
- *adequate;* that is, goals that are substantial translations of the mission of the system and that *de facto* satisfy real needs and wants.

Furthermore, in a well designed and functioning system, these goals are communicated clearly to the members, and system members are committed to the goals. Many systems, especially those that deliver human services, find it difficult to spell out clear, behavioral goals. Since goal clarity affects every other aspect of the system and its ability to function, the ability to establish realistic behavioral goals is not a luxury for any system.

It is easy to see that "hard" systems, such as manufacturing concerns and other for-profit businesses, cannot succeed if they have fuzzy goals. "Softer" systems, including human-services-delivery systems (schools) and community-living groups (families) are not pressed into goal setting. They seem to go on and serve their purpose without setting clear-cut behavioral goals in any explicit way. Some people even think that it is somewhat inhuman to demand clear-cut goals of community-living systems; we believe, however, that failure to establish and pursue concrete goals contributes to the "psychopathology of the average" of a system's members. The question is not *whether* behavioral goals should be established, but *how*. Obviously, families set and pursue goals in ways that differ from the more impersonal goal-setting process we find in the business world. A family that sets behavioral goals for itself in explicit, systematic ways will be better able to meet its needs more effectively. Figure 8-3 is an illustration of the importance of clear and concrete goals.

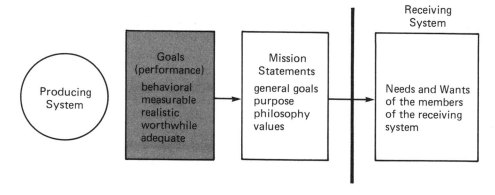

Figure 8-3

Programs—The Means for Achieving Goals

In a well designed and functioning system, systematic, step-by-step programs (means) are established to achieve clear, behavioral goals (ends). *Shaping* is the key behavioral term here; in this context it means that:

- each program moves step-by-step toward the goal,
- no step is too complicated or too difficult, and
- the connection of one step to the next is logical and clear.

If volunteers for a hot line are told "Just be a warm human being to the person who calls," they are being asked to engage in a program that is neither clear nor systematic, and it is unlikely that they will be very helpful to the caller.

In Figure 8-4, each step of the program is indicated by a number. The letter n refers to whatever number of steps any given program ultimately calls for. Simple programs might be carried out in a couple of steps, whereas complex programs might call for extensive chaining of steps. There might be many goals or subgoals in a complex system, in which case there would be a program for the accomplishment of each goal or subgoal.

The principle of shaping applies to the coordination of goals, subgoals, and programs in order to achieve some final overall goal, such as the production of an automobile. Extensive chaining of programs and subgoals is more common in the manufacture of products than it is in the delivery of human services such as counseling, but effective counseling involves shaping and program development, too. Some wonder why people can shape the complex goals, subgoals and programs that put a person on the moon but still find themselves unable to get eighth-grade students of some school districts to read at a sixth-grade level. There is no simple answer to such a problem, but part of the problem is often related to poorly devised and poorly shaped programs or to programs unrelated to clear, behavioral goals.

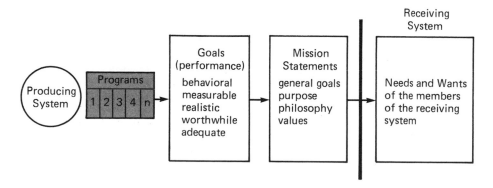

Figure 8-4

Families can also use well shaped programs to accomplish behavioral goals. For instance, if a goal is to give each of four children an opportunity to attend college without destroying the basic economic viability of the family, then the members of the family need to do some planning, including some serious program development. This program development might include sensible savings programs for both parents and children, part-time jobs for the children, and a reasonable division of the jobs that must be done around the house—all steps that lead to the family goal. Achievement of the goal is more likely if the family sees itself as a system cooperating to attain its goals and if it spells out its goal-related programs carefully. The ability to work together, mutual care, and successful achievement of intermediate goals are examples of the kinds of rewards or reinforcements families experience when they enable their members to commit themselves to long-range goals.

Education and Training—Working Knowledge and Skills for Program Implementation

In a well designed and functioning system, those responsible for the execution of any given program have both the working knowledge and the skills they need to carry out the programs effectively and efficiently; members are not asked to perform unless or until they possess both the working knowledge and the skills called for by the program. Therefore, well designed systems either select people who already have program-oriented working knowledge and skills, or they educate and train members to carry out programs efficiently. Volunteer programs sometimes collapse, not because the volunteers lose their sense of commitment, but because they do not have the necessary working knowledge and skills; they lose heart because they see themselves as inadequate for the task. Simple education and training programs could prevent this kind of failure in programs. In a well designed and functioning system, program-oriented working knowledge and skills are not taken for granted.

If the needs of the members of a family and of the family as a system are to be met, the members need the kinds of life skills described in Chapter 3. Ideally, these skills are first learned in the context of the family, and the first "internship" for their use occurs in this same context. School personnel find it difficult and frustrating to teach interpersonal skills to primary school students if these skills are not taught, modeled, encouraged, and rewarded in the real-life setting of the home. Some people fear that emphasis at home on training in life skills would be artificial and would make the home an uncomfortable place: "At home I want to be myself and not have to live up to anyone's expectations." Again, it is a question of how this education and training takes place. Imitation is a potent form of learning, especially at early developmental stages (Bandura, 1969, 1977); therefore, children will learn a great deal about life skills if their parents model these skills consistently. Explicit skills training in the family may be novel, but it can be as natural as other forms of education and training. Since

parents give children systematic training in such things as bicycle riding
and complement the school by doing tutorial work in reading and writing,
why should they neglect other life skills? Earlier, we gave the example of
the parents who had to train their children in the skills of budgeting and
saving. If the family is to provide, in part, the intimacy, support, and challenge its members need, then the skills required to implement programs
and the behaviors that achieve goals must be learned. Figure 8-5 illustrates
the importance of working knowledge and skills in the achievement of
goals.

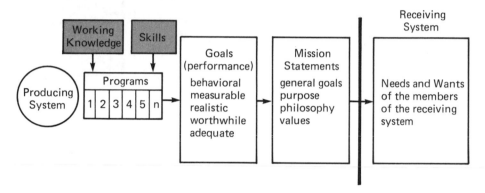

Figure 8-5

Other Resources Needed for the
Implementation of Programs

In a well designed system, resources that members need to execute
programs effectively and efficiently are provided at the time they are
needed. For instance, a highly skilled typist will do poorly if he or she must
use a defective typewriter or work in a poorly lighted and poorly ventilated
room. These "other resources" differ greatly in different organizations and
communities. Programs, then, are developed to make sure that resources
are available when needed; in a community mental-health clinic, this
might mean that rooms of adequate size, light, ventilation, cleanliness, and
comfort are available for group sessions; in a factory, it might mean that
effective machine-maintenance programs are developed so that "down
time" during regular working hours is avoided or minimized. When children are encouraged to develop good reading habits at home, they need
time to read, a place where they can read without being disturbed, and
adequate reading materials; without these "other resources," they cannot
develop and exercise their reading skills.

High-quality resources cannot substitute for working knowledge and
skills on the part of the system members. If teachers lack adequate teaching
and human-relations skills, then air conditioning, videotape equipment,
aesthetic buildings, and high-quality multimedia packages won't make up

for their basic deficiencies. On the other hand, highly skilled teachers can do excellent work without the benefits of sophisticated "other resources."

In Figure 8-6, *Other Resources* has been added to the model.

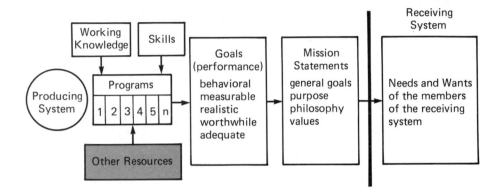

Figure 8-6

Structure—Division of Work That Serves Program Execution

If a system has more than one member, the work of the system must be divided. The term *structure* refers to the way in which the work or tasks of a system are divided among its members. In Figure 8-7, members A and B must cooperate in order to get Task 1 accomplished, but the remaining tasks of the system are divided between them.

In a simple system, structure might be very simple. Suppose Gary and Audrey cooperate to make rag dolls and sell them to novelty stores. Even in this simple system there are a number of structural possibilities:

- Gary makes the dolls, and Audrey sells them.
- Audrey makes the dolls, and Gary sells them.

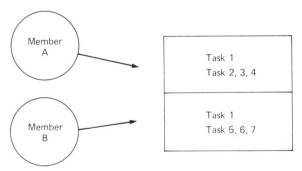

Figure 8-7

- According to an agreed upon schedule, sometimes Gary makes the dolls, whereas sometimes Audrey does; and sometimes Gary sells, whereas sometimes Audrey does.

However, in large systems that turn out complicated products such as automobiles, structure can be quite complex.

In a well designed and functioning system, whether it is small or large, structure exists so that programs might be executed and goals achieved as effectively and efficiently as possible. Structure is related to and determined by the goals and the goal-related programs of the system. Structure is not an end in itself (though it can become so in bureaucratic systems), but rather it exists in order to get the work of the system accomplished. Work should be divided fairly and in ways that respect the humanity of system members, but it should also be divided in such a way that it is done efficiently. If the structure of a system is clear to its members, then roles are also clear; members know what is expected of themselves and what to expect of others. Clarity of roles helps members invest themselves in programs more effectively.

One of the roles that arises from clear structure is that of leader. In corporations, the role of leader refers to the president, manager, supervisor, foreman, and the like. In the family, parents naturally assume leadership roles with respect to their children.

The family has a natural structure of parents and children that doesn't exist primarily "to get the work of the system accomplished," unless this work consists of living together, relating, and providing mutual services. However, the family *does* have tasks that should be divided among its members. Since structure—even natural structure—produces roles, role expectations among the members of a family should be clear. Families that examine their structures and roles don't necessarily develop stereotyped role expectations: "I'll earn the money, you take care of the children." As both children and parents advance to different developmental stages with different tasks and crises, their roles and role expectations change. The family in which open communication is normative has a chance to examine and handle the problems and possibilities that emerge from role transitions.

Structure Leads to Relationships

Structure, or the division of labor, leads to relationships. Relationships can be relatively simple in simple systems but in complex systems they are more numerous and more intricate. In well designed and functioning systems, relationships serve the effective and efficient execution of programs. Roles that arise from structure and relationships between roles are clear and clearly related to both programs and goals.

Good human relations within a system are not incompatible with high productivity; therefore, they should not be offered as an excuse for inefficiency. In a well designed system, there is a basic harmony among goals, programs, structure, and relationships; while fulfilling some of its members' needs for relating, the system does not place a disproportionate emphasis on meeting these needs. In a well designed work setting, people relate with respect and decency but ordinarily do not look for the intimacy of close friendship; however, they might well look for the kind of intimacy that comes from working closely with someone on a project.

In a well designed and functioning system, both structure and consequent relationships are *clear*—relationships between coworkers, between supervisors and workers, between workers of the producing system and members of the receiving system, between teams and departments, and between management and nonmanagerial personnel. Fuzzy relationships can lead to misunderstandings and unnecessary conflict and can stand in the way of efficient execution of programs. On the other hand, if goals and programs and structure are not clear, then relationships cannot be clear.

Technologies, such as human-relations training, team building, and conflict management, can be used to develop relationships, but those who use these technologies shouldn't lose sight of the purpose of relationships. These technologies are most useful when they are *systematic*—that is, related to the mission, goals, and goal-oriented programs of the system. The efficiency of a system can be hampered if people who don't need to relate to one another try to do so; in such a case, structure and the relationships that arise from structure need to be clarified.

Relationships in communities. Since one of the functions of a community is to foster relationships of various kinds, relationships in communities differ from those in organizations. Relating in communities is one of the *goals* of the system and not merely a means for achieving some other set of goals. The community or setting determines the kind of relationships that will develop; relationships obviously differ in family systems, self-help systems, friendship systems, and neighborhood systems.

In Japan, a great deal of effort goes into making the workplace a kind of community so that the distinction between organization and social community begins to blur. Workers meditate and recreate at the workplace and generally fulfill many of their social needs there. At times, the workers' families participate in the social life of the work "community." Workers often develop a deep sense of loyalty to the organizations for which they work.

For the last 20 years, there has been a movement in the West to humanize work settings without turning them into the kind of organization/communities found in Japan. The feeling is that, since work settings are *human* systems, they should fulfill some social needs. Strategies aimed at making organizations more responsive to the social and developmental needs of their workers without sacrificing production efficiency are constantly being tested. The issue of production efficiency versus the quality of the work setting is the object of a great deal of discussion and experimentation (see Heisler & Houck, 1977; Morrow & Thayer, 1977; Trist, 1977).

Effective Communication, Including the
Ability to Share Needed Information and
Give Evaluative Feedback

Structure leads to roles and relationships, and relationships demand communication (see Rockey, 1977). Communication in work settings does not exist for its own sake; it needs to be systematic—that is, related to getting the work of the system done. But the situation is different in community systems such as the family, where relating, and therefore communicating, is one of the goals of the system, since communication helps foster closeness. However, even community systems must organize themselves to get certain tasks done and in this respect become more like work systems. In this section we discuss two basic kinds of communication individuals need in order to pursue goals—information sharing and feedback.

Information sharing. In a well designed system, members freely share with one another the program-related information necessary to get the work of the system done. System members need to be reinforced for sharing relevant information if their system is to function properly. For instance, if subordinates are ignored or punished when they share negative information with management (a new product being developed is going to be too expensive or too unreliable for the present market), then information-sharing behavior decreases and the system suffers. Information should move freely both vertically and horizontally within a system, and people should receive positive recognition for sharing essential information, even when that information is "bad news." The resulting benefit of freely shared information is that the work of the system is done more effectively and efficiently. Withholding essential information from coworkers is a pet strategy in a system pervaded by a competitive, win/lose climate (see Argyris, 1976a, 1976b); members are concerned only for themselves, and withholding information, if it leads to personal advancement or gain, is reinforced. Obviously, these attitudes and practices impair the effectiveness of a system.

Feedback. A well designed and functioning system engages in ongoing evaluation. The term *evaluation* refers to a recognition and a reinforcement of what is going right and a recognition and a correction of what is going wrong. Since evaluation is a function of the system as a whole, all the members of the system should be part of the evaluative process, not just managers and supervisors. Individual system members can be important sources of feedback and evaluation for themselves. If frequent feedback from coworkers and supervisors is added to self-feedback, then ongoing evaluation becomes a reality. Ongoing feedback, then, rather than feedback at the end of a process, is essential. As we have seen, recognition for work well done is generally a potent reinforcer or motivator in systems. "Good job" is perhaps one of the most underused statements in systems.

Individuals often fail to give such feedback even to themselves in many situations.

Since relating is a goal in the family, the kinds of communication that characterize a family differ from those that characterize organizational systems. There is a great deal of conversation for the sake of conversation as a mode of relating among the members of a family. Still, sharing information and ongoing feedback can contribute to full family living if challenge rather than support alone is to characterize the family. In order to relate intimately and provide support and challenge for one another, the members of a family need the kind of interpersonal-communication skills discussed briefly in Chapter 3. The fact that family members possess these skills does not mean that communication must be deep and intense at all times; rather, it means that family members are capable of intensity and that they enjoy intense interactions from time to time. If parents are to help their children face developmental tasks and move through developmental transitions, they need to be able to share themselves and to help their children verbalize the problems related to these transitions.

Climate—The Quality of a System's Internal Environment

When we ask people "Is this a good place to work or to live?" we are asking them about the climate of a system—that is, the quality of its internal environment. Is the system structured to meet the legitimate needs of its members, and does it function to meet these needs?

Argyris and Schön (1974; Argyris, 1976a, 1976b) distinguish between what they call Model-I and Model-II systems. In Model-I systems, certain self-defeating assumptions or *governing variables* are operative and have a negative impact on the climate of the system. The following is a list of some common Model-I governing variables.

- It is important to win and not to lose.
- In the running of a system, rationality is to be encouraged, and emotions are to be discouraged.
- It is better to minimize or eliminate the expression of negative feelings.
- It is better for the system when all decisions come down from the top.

Certain *strategies*, such as controlling information flow in the system and withholding feelings, are used to implement these Model-I variables or

assumptions. Argyris and Schön claim that the results of the implementation of Model-I variables are predictable: system members become cautious and self-protective, competition replaces collaboration and cooperation, sources of information needed for learning dry up, public testing of
theories diminishes, overall system effectiveness decreases, and the climate
of the system contributes little to the development of its members.

Model-II governing variables or assumptions are different from (but
not the opposite of) those of Model I. The following is a list of some
Model-II variables.

- Information should be shared freely.
- Appropriate expressions of emotion, including negative emotions,
  are part of full human living and have a function in the life of systems.
- Positive reinforcement is more effective than negative control.

Predictable strategies emerge to implement Model-II assumptions:
asking for feedback, giving ongoing feedback, expressing negative feelings
in assertive rather than aggressive ways, surfacing and facing conflicts,
and seeking valid information from any source inside or outside the system. Argyris and Schön suggest that Model-II governing variables and
strategies lead to increased trust, heightened internal commitment to the
system and its goals, free flow of essential information, public testing of
opinions and theories, and increased long-term effectiveness.

Even though the world consists predominantly of Model-I systems,
Argyris (1976a, 1976b) suggests that an effectively designed and functioning system is based on Model-II governing variables and makes every attempt to implement these through Model-II strategies. He claims that
there is evidence showing that, although Model-I systems are initially
more efficient, Model-II systems are both more human and more efficient
in the long run.

When we talk about the need to develop a working knowledge of systems and systems-involvement skills in order to *cope* with systems, we
have in mind Model-I systems or the Model-I dimensions of the systems
with which we are involved. When we talk about acquiring working
knowledge and developing skills in order to help *change* systems, one kind
of change we have in mind is the movement from Model-I to Model-II systems. Argyris presents methods for improving the climate and, therefore,
the effectiveness of a system; however, he has discovered that changing a
Model-I system to a Model-II system is, under the best conditions, difficult
work that requires a long time frame.

Some people expect community systems such as families and friendships, in which caring and trust are supposedly normative, to be Model II
systems; however, families (and other community-living systems), like
organizations, can develop into Model-I systems in which human development is not fostered. Whether their members reflect on it or not, families

develop climates—close or distant, tense or relaxed, intense or bland, open or closed—through the behavioral correlates of these rather abstract terms. The family climate affects task accomplishment, the quality of relating, the ability to learn, and the general development of its members. We suggest that families develop a working knowledge of their own internal environments using models similar to those elaborated by Argyris and Schön to analyze the relationships among their members.

The Ability to Manage the Relationships between the System and the External Environment

We intimated in Chapters 4, 5, 6, and 7 that an effectively designed system has a working knowledge of its environment, which means that a system knows how it influences the receiving system as well as other systems in the environment. A steel company should be aware of how its pricing policies influence the economic climate of the country, how its pension policies affect not only its own employees but the climate of labor relations in the industry, and how its plants affect the physical environment. A well designed system also knows how it is being influenced by the other systems of the environment. A school or a school district should be aware of how the family life of its students affects the day-to-day functioning of the school, what impact the sociology of the neighborhood has on hiring teachers, how conservative or liberal political climates affect the curriculum, and how state fiscal policy affects extracurricular programs. A system that has clear goals, well shaped programs, and skilled workers who relate and communicate well can still cease to function if it hasn't taken into account the ways in which it is being influenced by the other systems of the environment. In Chapters 5 and 6, we suggested ways in which systems can acquire a working knowledge of their relationships with other systems of the environment. A working knowledge of the interaction of systems enables a system to meet the needs of its own members, protect itself from destructive environmental stress, and contribute to the growth and well-being of other systems in its environment. A system that is trying to transform itself from Model I to Model II might be particularly vulnerable to environmental influences, since the environment is filled with predominantly Model-I systems. If a Model-II system is one that is sensitive to whatever negative impact it might have as it pursues its goals, then it is at a disadvantage when it competes with Model-I systems that lack this sensitivity. In the case of such a disadvantage, the Model-II system cannot protect itself fully and needs the help of a *society* sensitive to environmental damage.

In Chapters 4, 5, 6, and 7, we pointed out that families need to acquire a working knowledge of themselves as systems and of the various ways they are affected by other personal systems, by the large institutions of society, and by the surrounding culture. If families are to protect themselves adequately from destructive influences, they need to join together in larger coalitions, such as church and neighborhood groups, that can provide rich resources for both development and defense.

Conclusions

Systems, like people, fall short of ideals and are in constant need of renewal. In the business marketplace, ineffective organizations sink. For instance, many newly established restaurants and magazines fail because they do not meet the needs of the public. But the situation is different with community-living and human-services-delivery systems. Although many married couples and families break up, it is also true that many stay together even when destructive or bland interactions predominate. Organizations that deliver services (governments, schools, churches, and many of the helping professions) remain intact even when they become ineffective, because their alternatives are unthinkable (anarchy, ignorance, "damnation," and "illness"). Since even inept delivery systems do provide needed services, however inefficiently, they are supported; therefore, such systems are very difficult to change.

As the members of a system increase their working knowledge of the logic of system design, they increase their ability to help a system discover its illogicalities. Model A provides the framework for a system "checkup." As Weisbord (1976) suggests, Model A can be placed over any system like a template or a radar screen. The "blips" are the inconsistencies, the trouble spots, the danger points, the "soft" areas needing attention and change. Model A, then, is the first step of Model B in that it provides a framework for system-wide diagnosis.

Model A also suggests the specific technologies needed to handle a system's problematic areas. For instance, if relationships and communication are poor within a work team, then team building is called for; if the members of the system are making a lot of mistakes in attempting to execute otherwise well shaped programs, or if other "blips" such as vague, nonbehavioral goals do not show up on the screen, then educational and training programs may be called for; if marketing and sales are fighting each other, then conflict management is called for. A working knowledge of Model A helps members see what types of technologies and skills they need to help the system renew itself. Model A, then, is a prerequisite for and leads into Model B. A systematic model for change can be applied to any "blip" that appears on the screen.

Model A is important for families, since they, like other systems, have a mission, however personal, and pursue this mission through concrete goals and programs, however informally. Model A can be useful for families as they organize themselves to accomplish tasks. If family members ignore the principles of effective organization, they can expect the consequences suffered by other systems that fail to coordinate mission, goals, and programs.

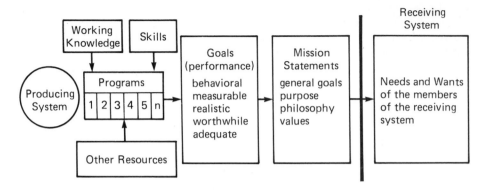

Figure 8-8

Summary

Figure 8-8 is an illustration of the principal features of Model *A*—the characteristics of a well designed and effectively operating system. In designing a system, we proceed from right to left; in working within a system, we proceed from left to right. In a well designed and functioning system:

1. *The basic principles of behavior and behavioral change* are understood thoroughly, respected, and used; they include such principles as reinforcement, shaping, modeling, punishment, and aversive control and conditioning. These principles are operative in every aspect of the system's functioning.
2. *The needs and wants of the receiving system* are assessed, and the output of the producing system is geared to meeting these needs and wants.
3. The members of the system know what the enterprise is about; *mission statements* embody general goals and purposes related to the needs and wants of the receiving system, system philosophy, and system values.
4. *Goals* are clear, concrete, specific, behavioral, operational, realistic, worthwhile, and adequate; they are communicated clearly to system members, and system members are committed to them.
5. *Programs* are designed to achieve each goal or subgoal. Multiple goals and subgoals are clearly coordinated with one another. Programs are well-shaped, clear, step-by-step processes that lead to goal achievement.
6. Those in charge of the execution of programs have the *working knowledge and skills* needed to do so; education and training programs are available to keep system members updated.

7. *Resources* (other than working knowledge and skills) are available when needed.
8. *Structure* serves goal achievement; work is divided up in ways that make the implementation of programs more efficient; roles are clear.
9. The *relationships* between roles that arise from structure are clear; system members know what they are about and how they relate to others. Team and department relationships are clear. All relationships serve program implementation and goal fulfillment. System members respect one another.
10. The *communication* needed to carry out programs and get the work of the system done is carried out in a direct way. Information is shared vertically and horizontally; all sources of feedback are operative.
11. To enhance the *internal environment* or *climate* of the system, Model-II governing variables and strategies are pursued for the sake of both good human relations and productivity.
12. The system is aware of the impact that other systems in the *environment* have on it and knows how to protect itself from a hostile environment. The system also knows what impact it has on the environment, including the receiving system, and it monitors this impact lest it be destructive.

Model B: A Systematic Approach to System Change

Once we have a clear picture of an effectively designed and functioning system to serve as a guideline or map, we can begin to make any system or subsystem look more like this ideal; in order to do this, we need a systematic, step-by-step model of change. Model *A*, then, is used for both designing and diagnosing a system, while Model *B* is used to change a system or any part of a system.

The Basic Problem-Solving Model Revisited

Many different models of change and organizational development have been described, but almost all of them are versions of what could be called the basic "folk model" of problem solving, which is nothing more than common sense or problem-solving logic. We discussed this model in Chapter 3, but now we want to take an extended look at it in the context of system change. As we have seen, the basic problem-solving model consists of the following steps:

- Diagnosis: find out where you are, what is going right and what is going wrong with the system.
- Goal setting: find out where you want to be. (The order between these first two may be reversed.)
- Program development: find out what means are needed to get you where you want to go.
- Program implementation: use these means.
- Evaluation: find out whether you've gotten where you wanted to go.

Then, since systems are in constant need of renewal, this process is recycled.

Change, in the sense of renewal, is a form of learning; it means learning how to do things better, more effectively, and more efficiently. It means learning how to meet the needs and wants of the members of the receiving system in better ways, how to face influences from the environment more constructively, and how to pursue system goals without harming the environment.

The following model of change is an expanded version of the problem-solving model we have already seen. The basic steps are:

- diagnosis,
- goal setting,
- program development, and
- implementation/evaluation.

Moreover, each step has been subdivided into an "expanding" and a "contracting" phase. For instance, in Stage I (Diagnosis), the "expanding" phase refers to a system-wide checkup, whereas the "contracting" phase, or "focusing," refers to the identification of the specific elements of the system that need change or reform. At the end of this contracting phase, we know what specific areas need attention; goals may be too fuzzy, programs may not be well shaped, the system members may not have the information and skills they need to carry out programs, and so forth. Figure 8-9 is an illustration of an overview of Model B.

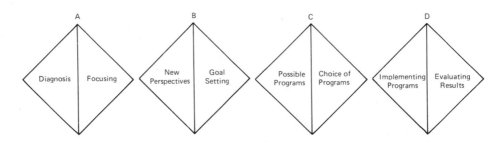

Figure 8-9.
An Overview of Model B.

The model depicted in Figure 8-9 has four stages: (A) Diagnosis, (B) Goal Setting, (C) Program Development, and (D) Implementation/Evaluation. Each phase has an "expanding" and a "contracting" subphase or step.

1. *Diagnosis:* the system, using Model *A*, takes its pulse.
2. *Focusing:* the system centers on elements in need of renewal.
3. *New perspectives:* new ways of carrying out the activities of the subsystem in need of renewal are considered.
4. *Goal setting:* behavioral goals are set, based on the new data considered in Step 3.
5. *Possible programs:* different means for achieving established goals are considered.
6. *Choice of programs:* the system commits itself to specific programs in order to achieve goals.
7. *Implementation:* the programs are carried out.
8. *Evaluation:* the system determines the effectiveness of programs in light of behavioral goals.

If the results are negative or only partially positive, the entire process, or part of it, is repeated; this is called *recycling* the change process.

Since change, like learning, is an ongoing, cyclic process, Model *B* can also be presented, like the learning model in Chapter 3, in the form of a circle. Figure 8-10 is an illustration of the circular form of Model *B*. The movement here is clockwise.

Let us take a look at each of the eight steps of the model.

Diagnosis—Reviewing the System and Focusing on Critical Areas

Step 1—System checkup. The system member with a working knowledge of Model *A* can use that model as a template or radar screen over the system or subsystem being diagnosed; the "blips" on the screen are trouble spots (see Weisbord, 1976). Some examples of trouble spots are: goals or subgoals are not clear, behavioral, and measurable; teams do not share essential information with one another freely; a husband fails to share essential information about his job—his discontentment with his work, the possibility of his being laid off, and so forth—with his wife. These will appear as trouble spots to a person with a working knowledge of Model *A*.

Step 1 is an expanding step; this means that one should not be too hasty in determining what is wrong and what needs changing in a system. For instance, the workers on a large machine in a manufacturing concern were not getting along with one another. The diagnosis of interpersonal conflict was quickly made and human-relations training programs were used to try to remedy the conflict and improve production. However, these programs didn't resolve the conflicts. Well into the human-relations training sessions, it was discovered that something was wrong with the machine! In Model *A*, such a problem with a machine would be in the

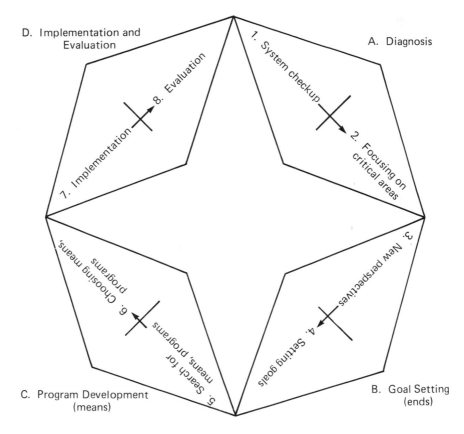

Figure 8-10.
The Process of System Change: A Systematic Model.

category of other resources, not in the category of relationships and communication. In the case of the workers on the machine, poor relating was a consequence, not a cause. Once the machine was repaired, harmony was reestablished.

General diagnosis includes the evaluation of not only the readiness or motivation of a system to change but also the capacity of a system to change. For instance, if change in a family system is predicated on the employment of both spouses, the economic status of the country may make such change temporarily impossible. Step 1 is an "expanding" step because it takes into consideration the whole picture—the entire system and its environment.

Step 2—Focusing. Once the "blips" appear on the radar screen— whether they arise from an assessment of the general functioning of the system, a consideration of the motivation of the system to change, or a determination of the ability of the system to change—the next step is to decide what facet of the system is most in need of attention.

When a number of "blips" appear on the screen, where should system members start? Where should they focus their energies for change? One answer is to start with crisis areas. If a "blip" spells danger for the very existence of the system, then crisis intervention is called for. If the administration and staff of a mental-health agency are in such conflict over the very mission of the agency that clients are being served poorly and the agency itself is in danger of collapsing, conflict-management procedures are called for. However, crisis intervention should not be the normal approach to change. Such "management by crisis" is both expensive in every sense of the word and, in the long run, ineffective.

Attempts at noncrisis change are best directed toward areas in which change is quite possible, toward changes that will have a positive system-wide impact, and toward areas that are relatively easy to handle. Meeting these three conditions simultaneously constitutes an application of the behavioral principle of shaping to the change process. Step 2 becomes easier as members' experience with a system grows and they develop a sense of "clinical judgment," or the ability to identify which areas need immediate attention and which changes can be postponed. Clinical judgment requires both experience and decision-making skills.

Attaining New Perspectives and Establishing Goals

Step 3—New perspectives. A careful diagnosis of the problems and needs of the system leads to goal setting—determining what, concretely, will make the system more effective. Step 3 is an expanding step, which means that alternatives should be considered and goals should not be set too quickly. The new-perspectives step suggests the use of such techniques as divergent thinking, brainstorming, scenario writing, and fantasy in order to discover new goal possibilities related to the problems or potentials of the system. For instance, when students in a classroom aren't committed to the goals of the system, one way to capture their interest is to "give them a piece of the action"—that is, to get them involved in the teaching process as a way of getting them involved in learning. The problem is apathy; the need is for interest, initiative, and commitment. One possible goal is to use students as interns, teaching one another or teaching younger students as a way of learning themselves (see Rogers, 1969, pp. 11–27). As more goal possibilities are uncovered, it becomes more likely that the goal finally chosen will most creatively satisfy the needs of the system.

Step 4—Establishing goals. Decision-making skills are needed in order to choose the best among possible goals. As we have already seen, to be effective, goals must be clear, concrete, specific, behavioral, attainable, and adequate to handle the problem calling for attention. If the members of a curriculum committee for a school of nursing are faced with the fact that their graduates go into hospitals without adequate human-relations skills, their goal cannot be "to do something about developing human-relations skills in nursing trainees"; this goal is too vague. The requirements for goal setting would be fulfilled if the committee members determined to establish a human-relations training curriculum to parallel the medical and nursing-skills curriculum. The goal or goals should state what skills will be taught and indicate how proficiency is to be evaluated. If an overriding goal includes subgoals, then these subgoals should be spelled out clearly together with their relationship to the overriding goal.

Program Development—Searching for Means and Choosing Means

Step 5—The search for means. Since this is an "expanding" step, care should be taken not to choose means too quickly. If the goal is to establish an internship program through which students learn by teaching other students, care should be taken to consider how many different ways this goal might be accomplished. If the goal in a family is to increase the amount of time spent together, one parent may decide unilaterally that all day Sunday every Sunday is to be a family day, but this would be a disastrous means. There is much greater commitment both to goals and means when those who are affected by them have a say in establishing them. The skills of brainstorming and divergent thinking and techniques such as forcefield analysis (Egan, 1975) are most useful in the search for means.

Step 6—Choosing means. In order to choose means wisely, the members of a system need decision-making skills. These skills include: the ability to clarify values and apply them to the choosing process, the ability to evaluate means according to the task and "people" needs of a system and the possible conflicts that exist between the two, and the ability to see programs as means and not as ends in themselves. In human-services delivery and community-living systems, programs or means are frequently chosen because they are attractive in themselves and not because they are the most likely means to achieve the behavioral goals that have been established. It is a mistake to move from mission to means or programs without going through the agonizing process of establishing behavioral, measurable goals. A person working for the welfare board of an eastern seaboard state told us that this is precisely what happens in her agency. Each bright new program that comes on the scene is tried, but little effort is expended in the behavioral clarification of goals. Programs come and go, but the system itself does not improve.

Implementation/Evaluation

Step 7—Implementation of programs. Implementation includes launching a program and maintaining momentum in it; this depends on how well shaped the program is—whether it is a clear, step-by-step progression toward the goal—and how well other basic principles of human behavior, such as modeling and reinforcement, are used to maintain the program.

A weight-loss group is a system in which the goal is clear: each member wants to lose a certain number of pounds in a specific amount of time without taking the health risks involved in unsupervised crash diets. In one weight-loss program, the members were told that they would lose weight if they observed two rules. (1) Obey the contract: eat formally whenever you eat anything (for example, set the table and use a knife and fork to eat a candy bar), eat alone (except for the main meal), and do nothing else while you eat. (2) Come to the weight-losers meeting every other week to report on fidelity to the contract and on weight loss or gain. These two stipulations constituted the program. At the meetings, members were praised for keeping the contract and encouraged to continue to do so for the next two weeks. Of course, people tired of eating formally, alone, and without other distractions. With greater and greater frequency, members deicded not to snack, because it was too much trouble. At the meetings, people were praised, or reinforced, when they reported weight loss. For many, the program worked. It was novel enough to sustain interest; it was simple, straightforward, and sufficiently reinforced. Eventually, losing weight itself became the principal reinforcement.

Unforeseen problems often arise when an attempt is made to implement programs. The programs may prove to be too difficult, they may fail to achieve goals, or system members may not have the skills necessary to execute them. But problems that arise can themselves become objects of the problem-solving process. For instance, when programs are diagnosed as being too difficult, the goal is to shape them more effectively. Ways of reshaping programs are considered and implemented in the problem-solving process.

Step 8—Evaluation. Program evaluation is possible only when goals are behaviorally clear and thus provide clear-cut criteria for evaluation. Evaluation, therefore, is tied intimately to goal setting. If goals are fuzzy, evaluation will be just as fuzzy. Unfortunately, some human-services delivery systems, such as schools, government agencies, and religious organizations, rarely evaluate themselves closely and therefore fail to set concrete behavioral goals for themselves.

Finally, it should be noted that Model *B* can be used in either an authoritarian or a participative way. External conformity without real commitment often results when change is forced upon people with little or no opportunity on their part to participate in the decision-making process. If members are to commit themselves to the goals and programs of the system itself (Model *A*) or those of a process of renewal or change (Model *B*), then their participation in the establishment of these goals and programs is important.

Recycling

One of Bronfenbrenner's (1977b) mentors once told him "If you want to understand something, try to change it." This statement can be applied to attempts to change systems, because every attempted change is a source of new knowledge about the particular systems. Any rigid use of Model *B* is impossible; effective agents of change move back and forth between the steps of the model. For instance, when people begin to look for possible ways of achieving goals that have been set (Step 5), they might discover that their diagnostic procedures were inadequate and find themselves forced to repeat some of Step 1.

Since renewal is an ongoing process, recycling is necessary even after successful efforts to change systems. If an organization remains static while its internal or external environment undergoes change, the organization will be in trouble. An effective system doesn't merely react to environmental changes; rather, it monitors both its internal and external environment. This does not mean that systems become the playthings or victims of their environments, for every system needs a degree of stability in order to organize its forces in pursuit of its goals. The family that is open to every new fad will dissipate its energies and fall apart. On the other hand, the family that remains ignorant of significant cultural changes and the demands these changes make on the family as a system might not realize the need for change. For instance, if family members believe that males are still the sole breadwinners and urge them to find employment while encouraging the females to learn household tasks, they might find themselves in a bind in a culture that expects women to fill some of the jobs men have traditionally held. And the women of the family might not be ready for men who expect both partners to work during the early years of marriage. In other words, the family's ignorance of cultural changes can impede the progress of the children through developmental transitions defined by the culture.

A working knowledge of Models *A* and *B* and the technologies and skills needed to apply them make up the central systems-involvement skills. Individual members who possess these skills will know how to cope with repressive systems, even though they may not have a power base to influence changes in the systems. If a system is open to change, then individual members who have a working knowledge of the basic logic of systems and possess systems-involvement skills can become contributors to the process of change. Obviously, a brief review of these two models does not give individuals the skills needed to implement them, but these models do provide a framework for determining the kinds of technologies and skills people need to invest themselves more fully in systems.

Other Systems-Involvement Skills

Helping Skills

Since individuals experience crises as they move through developmental stages and face developmental tasks, and since they experience these crises in the context of (and sometimes because of) the systems of their lives, these systems should be able to provide individuals with whatever help they need in terms of support, challenge, and problem solving. If individuals are to be helped in the context of family, peer systems, work situations, church groups, and the like, the members of these systems

Models and Skills for Effective Involvement
within the Social Systems of Our Lives
147

need the models, techniques, and skills of helping (Egan, 1975). We believe that helping need not be left entirely to professionals but that a great deal of it can take place within the context of the systems that constitute much of people's lives (Gartner & Riessman, 1977).

The peer self-help movement is probably providing more help than all the helping professions combined, and helping is seen more and more as a process of equipping individuals and systems to help themselves. School systems are developing peer-counseling programs, businesses are attempting to rehabilitate the alcoholics who work for them, supervisors, foremen, and managers are taking courses in helping skills, group counseling is flourishing, and some family therapy is geared to giving the family the kinds of skills it needs to face its own problems. Not only is helping in the form of models and skills being "given away," but it is taking place more and more in the contexts of systems. Therefore, these systems and their members should school themselves in the models, techniques, and skills that make peer helping at all levels an informed and effective process.

Education and Training Skills

Human development depends a great deal on education and training. We suggest, therefore, that these skills of educating and training also be "given away" (Aspy, 1972; Aspy & Roebuck, 1977; Carkhuff & Berenson, 1976; Carkhuff, Berenson, & Pierce, 1977). Nonprofessionals, of course, educate and train constantly. Parents, for example, are entrusted with the education and training of their children, but they often perform these tasks poorly because they lack models and skills. The same can be said of many teachers: they come away from formal training institutions poorly equipped to educate and train. Thomas Gordon has established education and training systems to give skills away to parents (1970), educators (1974), and those responsible for the management of systems (1977).

Three principal ingredients of effective training are: (1) a systematic model, (2) skills, techniques, and methodologies, and (3) training systems. If people are being trained in helping skills, then a comprehensive model for helping is in order—a model solidly based on theory and research (Carkhuff & Berenson, 1977; Egan, 1975). Moreover, people must be trained in the skills, techniques, and methodologies that make each phase of the model operative. In the helping model, for instance, people are trained in the skill of confrontation as a way of helping others discover new perspectives and new possibilities for action. Finally, systematic training methodologies need to be established to give those who educate and train others step-by-step programs through which they can impart skills (Carkhuff, 1977).

We firmly believe that training people in skills and in the models, techniques, and training methodologies they need to train others will humanize rather than mechanize both people and systems. Even highly systematic approaches to training and training methodologies are only as rigid and mechanistic as the trainers who use them. Life, from one point of view, can be defined as learning; giving people learning, training, and teaching skills can provide them with freedom from haphazard living, opening the way to the freedom of spontaneous living.

Conclusion

In this chapter, we have presented a brief overview of some of the kinds of working knowledge and skills individuals need to involve themselves creatively in systems. The emphasis here has been on rational and systematic means of fostering organizational goal attainment. We are aware, however, that much of human life is concerned neither with rationality nor with explicit goals. People need a quality of contact and interaction that is not necessarily directly related to efficiency or achievement. The need for human support and mutuality and how this need can be addressed by those whose task it is to foster human development is treated more fully in Chapter 11. In the following chapter, we discuss what systems can do to foster the development of their members.

Chapter 8: Additional Resources

Alternative Institutions. *Journal of the Applied Behavioral Sciences* (Special issue), 1973, *9*, 2–3.

Havelock, R. *The change agent's guide to innovation in education.* Englewood Cliffs, N.J.: Educational Technology Publications, 1973.

Luthans, F., & Kreitner, R. *Organizational behavior modification.* Glenview, Ill.: Scott Foresman, 1975.

Sperry, L., Mickelson, D., & Hunsaker, P. *You can make it happen.* Reading, Mass.: Addison-Wesley, 1977.

Thompson, J. *Organizations in action.* New York: McGraw-Hill, 1967.

9

How Human Systems Can Foster Human Development

Beyond Individual Coping

In this chapter, we would like to turn our attention from what is to what might be. Can human systems be more than something to be understood and coped with by individuals? Can they carry out their various missions *and* offer their members the challenge and support necessary for human development? If you have accepted our premise that human development is continuously affected by systems, you will readily see that these two questions are of fundamental importance to a society with a commitment to the development of individuals who are capable of competent and responsible social living. Human systems are the classrooms of life within which competence for social living is attained, attenuated, or destroyed.

In recent years, the issue of "corporate social responsibility"—which refers to the obligations the business world has, beyond making a profit—has been widely examined (Buchholz, 1977; D. Jones, 1977; Purcell, 1976). Air and water pollution, abandonment of our urban centers, and unequal employment opportunities are among the issues that have called attention to the societal ramifications of corporate policy. Moreover, questions have been raised concerning the policies of governmental, educational, and religious institutions (Berger & Neuhaus, 1977; Lakoff & Rich, 1973). We would like to address the issue of the social responsibility of systems by posing the following question: what are the responsibilities of human systems at all levels to their members and to society as a whole? Our provisional answer to this question is twofold. First, systems are responsible for assessing the *direct* effects of their policies and practices ("bottom line" issues of productivity and profit in corporate systems; numbers of contacts in a community mental health center) on the development of their members as well as the effectiveness of the system in accomplishing its mission. One purpose of this chapter is to indicate how this assessment might be made. Second, systems are responsible for assessing the *indirect* effects of their policies and practices on the development of their members. The practices of a system that diminish or destroy the capacity of an individual person to participate effectively in the other settings of his or her life contribute to the weakening of the social fabric of our world and must be questioned for the sake of the commonweal.

We will cite two examples to illustrate what we mean by indirect developmental effects. In the first example, we examine these indirect effects in an immediate setting. Individuals may have little or no energy left to invest in family living if they are regularly required to take home a great deal of work in order to succeed in their jobs. This lack of energy will have an impact not only on the development of the workers but also on their families. Their marriages, as well as their children's experiences in the classroom, will suffer as a result of the negative impact on the development of the family. And all these negative effects will, in turn, make it more difficult for the individuals to return to the workplace rested and capable of quality investment in its mission.

Our second example of an indirect developmental effect refers to the impact of one of the larger systems—the economy—on immediate settings and individuals. The recent report of the Carnegie Council on Children (Keniston, 1977) suggests that a society can give fundamental assistance to the development of its children by implementing policies that make employment available to the heads of families. The debate over how employment should be made available—by the private or the public sector—will no doubt continue. In the interim, the children of families living with severe and chronic financial instability are victims of developmental tragedy. The specific outcomes of this tragedy—crime, broken homes, delinquency, and educational failure—and their ramifications throughout our society illustrate the interdependence of systems.

Individuals who shape policy and practice in systems—parents, teachers, supervisors, managers, and informal leaders—are faced with two main questions regarding both direct and indirect developmental effects of systems. (1) Does membership in their system hurt individuals as human beings? (2) Does membership in their system tend to foster the development of individuals as human beings?

It is possible to answer these questions by examining the daily experiences of people in systems. The first question concerns the results of system functioning from a preventive standpoint: can people participate in the system from day to day, month to month, and year to year without being ground up as human beings in the process? Do they move from the system to the other areas of their lives in at least as human a condition as when they arrived? The second question concerns the issue of development: is the system a positive source of challenge and support for its members? Do they move from the system to the other areas of their lives more fully human than when they arrived? An analysis of the first question can lead to prevention strategies; an analysis of the second can lead to developmental approaches within the system.

The Human Side of Human Systems: A Retrospective

In his seminal work on organizational theory, Douglas McGregor (1960) outlined several basic assumptions of a new theory of behavior in organizations:

- A primary function of management is the organization of people and resources to meet the goals of a system.
- People learn passivity and resistance to organizational goals as a result of prior experience.
- Management's task is to assist individuals to elicit motivation, potential for development, readiness to participate in organizational goals, and capacity to assume responsibility, which are present in all people.
- The organization's basic task is to arrange conditions so that individual and organizational goal attainment are combined.

McGregor cites decentralization and delegation, job enlargement, participative management, and new approaches to performance appraisal as possible improvements in system functioning. We refer here to McGregor's work because he took as his explicit concern "the human side of enterprise." McGregor's approach constitutes an initial attempt to focus simultaneously on human *and* organizational needs—a recognition of the fact that a unidimensional perspective of people or systems is limited, because people and their systems are intertwined. In the years that followed McGregor's initial work, interest grew in the individual/organization question. Writing in the early 1960s, Argyris noted:

> Organizations and personalities are discrete units with their own laws, which make them amenable to study as separate units. However, we also believe that important parts of each unit's existence depend on their connectedness with the other. We hypothesize that one cannot fully understand the individual without understanding the organization in which he is embedded and vice versa. We are not negating the value of studying individuals or organizations. Our primary interest is at the boundaries of both—at the points where they overlap and are interrelated [1964, p. 13].

The title of Argyris' work, *Integrating the Individual and the Organization*, suggests the simultaneous person/system focus that we alluded to in reviewing McGregor's work. Argyris' description of the "organization of the future" (1964, p. 273) seems to build on and amplify McGregor's assumptions:

- Values will be central to overall organizational planning.
- The importance of human relationships in the organization will be emphasized.
- Independence and commitment on the part of system members will be encouraged.
- New ways of fostering members' interest in the "health" of the system will become important.
- Alternative, nonhierarchical ways of structuring the organization will emerge.
- Emphasis will be placed on feedback and performance rather than on controls.

Argyris deepens and expands McGregor's perspective by stressing the importance of members' authentic commitment to system goals. He suggests that members who are committed to goals require their system to address itself to three key issues:

- the system's values and how they are implemented,
- interpersonal relationships in the system, and
- shared decision making in the system.

In recent work on effective organizations, Argyris' thought has further evolved, and a deepening emphasis on the human climate of the organization is observable (1976a, 1976b). The following assumptions about organizational functioning will give you the flavor of this evolution:

- Cooperation is more productive than competition.
- The free sharing of information leads to enhanced organizational performance.
- Free and informed choice is to be encouraged among members.
- Self-directed behavior by system members is preferable to external controls.
- Positive reinforcement is more effective than punishment.
- The expression of emotion is part of full human living.
- Safety and security are most often found in a supportive group.

There is a great difference between McGregor's "organization of people and resources to meet systems goals" and Argyris' "the expression of emotion is part of full human living." And yet, both McGregor and Argyris are clearly members of an emerging school that emphasizes the human aspect of organizations rather than human development or potential per se.

Model A: Implications for the Development of System Members

When we first outlined Model A, we focused on how a system might use the model to effectively accomplish its particular mission. In this chapter, we would like to emphasize how a system might use Model A as a guide in providing conditions that are likely to enhance the development of its members. Our intent is not to suggest a prescription for a finely calibrated developmental environment that is responsive to the needs of everyone. The relative lack of information about development, especially adult development, makes such a prescription unrealistic. Even if our knowledge were adequate to the task, the question of what values should be used to structure such an environment would be a difficult one (see Perry, 1977). Our goal, which we believe to be realistically hopeful, is to determine what conditions a system can provide that will have appreciable effects on the well-being and development of its members, irrespective of their age, sex, race, socioeconomic status, or educational level. We concentrate here on general principles that will assist any system in determining how it affects the development of its members. Systems whose members tend to have specific developmental needs (such as preschools, high schools, issue-centered support groups, and homes for the elderly) and systems that include highly diverse groups (such as religious congregations, neighborhood organizations, and large corporations) will find different uses for developmental analysis.

The following elements of Model *A* (see Chapter 8) are especially potent in their effects on the development of a system's members:

- Principles of behavior
- Goals
- Programs
- Working knowledge and skills
- Other resources
- Structure
- Communication
- Climate

Each of these items will now be considered in detail.

The Principles of Behavior

Whether or not the principles of human behavior are respected in a system affects everything that occurs there. A system in which people are punished for negative behavior rather than reinforced for maintaining desired behavior may accomplish its mission—though perhaps not as effectively as it might (see Argyris, 1976a)—but it probably won't contribute to the well-being or development of its members. For example, teachers who attend only to negative behavior, and who do so principally by applying punishment, tend to foster two conditions in their classrooms. First, students are likely to prefer negative attention to no attention; as a result, negative behavior is actually reinforced by the attention it invariably evokes from the teacher (Patterson & Gullion, 1971). Second, punishment is likely to create emotional avoidance of the situation to which it is related (Watson & Tharp, 1977). Teachers' use of punishments, in other words, conditions a negative emotional response to learning in people who spend ten or fifteen years in formal learning settings.

The developmental implications of the principles of human behavior can be seen clearly in relation to the concept of shaping. A human system can shape the tasks of its members in many ways, but the basic issue is this: how can a system break down complex tasks—self-management in the classroom, independent living, work behavior, career decisions, intimate communication, and system involvement—into subtasks that can be mastered in a step-by-step fashion?

Our society has assiduously applied the principle of shaping to problems of high technology, such as manufacturing an automobile or learning to fly jet aircraft, but it rarely considers its utility in coping with the skills of effective living. Examples of recent attempts to apply shaping principles to tasks relevant to system functioning can be found in the areas of decision making (Kaufman, 1976), problem solving (Carkhuff, 1973), interpersonal-relationship enhancement (Egan, 1976, 1977; Gazda, 1973), and teaching and supervision (Carkhuff, Berenson, & Pierce, 1977; Gerhard, 1971). These shaping programs are examples of concrete steps that systems can take in order to break down complex developmental tasks into manageable subtasks.

As an example of how the principle of shaping can be used, a business firm that desires to provide adequate and decent feedback to its members through its supervisory personnel might initiate the following program:

- *Phase 1.* Train supervisors in the basic interpersonal skills of self-disclosure and accurate empathy. (See Egan, 1976, 1977.)
- *Phase 2.* Train supervisors in advanced interpersonal skills of responsible challenge. (See Egan, 1976, 1977.)
- *Phase 3.* Train supervisors in the rudiments of assisting someone to change behavior in a desired direction. (See Watson & Tharp, 1977.)
- *Phase 4.* Train supervisors to apply learned skills to selected real-life tasks, to report on the results, and to receive feedback on their efforts.
- *Phase 5.* Provide an ongoing source of consultation and support, including additional training if necessary, to supervisory personnel through a chief supervisor.

A letter from management to supervisors mandating effective supervision is an approach that violates the principle of shaping, however laudable the motive may be. A well-shaped program for enhancing the effectiveness of supervision uses shaping to significantly increase the probability of attaining the desired goal.

Systems that do not reinforce effective task behavior of their members cannot hope to see that behavior maintained (Egan, in press; Watson & Tharp, 1977). In short, a system will find that it gets from its members the behavior that it shapes and reinforces. The principles of shaping and reinforcement have been applied to child rearing and family living (Patterson, 1973; Patterson & Gullion, 1971), the classroom (Carkhuff, Berenson, & Pierce, 1977; Gerhard, 1971) and organizations (Sperry, Mickelson, & Hunsaker, 1977). The principles of human behavior are a fundamental source of developmental challenge and support to human beings and to systems, and as such, they constitute a basic working knowledge for effective systems.

Goals

When system members are committed to the system's goals, a sense of participation in a significant or meaningful activity is made possible. How is such commitment to be fostered?

Minimal and maximal degrees of participation by system members are possible with respect to goals. Minimally, members are clearly informed of the system's behavioral goals and where their particular tasks fit into these goals. Maximally, they collaborate in the elaboration of goals that translate the system's mission into specifics. The extent to which members should be involved in the elaboration of goals varies with the mission of a particular system; however, in our view, the potential for involving system members in this process is rarely explored.

A family that encourages the input of its members regarding a variety of goals—housekeeping, finances, recreation, community involvement, or religious training—is likely to increase its members' sense of responsibility as well as facilitate the development of their decision-making skills and awareness of others' views and rights (Newman & Newman, 1975). On the other hand, a family whose goal-setting and goal-sharing procedures are unilateral and nonnegotiable often finds itself in the position of exacting compliance from family members, thus reducing the opportunity of encouraging voluntary involvement in family activities. Unilateral goal setting and goal sharing are, of course, relevant to other important personal systems, including the school, the workplace, the parish, and the neighborhood. Participative management programs (Drucker, 1974; McGregor, 1960; Susman, 1976), in which system members collaborate with management in arriving at certain policy choices, are examples of how systems can attempt to actively engage their members in setting and sharing goals.

Although no one approach to the involvement of members in meaningful ways with the goal-setting process will serve the great diversity of human systems, any system that prizes the development of its members would do well to seek ways of involving them in setting the system's goals. Individual involvement is of particular importance to those systems whose *raison d'etre* is the development of their members, such as families, schools, and religious congregations.

One of the authors, for example, has found that calling the attention of junior and senior undergraduate seminar students to the covert effects of the college curriculum (see Chapter 7; Giroux & Penna, 1977) and encouraging them to take responsibility as a group for setting learning goals and means initially results in a mixture of anger, excitement, and confusion on their part. When these feelings have been resolved, however, the seminar tends to proceed in a manner that suggests a heightened sense of "ownership" on the part of many of the students—an observation supported by their later evaluations of the seminar.

Programs

Effective programs permit a human system to translate clear goals into purposive action. The basic issue is this: a system that wishes to engage its members effectively in complex behavior must break that behavior down into step-by-step subunits. These subunits must then be linked to form a meaningful whole. Programs are the concrete steps that human systems take to attain their goals.

A system's programs are critical to the well-being and development of its members, because they dictate the specific tasks members will engage in day after day. Most adults spend the greater part of their waking hours engaged in the programs of their workplace. Much of the remainder of their time is spent in the programs of other immediate settings—families, religious congregations, organizations, and communities. When people spend the bulk of their day engaged in these programs, how can the programs fail to significantly affect the quality of their lives?

Some "diagnostic" questions regarding the impact of the programs of immediate settings on the well-being and development of members may be helpful at this point.

- *The family.* How does the role played by each member of the family—breadwinner, disciplinarian, nurturer, free spirit, scholar—affect his or her development? Are there alternative ways of involving the individual in family life that would be beneficial?
- *The workplace.* How does the repetition of particular tasks over an extended period of time—clerical work, technical planning, operating a punch press, supervising production, counseling others, accounting, managing a home—affect those who engage in them? What means do people have of minimizing the negative effects of their work while maximizing the positive effects?
- *The classroom.* How does the form of education—lecture versus discussion, competition versus cooperation, democratic versus autocratic decision making—affect the development of students? What relevance does the curriculum have to the development of the students? Have teachers made it possible for students to tell them how they are affecting the students? Do teachers listen when students tell them how they are being affected?
- *The religious congregation.* Do people experience this setting as a real, personal, and significant one? Are the members of religious congregations aware of a meaningful and integrated set of communal activities or programs to which their commitment is essential if the congregation is to succeed in its mission? To what extent are members involved in shaping programs?

Systems, particularly those with fundamental commitments to people, can ask themselves no question more basic than this: what happens to a human being who participates day after day in the programs of this system?

Working Knowledge and Skills

Our educational system is geared largely to cognitive competence and the mastery of information. We would never assent to the proposition that a high school graduate need not have an understanding of mathematics or basic competence in reading. However, basic skills required for effective living, such as the ability to listen accurately to another human being, are left to be acquired randomly, if at all. As a result of this bias in favor of cognitive/technical competence, human systems—from the family to the corporation—have neglected other significant types of human competence.

The notion of a deliberate approach to social/psychological education—education for effective living—was discussed in Chapter 3. We maintain that the acquisition of certain skills and knowledge crucial for competent living in a complex society—self-management, problem solving, decision making, and system involvement—should no longer be left to chance. Systems that wish to foster the development of their members must provide these basic skills of effective living in the event that members do not already possess them. Examples of how social/psychological education and training might be provided for system participants include:

- training programs in human-relations skills for employees, students, and congregations,
- parenting education programs,
- education of teachers, employers, and ministers regarding the developmental events of particular life stages, and
- training programs for agents of system change.

It should be noted that all of these programs, and many others that could be added to the list, are currently available in many homes, schools, work settings, and religious congregations. Training and education programs for effective social living are available to the system that desires them.

Other Resources

It would be absurd to equip people with adequate knowledge and skills and then fail to provide the tools they need for task accomplishment. Providing a pool of trained typists with faulty machines or inadequate lighting is an example of a situation in which knowledge and skills are available but other resources are not.

Herzberg (1966) has suggested that working conditions are important but not essential to satisfaction in a work system. In our view, adequate supporting resources play a similar role in effective systems; they can facilitate but do not of themselves account for system effectiveness and member development. Maslow's hierarchy of needs (Maslow, 1968; McGregor, 1960) suggests that more complex human needs surface only after more basic needs are met. Other resources constitute one type of basic need, and their absence has a significant negative impact on the development of system members. Although the workplace typically creates its own supporting resources and environment, other key personal systems, such as families and schools, are extremely vulnerable to the policies and practices of institutions with regard to the supporting resources they are able to offer their members (see Berger & Neuhaus, 1977; Keniston, 1977).

Structure

The need for structure raises the issue of division of labor in systems and its impact on the development of system members. A basic dilemma that illustrates the interrelatedness of system functioning and member development emerges here. It often seems most efficient to devise a division of labor for a particular task on strictly logical, rational, and technical grounds—what is the quickest and least expensive way of getting this task done? However, this strictly rational approach disregards the fact that human beings operate on a psychological as well as a logical basis (Ausubel, 1968). Systems should effectively merge decisions regarding task efficiency with awareness of their members' needs, understanding that, if either is neglected, the system's effectiveness is likely to be compromised. A case in point is the Scandinavian automobile company that trains workers in a variety of jobs and then rotates work scheduling so that workers engage sequentially in several tasks rather than repeat one task day after day (Goldman, 1976).

While the balance of efficiency and human needs is important in any system, it is basic in those systems whose primary role is the development of human beings. It may seem efficient when parents make all family decisions or when teachers establish a strict methodology for the classroom, but this "efficiency" proves to be illusory when it produces persons who have little capacity for effective self-directed learning and little or no ability to involve themselves meaningfully in the lives of others.

Douglas Heath (1968, 1977a) has engaged in research that illustrates the effects of the structure employed by personal systems on the development of their members. Heath's longitudinal study of the impact of higher education on the development of college students (1977b) suggests a startling conclusion: the more capable students are in terms of academic competence, the more likely they are to experience difficulties later in nonacademic aspects of living, such as marriage and family life. Heath suggests that contemporary higher education tends to produce people who are interpersonally immature, and he maintains that this immaturity is caused by a major aspect of the typical classroom experience—competition. It must be noted that an ethos of competition is characteristic of our culture and that it is therefore unlikely that significant lower-level systems—institutional and personal—would not be subject to this same ethos. At the same time, it is ironic that higher education, with its primary commitment to the "examined life," reinforces competitive behavior uncritically.

Programs (tasks) and structure (how tasks are accomplished) affect the well-being and development of system members. The question is not whether the development of members is affected by the program/structure combination, but how it is affected.

Communication

Decent relationships are a fundamental requirement for the development of people and systems. Basic decency in interpersonal communication means that persons are capable of presenting their perceptions, thoughts, feelings, and values to one another in straightforward and non-destructive ways and are capable of listening to one another and of viewing the world from the frame of reference of fellow system members (see Chapter 11 and Egan, 1976, 1977). In no sense should this be construed as a plea for an "encounter group" model of human systems functioning. The extent to which relationships are central to the mission of a system varies with the system's purpose. Relationships assume a central role in families and other living communities. In a factory, relationships are important but clearly subordinate to production tasks. The classroom might be cited as an example of a system in which a balance should exist between the importance of relationships and the importance of tasks.

Once basic human decency has been established in relationships, information sharing and feedback must occur if system goals are to be met and member development is to be fostered. The information needed to engage effectively in one's role and to see how that role fits into the overall goals of the system is a basic resource for the development of persons; without such information, it is impossible for the individual to engage in purposeful and self-directed behavior. Those who lack the information needed to engage effectively in roles and understand goals are not likely to experience the growing sense of autonomy characteristic of development (Newman & Newman, 1975).

Feedback is also basic to the development of system members. Systems theorists (Ashby, 1956; Buckley, 1968) have suggested that feedback is the basis of goal-directed behavior of individuals and groups. They argue that the concept of feedback is an extremely valuable tool in understanding human motivation, because it provides analysis of behavior in terms of immediate, here-and-now causes rather than in terms of historical determinants (Rapoport, 1967).

Systems that fail to provide adequate feedback to their members rob them of the basis on which they can evaluate the adequacy of their behavior. In a recent article, Cassel (1973) concludes that, without adequate feedback concerning how well an individual's behavior fits the expectations of a particular system, the individual becomes vulnerable to debilitating physical and psychological stress. Feedback, then, not only is a requisite of effective task behavior but also meets a basic psychological need of human beings (see Chapter 11).

A family, classroom, workplace, or other system that wishes to assess the quality of its feedback can consider several sources from which feedback is potentially available to system members (see Cowan, Egan, & Bacchi, 1978):

- *Self:* are members of this system capable of evaluating their own behavior effectively?
- *Peers:* do people with similar roles, such as coworkers, siblings, or team members, offer one another useful feedback as a matter of course?
- *Leaders:* do leaders, such as managers, supervisors, parents, teachers, and pastors, offer effective feedback to members?

A system characterized by decent human relations that lead to effective sharing of information and active feedback provides its members with an invaluable set of resources for their development and maximizes the effectiveness of its goal-seeking behavior (see Argyris, 1976a).

Climate

The climate of a system refers to the overall quality or atmosphere that characterizes that system. In a Model-II climate, individuals are committed to the goals of the system, share information freely, allow emotion as well as rationality a place in system functioning, and rely on positive reinforcement to sustain goal-directed behavior (see Chapter 7; Argyris, 1976a, 1976b; Argyris & Schön, 1974). Because the concept of climate is meant to focus on the overall picture of a system's functioning, it is much less specific than the other dimensions of Model A. The climate of a system may result directly from its success or failure in implementing the other dimensions of the model. Climate provides a kind of composite picture of the functioning of a specific system and exemplifies and reinforces the way in which it operates. We maintain that it is the responsibility of every system to assess the effects of its climate on the development of its members, since the composite of climates in the systems of each individual's life constitutes the basic matrix within which his or her development is supported, limited, or destroyed.

A Model-II climate tends to foster autonomy, commitment, and the ability to work cooperatively in achieving a goal (Argyris, 1976a, 1976b). Autonomy, commitment, and interdependence are landmarks in human development through life (Chickering, 1969; Heath, 1977a; Newman & Newman, 1975; Perry, 1970). Therefore, a Model-II climate might also be described as a developmental climate.

We refer to the work of Argyris because of his explicit concern with the *human* dimensions of organizational behavior. We are far from the point of having clear evidence that any model of human organizational behavior has successfully resolved the issues discussed here. Argyris (1976) has clearly indicated that real difficulties emerge in attempting to move an organization toward the type of functioning described as Model II.

Renewing Systems as Contexts for Human Development

Model *B*, a model for organizational change, was presented in Chapter 8 where emphasis was placed on effective task accomplishment. At this point, we would like to say a word about Model *B* with regard to its developmental implications. Models *A* and *B*—indeed, any working model—can be applied according to the agenda of the user. Model *A* or Model *B* could be used by leaders of a system to drain every bit of human energy from their members by focusing strictly on tasks and ignoring the members' developmental needs. Model *B* could be similarly employed. How long such a system might last is open to question.

Our point is this. The ultimate use to which models are put depends on the values of those members who shape policy and operation in the system. Model *B*, in other words, can be applied in a Model-I or a Model-II fashion. The system's task can be considered strictly in terms of logic and efficiency, thus ignoring the "psychologic" of human development. An alternative approach is being advocated here—namely, that those responsible for shaping policy and practice within systems should face the continual challenge of merging task accomplishment with member development. The values assigned to tasks and development vary with the system's mission, but, in principle, they are as real for corporate leaders as they are for family heads.

Model *B* is intended to foster a collaborative, democratic process of renewal and a developmental, Model-II climate in systems. Whether the model is used in this fashion depends ultimately on the personal and societal awareness and values of key system members—parents, teachers, government officials, and corporate and religious leaders.

The Human Potential of Systems

We believe that a great deal of social demoralization is rooted in the fact that people fail to understand and approach the world as a systems world—a world characterized by complex interdependencies. The fact that one thing leads to many others—a basic systems concept—often seems to be taken as a counsel of despair; however, it is simply a statement of how things work in the world and constitutes grounds for despair only when we explicitly or implicitly translate it to mean that one thing leads to many other *unanticipated and destructive* things.

Systems constitute the basic contextual reality of our lives from birth to death; therefore, a commitment to the development of human beings has little meaning without a concomitant investment in the development of human systems. We know that organizations and communities influence people's lives profoundly. The tragedy is that, although this influence is often negative, it need not be so. Paradoxically, the ability of systems to harm their members is a sign of the power they have to contribute constructively to their development. It remains for us as a society to develop persons and methodologies capable of renewing systems. In Chapter 10, we examine alternative approaches to this task of renewal based on the people-in-systems model.

Chapter 9: Additional Resources

Argyris, C. *Increasing leadership effectiveness.* New York: Wiley-Interscience, 1976. (See Chapters 12 and 14.)

Argyris, C., & Schön, D. *Theory in practice: Increasing professional effectiveness.* San Francisco: Jossey-Bass, 1974.

Heath, D. Academic predictors of adult maturity and competence. *Journal of Higher Education,* 1977, *48,* 613–632.

Schein, E. *Organizational psychology.* Englewood Cliffs, N. J.: Prentice-Hall, 1970. (See Chapter 2.)

10

Toward an Upstream Approach: Applications of the People-in-Systems Model

Introduction

In the previous chapter, we suggested a number of concrete ways in which systems can contribute to the development of their members. In this chapter, we examine in a preliminary way the implications of the people-in-systems model for individuals and for those who work in human services. We look first at one person's effort to systematically assess the key systems of her life; then we consider some potential applications of the model to the work of those in mental health, education, ministry, and training for the helping professions. Finally, we offer a set of suggestions to serve as guidelines for "upstream" agents of human development.

The Individual: A Walk through the Human-Systems World

A working model of people in systems that individuals can use to shed light on their day-to-day experiences in the key settings of their lives is ultimately meant for systems as well as individuals. A working model is not something that merely satisfies intellectual curiosity; it is an instrument that has implications for self-directed behavioral change. We asked Sara, a graduate student in one of our classes, to use the material presented in this book to assess what goes on in the systems of her life—that is, to "walk through" the various levels of the systems world described in Chapters 4, 5, 6, and 7. Sara is 39 years old, married, the mother of three teenage children, and an employee in a public-accounting firm.

Level I: Immediate Settings

Immediate settings are the directly experienced systems of a person's life, including the family, the workplace, school, friendship groups, and the neighborhood. As we have seen in a previous chapter, Berger and Neuhaus (1977) note that immediate settings have a "private face" and a "public face"; that is, they mediate between the individual and the larger systems of life.

After using the Model-*A* checklist in Chapter 7 to assess the immediate settings of her life, Sara had this to say about her workplace:

> I saw both good things and bad when I used your model to look at my company. We do have clear, behavioral goals as a firm. Feedback as to my performance is swift and accurate, but often delivered in a way that leaves me feeling like a child. It's not *what* is said but *how* it is said that I think offends me. I guess our firm's climate could be described as Model I. A real emphasis on control. I am financially secure because of my job, but I don't feel nourished as a human being there. Somehow I don't feel trusted.

Sara then made the following comments about her family:

> It occurred to me when doing this task that my situation at home is almost the reverse of what I described at work. The climate there is much more like Model II—collaboration, trust, democratic decision making. On the other hand, I often have the sense that our goals are ambiguous and that it's difficult for us to accomplish concrete tasks as a group. Somebody always has to nag. This can take the satisfaction out of things for everyone at times. One other thing. When I read in Model A about working knowledge and skills, it dawned on me that, during my education, no one ever mentioned either of these as they apply to family life. There are some family-living skills such as self-management and group program-development skills that we could use.

Finally, Sara made the following observations regarding her friendship group:

> I had never thought of my friends as a unit—a human system—in my life. But we do interact a lot and have powerful effects on one another—on each other's development. We talk about how important it is to spend time with one another; we talk about our values and what shape our lives are taking. But we leave getting together to chance so often. In terms of Model A, I think I would like something like systematic programs to help us get more out of our friendship. For instance, I wish that some of us would meet every other week, say, in some kind of life-style group; that is, a group in which we would explore our values and our behavior, what we'd like to achieve in life—some of the bigger issues.

Sara's thoughtful and systematic assessment of her personal settings provides valuable clues that help her understand how systems function and how that functioning affects her development.

Level II: The Network of Personal Settings (the Mesosystem)

In order to assist Sara in developing a concrete understanding of the network of her personal settings, we suggested a role-stripping analysis.

- Step 1: List the roles that have some significance for you.
- Step 2: Order these roles from the most to the least important, and indicate what percentage of your available energy you would choose to invest in each, given your personal values.
- Step 3: Now list these roles again from the most to the least important based on the percentage of energy you actually find yourself investing in each.

Sara's response to this role analysis is summarized in Figure 10-1.

Roles	Value Rank Order		Behavior (energy spent)	
wife	1–2. wife and mother	(40%)	1. worker	(50%)
worker			2. mother	(20%)
mother	3. worker	(40%)	3. friend	(15%)
friend	4. friend	(10%)	4. wife	(10%)
pianist	5. pianist	(5%)	5. pianist	(5%)
community-council volunteer	6. community-council volunteer	(5%)	6. volunteer	(0%)

Figure 10-1.
Sara's Role-Stripping Analysis.

The data provided by Sara illustrate in a graphic way the constant pulls and tugs that result from being a member of several important personal systems simultaneously. In Sara's case, because the demands of the workplace encroach on her roles as wife and mother, her availability to her children and to her partner tends to diminish. Sara's work often makes it difficult for her to participate in family life as fully as she wishes, and this difficulty at home may affect the quality of her work. Sara's role-stripping analysis indicates that her friendships are more important to her than she had thought and that she finds no time to invest in the community council.

When asked about the schools her children attend, Sara had this to say:

> I feel guilty sometimes because I don't know much about the schools. I guess I trust the schools and leave everything to them. They [the children]

don't come home with wild ideas and, as far as I know, they don't engage in very wild behavior. The schools don't seem to make many demands on parents aside from paying the tuition.

This statement indicates a case of compatibility between systems (see Chapter 5): the school system and the family system do not make widely divergent demands on the children—the "linking pins" between the systems—and, therefore, these systems typically do not engage each other in noticeable ways.

Once Sara has become aware of her world as a systems world and of what she is doing and what is happening to her in these systems, she is in a better position to reorder her priorities and to engage in more systematic life planning.

Level III: The Impact of the Larger Institutions of Society

The economic system, the media, and the government are institutions of the exosystem that affect Sara's life. She expressed her feelings about these three institutions by saying:

> I feel that, financially, we're treading water. The steady rise in the cost of living seems to leave us working harder and harder just to stay even. I thought that I might work only part-time, but that doesn't seem possible now, unless the family wants to give up some of the comforts we've gotten used to.
>
> I see the media as important mainly because of my kids. They spend too much time in front of the TV. I've tried to read a few articles about violence and sex on TV, and I've begun to monitor a little more what they watch. We talk about it more than we have in the past.
>
> And government—I guess we're all caught up in that, like it or not. My main feeling there is discouragement. Sometimes I feel that we are the last to be considered. Some senators say there is no energy crisis. They didn't have to pay our oil bills last year! If all the experts in Washington can't decide where to go and what to do, where does that leave me and my family?

Clearly, institutional realities affect Sara's life. It is our belief that the first step available to her in confronting this complex level of systems is *awareness*. Effective and systematic action is impossible without awareness, but awareness in and of itself does not automatically lead to effective action; action also requires the skills and value commitments that can mobilize Sara. The alternatives to awareness and subsequent action are demoralization and a retreat into narrow self-interest.

Level IV: Cultural Influences

Cultural influences affect Sara through the economic, legal, social, and educational settings in which she spends her life. She was intrigued with the notion of culture, or the macrosystem. On reflection, she saw cultural influence as both the most difficult to pinpoint and, paradoxically, the most potent in her life. This is what she had to say concerning culture and its influence:

> I feel that our society is almost self-destructively individualistic, and I find myself getting caught up with it, too—individualistic and self-centered. At least I feel these values blasting out at me every day. At work, everybody's competing to move up the corporate ladder. Advertising tells me—almost screams at me—that my pleasure, my personal pleasure, is just about the most important thing in life. We can't get car pools going because everyone wants to run his or her life apart from everyone else. Books talk about the disintegration of community. I feel infected by my culture at times. I feel my family is infected. I don't have time enough for my family or for community work. I don't often think about cultural influences. Culture used to mean "ethnic" to me. But I'm beginning to realize that I'm a child of my culture, and that's scary.

Our culture shapes the most intimate dimensions of living in potent ways. We are all culture's children to a greater or lesser extent, and we need a practical awareness of its workings that allows us to stand back from it in order to exercise freedom within it (Hall, 1977).

The people-in-systems model became an instrument of awareness for Sara; she felt somewhat overwhelmed but freed by some of her discoveries. Armed with an initial working knowledge of the systems of her life and a similar knowledge of her own developmental needs, Sara could meet developmental tasks more intelligently and more resourcefully. She said this about her own development:

> Erikson talks about generativity. Becoming generative with respect to the world in which I live is something that is more and more important to me. But I'm beginning to think that I can best become generative through the systems in my life. I express my generativity in caring for my family and in sharing values with my friends. Working for the neighborhood community council is another opportunity for generativity which I haven't taken advantage of. It seems that our family itself can be generative with respect to itself and get involved in a similar way with the neighborhood.

What happens in the systems of our lives shapes our human development and the development of others. After this analysis of the systems of her life, Sara felt more like an agent in her life rather than a passive onlooker or victim.

Human Systems: Upstream Approaches

We now turn to potential applications of the people-in-systems model in settings concerned with individual welfare and development—mental health, education, ministry, and training for the helping professions. We offer these applications as preliminary suggestions of the concrete utility of the model presented in this book.

Applications of the People-in-Systems Model
to a Personal Setting—
Family Problem Solving

In this chapter, we have been considering an individual who affects and is affected by the systems of her life. We now turn our attention to a personal system—a family. The Rubiano family consists of three members: Betty, 43 years old, Carlos, 45 years old, and Don, their 17-year-old son. It is a family in turmoil—a family looking for ways to help itself. Each member of the family has attempted to obtain help: Betty has talked over her problem with a friend; Carlos has talked to a counselor at work about his family problems and how they are interfering with his performance on the job; Don has talked to one of the counselors at school because of his poor academic performance and his surliness toward his teachers. However, none of these individual attempts at getting help have dealt directly with the family as a system that is being affected by other systems. Finally, at the urging of a friend who is on good terms with all three members of the family, the Rubianos agree to participate in a communications weekend as a family unit.

Without going into the history of their problem or detailing the course of therapy with the family therapist, we ask: What would increase the Rubianos' ability to face and deal with their family problems intelligently and resourcefully? The people-in-systems model suggests that the probability of growthful family interaction will increase if:

- Betty, Carlos, and Don develop a working knowledge of their own current developmental stages, tasks, and crises, a working knowledge of the developmental stages, tasks, and crises of each member of the family, and a working knowledge of how their developmental needs interact. For instance, Don might come to realize that, while he pursues deeper peer relationships and seeks more independence, his parents face the "crisis of the limits," feeling a sense of loss as their son moves toward greater independence.
- Each member of the family understands the family *as a system* in terms of its general mission, its practical goals, and its means to achieving these goals.
- Each member develops the life skills related to effective family living, such as self-management, interpersonal communication, empathy, and immediacy.
- The members of the family have some idea of the significant influences on the family from the other systems of their lives, including the network of personal systems, the exosystem, and the culture in which they live. They might ask themselves what influences they bring home from work and school and how each of them deals with the fact that Don comes from a youth culture that is different from that of his parents.
- The members of the family have a working knowledge of a problem-solving model and the skills they need to engage in interpersonal and system problem solving.

The people-in-systems model isn't intended to transform people into psychologists or sociologists, but it is intended to give them the ability to face and solve their own problems rather than see them as unsolvable. If the Rubianos are equipped with the working knowledge and skills of effective living, then the therapist needn't be a miracle worker but rather a consultant to the human development of the Rubiano family system. Through consultation, the family members come to understand what they need to face their problems intelligently and resourcefully and to help one another acquire the working knowledge and skills they need to face problems, develop competencies, and pursue developmental goals.

Applications of the People-in-Systems Model to a Larger System—A Hospital

Larger systems such as hospitals are obviously more complex than families and other personal systems. Hospitals deal with people in various crises and at every developmental stage from birth to death. The hospital itself has great internal complexity, with many different departments providing many different services. The changes and advances that occur in medical technology lead to financial problems, the continuous need for retraining programs, and the complexities involved in making prudential judgments concerning the necessity of the latest technological developments. Moral questions concerning abortion, sterilization, the right to die, and medical services for the poor are questions that must be faced daily by hospital administrators and personnel. Although Illich (1976) questions some of the assumptions underlying the existence of hospitals, they do exist and will continue to exist as important systems in the lives of almost everybody.

(1) The people-in-systems model has a number of applications in a hospital setting. For instance, it suggests that doctors and nurses should become aware of the developmental stages, tasks, and crises of their patients and how the patients' developmental needs interact with the delivery of medical services. The way in which people conceptualize their illness or disability and relate it to the rest of their lives is an important element in the treatment process. For example, serious illness can be a devastating shock to a 20-year-old youth who has never thought of himself as physically vulnerable and who tends to see life stretching endlessly into the future. A working knowledge of different kinds of reactions to illness at various developmental stages of life is important to the training of medical personnel.

(2) The people-in-systems model also suggests that medical personnel should develop the human-relations skills they need to communicate effectively with patients. These skills include the ability to give the patients whatever information they need to handle both their illness and the various forms of treatment, to communicate an understanding of how they feel about what they are going through, and to challenge their patients to become agents in their own treatment and cure. In many cases, poor communication skills actually stand in the way of effective delivery of medical

services. As we noted earlier, technologies for training medical personnel in human-relations skills are being developed (Anthony & Carkhuff, 1977; Gazda, Walters, & Childers, 1975).

(3) The people-in-systems model suggests that medical personnel should acquire a working knowledge of the hospital as a system, including ways in which a hospital systematically affects patients. Model *A* (see Chapter 8) is a blueprint for developing a working knowledge of the hospital system as a whole and of its subsystems, such as adolescent wards, intensive-care units, laboratory services, pastoral-care services, and other departments. A hospital, like any large system, can become departmentalized to such an extent that it begins to fragment its patients. If communication between departments is poor, both patients and medical personnel suffer. Again, every person working directly with patients in a hospital should be aware of the ways in which the hospital system affects its patients. A hospital system that operates efficiently *and* humanely can benefit its patients greatly, whereas an ineffective system can swallow up the individuality of the patient.

(4) Our model suggests that innovations in medical technology should be reviewed with regard to their impact on patients as total human beings rather than mere bodies and that hospitals should design systems to meet all the needs of their patients. Some hospitals have designed hotel- or motel-like facilities for patients who are not bedridden or who don't need constant attention or supervision. Since these patients are free to move around and go to a dining room for meals, they generally feel less captive. Moreover, the costs for such a room are substantially less per day than the costs for a regular hospital room. In some cities, outpatient-surgery centers have been set up for those who require minor surgery. Patients report to these centers early in the morning and leave by afternoon or evening. The costs, both physical and psychological, are relatively low in these centers. These are some of the ways in which a number of hospitals have broken away from the cultural "blueprints" (Bronfenbrenner, 1977b) that would make all hospitals and their procedures identical.

(5) The way in which a culture views death and dying obviously influences the way in which the people of that culture respond to a dying individual. The people-in-systems model suggests that programs for the terminally ill should be established that are either secular in character or related to religion and religious systems. Innovations in health care are significantly influenced by the macrosystem, and cultural influences—the norms, rules, regulations, values, and ideologies of the wider culture—reach down through health-care systems and touch even those who are dying.

(6) The people-in-systems model suggests that medical personnel should teach the art of self-care, insofar as this is possible, and should encourage and challenge their patients to practice it so that they might become responsible agents in their own healing. Since about half the population in our society suffers from some kind of chronic illness (Gerson & Strauss, 1975)—diabetes, heart disorder, hypertension, arthritis, and the like—self-help care is extremely important to a great number of people.

Gartner and Riessman (1977) discuss some of the reasons behind the growth of the self-help movement:

> The development of self-help is taking place among a population increasingly older, more afflicted with chronic illness, increasingly skeptical of both the efficiency and very foundation of present technologically based medical care, increasingly concerned about cost and effect, and more and more interested in doing things for oneself, as part of a broader anti-Leviathan ethos [pp. 95–96].

The trend toward self-help needn't be seen as an attack on the medical profession, but rather as a refreshing push toward greater individual responsibility.

Finally, a word should be said about the development of medical personnel. Constantly dealing with people in moderate to severe crisis takes its toll on health-care workers. A nurse in charge of an intensive-care unit in a large urban hospital discussed with us the tensions that arise among nurses in her unit. After involving herself in human-relations-training courses, she was convinced that intensive-care-unit personnel would benefit from having some kind of forum in which they could deal directly with the tensions created by their work setting. In our terms, these nurses would develop and share a common working knowledge of the intensive-care unit as a system, they would develop and use whatever communication skills they needed to deal with their tensions, and the hospital itself would provide them with time and a forum in which they could develop working knowledge and skills as important aspects of their professional development.

Model *A* can be used to focus systematically on the developmental needs of those who work in health-care delivery systems. Moreover, issues that deal with social systems and human development need to be addressed in medical and nursing schools, in university departments where administrative and health-care personnel are educated and trained, and in training programs located in hospitals.

Applications of the People-in-Systems Model to a Curriculum for Social/Psychological Education and Training

The people-in-systems model encourages the use of the kinds of education and training programs ordinarily included under the rubric *affective education* (see Thayer & Beeler, 1977). Affective-education programs are currently being used to help many students develop a sense of what it means to be human and acquire the skills they need to deal with social and emotional realities.

Cross (1976) wryly notes that "student development is a little like the weather. Everybody talks about it and is interested in it, but no one does much about it. . . . Like the weather forecaster, we enjoy modest success in predicting what will happen when certain elements are present in the environment, but we rarely know how to take the action that will increase the probability for bringing about desired ends" (p. 137). She reviews three general approaches to student development: the humanistic (O'Banion, Thurston, & Gulden, 1972), the developmental (Craig, 1974; Kohlberg, 1973; Kohlberg & Mayer, 1973; Kohlberg & Turiel, 1971; Perry, 1970), and the multidimensional (Alverno College, 1974; Chickering, 1969; Chickering & McCormick, 1973). Cross suggests that there are more commonalities than differences among these approaches and lists a series of propositions (familiar to us from Chapter 2) that proponents of all these approaches would be likely to agree with:

> 1. Development is a lifelong process occurring in sequences and spurts rather than in linear or regular progression. 2. Development involves the total being, integrating cognitive and affective learning. 3. Development involves active internal direction rather than "adjustment" to culturally determined criteria. 4. Development is stimulated when the individual interacts with an appropriately challenging environment. 5. The phenomena of developmental growth can be submitted to scientific study. 6. Educational programs and interventions can be designed to make an impact on the rate, levels and direction of development [p. 167].

The people-in-systems model is consonant with these propositions and attempts to integrate the humanistic, developmental, and multidimensional approaches. However, our model places much greater emphasis on the social environment, or the settings in which development does or does not take place.

The model presented here also stresses the acquisition of a working knowledge of human development and of the key systems in which this development takes place, as well as the acquisition of the life skills that facilitate interaction between individuals and systems. It thus offers a relatively comprehensive blueprint for developmental education and training. As we have noted, many of the technologies for imparting life skills have already been developed and now need adaptation to different developmental levels. The question is whether school administrations will institute programs in affective or "deliberate psychological" education (Mosher & Sprinthall, 1971; Sprinthall, 1973). Peterson (1973) found that even educators and administrators who considered "personal development" a high priority in college did little to make it a high priority in practice. We believe that they hesitate because they assume that personal-development programs are anti-intellectual and therefore opposed to traditional educational values, and because they are unfamiliar with social/psychological education and training.

As we have stated previously, direct social/psychological education and training for development in a systems context should begin as early as possible in life and should be a part of the school curriculum from the earliest years. Although it is true that education for development is necessary during the college years because these years represent an important developmental stage, it is unfair to ask colleges to make up for the deficiencies of primary and secondary schools. People should be equipped with the kinds of working knowledge and skills they need to face de-velopmental tasks *as these tasks arise;* otherwise, education for develop-ment takes on a remedial air that can dishearten both faculty and stu-dents. We have already discussed the initial resistance trainers often meet when teaching basic human-relations skills to adults (see Chapter 3).

If educational systems are to change, then the way in which teachers and educational administrators are trained must change. The people-in-systems model not only offers a curriculum for educating and training stu-dents in development but also provides a model for training teachers to deliver such a curriculum. Teachers should be trained in both the working knowledge and skills of the model as well as in the training methodologies needed to pass these on to students.

The implementation of the people-in-systems model shouldn't be left solely in the hands of school counselors. Although counselors may be in the best position in terms of professional background to learn and implement such a model, we fear that the present affective/cognitive dualism will only be perpetuated by a compartmentalization of roles. Moreover, because the school organization must change, administrators, teachers, and counselors must plan change collaboratively in the development of a curriculum for direct social/psychological education and training. School counselors, trained in theory, research, and the implications of the model, should be consultants to both administrators and teachers without taking over all the training functions themselves (see Moore, 1977).

Applications of the People-in-Systems Model to the Helping Professions

In our view, it is unrealistic to expect highly trained and relatively highly paid professionals to be the major providers of psychological ser-vices, such as counseling and other forms of helping. Moore (1977) cites the fact that there are too few professionals to deliver needed services:

> We are faced with a demand for quality, low-cost psychological services that are accessible to all persons, regardless of income level, race, religion, sex, or sexual preference. It is not feasible, or even desirable, that only a handful of individuals trained at the doctoral level be considered the exclu-sive providers of counseling services [p. 359].

In the helping professions themselves, we must work at giving psychology away and at developing the knowledge and skills that enable us to do so; the people-in-systems model is an attempt to facilitate the pursuit of these goals.

We feel that anyone who attempts to help others needs basic compe-tence in the three areas represented in the people-in-systems model—that is, a working knowledge of the developmental status and needs of those being helped, a working knowledge of the ways in which systems affect those being helped, and the life skills that make helping possible, including communication and problem-solving skills. Therefore, helper-training programs need to provide these skills and this knowledge in practical, systematic, and thoughtful ways.

The helper as consultant to human development. The people-in-systems model suggests new ways of providing help. We see helpers, ideally, as *consultants* to the development of those they are trying to help. Therefore, according to our model, a great deal of helping consists of the education and training of those being helped (Carkhuff & Berenson, 1976; Egan, 1975; Ivey, 1976). Very often, the most effective kind of helping equips people with the kinds of working knowledge and skills they need to pursue their own development in the context of the key social settings of their lives. Theoretically, people who are educated and trained at an early age in working knowledge and skills for development won't need help as often as people who lack such training, and at times of crisis they'll need help in using the resources they already possess rather than training in basic working knowledge and skills. Unfortunately, helping today is often a catch-up game: clients have to be educated and trained in working knowledge and skills and then guided in applying these resources to the troublesome areas of their lives.

Anthony (1977) faults the mental-health professions for not yet developing a viable approach to psychological rehabilitation. "The field of psychological rehabilitation," he writes, "has generated little talk, a great deal of rehabilitation environments, and very little energy directed at using those rehabilitation environments" (p. 662). He suggests that training patients lies at the core of more effective rehabilitation: "First . . . mental health professionals must learn to practice a rehabilitation approach to psychological rehabilitation; that is, an approach that diagnoses and teaches the skills the patient needs to live, learn, and work in her or his community" (p. 662). In order to involve themselves in a rehabilitation approach, mental-health workers need to develop training skills. The people-in-systems model amplifies Anthony's approach by suggesting that helpers acquire a working knowledge of the developmental needs of their clients and become skilled in systems analysis. Whether or not the helping professions move beyond mere tolerance to encouragement and support of the self-help movement depends upon the values of the members of the helping professions. The chosen methods of practice reflect the values of the practitioner in fundamental ways.

Applications of the People-in-Systems Model to a Community Mental-Health Center

Sarason's critique of community psychology (1974) underscores the importance of knowing more than psychology if community intervention is an essential aspect of an agency's mission; the diagnosis of a community *as a community* must also be undertaken. In Sarason's view, contemporary community mental-health centers have emphasized the provision of direct counseling and psychotherapy services to people; in doing so, they have had much to do with mental health but little to do with the community.

The people-in-systems model suggests that a substantial portion of available community mental-health center resources should be allocated to nontherapy endeavors. In Mills' (1959) terminology, mental-health personnel would invest significant amounts of their energy in dealing with *issues*, or social-systems events, rather than focus strictly on *troubles*, or individual difficulties. Examples of specific programs include:

- assisting persons to build support groups by linking them with others in need of support,
- educating and training people in the areas of family living and interpersonal living both within and without the formal educational system,
- consulting with and supporting other care-givers, such as ministers, doctors, teachers, parents, and community leaders,
- diagnosing community systems that seem to be chronic sources of developmental casualties, and
- assisting human systems of all types—families, schools, workplaces, and neighborhoods—in the task of becoming communities that are capable of fostering development as well as accomplishing their various missions.

In order to become involved in the community, mental-health-center personnel obviously need to spend substantial amounts of time in the community and less time in their own offices. In this regard, Sarason's basic guideline for effective work in human services seems particularly appropriate: "I consider the psychological sense of community to be the overarching value by which to judge efforts to change any aspect of community functioning" (p. 9). The people-in-systems model can be of concrete assistance to those mental-health personnel who wish to focus on fostering communities as a means of promoting human development.

Applications of the People-in-Systems Model to the Ministry as a Helping Profession

Even in congregations that have ministerial teams, ministers by themselves cannot possibly deliver all the services required by a congregation. Services could be adequately delivered, however, by "ministering congregations,"—that is, communities of believers who minister to one another (Egan, 1978). In such a congregation, ministry is regarded as the function of the community and its members and not merely the function of ordained or otherwise officially designated ministers. Ordained ministers do have special roles and functions in religious communities, but they needn't try to perform all ministerial functions themselves when the members of the community are encouraged to engage in what Fenhagen (1977) calls "mutual ministry." One of the most important functions of officially designated ministers is to see to it that mutual ministry takes place. Without surrendering the liturgical and sacramental roles and functions that are rightfully theirs, ministers could become ministerial enablers by establishing educational, training, and support programs to equip the members of their congregations with the working knowledge and skills they need to engage effectively in mutual ministry.

In Chicago, we have recently established a Doctor of Ministry program based on the people-in-systems and related models. In this program, we train both ordained and lay ministers who have had extensive experience in ministry to engage in what we call *lateral ministry*. Whereas *vertical ministry* refers to direct-delivery work such as visiting the sick and counseling, *lateral ministry* refers to promoting, developing, and encouraging mutual ministry in the congregation. As mediating structures, congregations that are supportive and challenging can have a powerful impact on the development of other immediate settings—specifically, on families and peer systems. The ministerial professionals in our program are becoming experts in establishing, implementing, and evaluating programs that encourage mutual ministry—a task that requires the working knowledge and life skills called for by the people-in-systems model.

Systems Intervention for Human Development: New Directions for Training

The people-in-systems model suggests the establishment of a new training program that is interdisciplinary. The following is a brief scenario of the program we envision.

A committee of three professionals—one in the area of human development, one in the area of social systems, and the third in the area of life skills—would determine the direction of the training program. These three professionals, each with his or her own specific contribution to make and each learning from the others, would constitute a learning community and a liaison between the resources of the university and the wider community. For instance, the professional in social systems would discover what resources such departments as anthropology, sociology, economics, urban studies, industrial relations, and political science have for the education and training of students to understand and deal effectively with systems at all levels. The purpose of this training program would be to produce what we have called "translators"; although these professionals would be equipped to help individuals as development consultants, they would work mainly with systems that deliver human services, such as schools, churches, governmental agencies, hospitals, mental-health centers, welfare systems, self-help groups, and community organizations. Their work with business systems would focus on what McGregor (1960) has called the "human side of enterprise" and on the relationship between the developmental needs of workers and the efficiency and profitability of organizations.

Graduates of the new training program would thus be human-development consultants to a variety of systems (see Dustin, 1974; Parker, 1975). They would help organizations to instill the concept of development in systems in their day-to-day operations and train people in its use and in the skills they need to implement it. Just as human-development consultants would work to make individuals more self-reliant rather than encourage their dependence on professional help, organizational practitioners would work to make systems capable of implementing and developing the people-in-systems model.

The training program would operate a "clinic" or center in which a great deal of the training would take place. This center would provide more than traditional helping services. It would provide workshops for individuals and families interested in their own development, the purpose of which would be to teach these individuals and families basic working knowledge and life skills. The clinic would also provide services to systems beyond the family. For instance, it could establish consultation and training services for workplaces and communities. Perhaps the principal function of the training center would be to provide consultation and training services for human-services delivery systems that want to function as resource settings for development. School administrators interested in developing and implementing deliberate social and psychological education and training programs for development to balance curricula that are intellectual and cognitive in nature could be helped in their pursuit by the training center. Faculty and administration would be trained in the people-in-systems model and in the skills needed to implement the model in their own schools.

The student trainees of the program would spend a good deal of their time in the training center, learning how to translate the concepts, models, theory, and research learned in the classroom into the development of programs and the delivery of services. The center, through its involvement with the community, would pursue ecological experiments and action-based research. The student trainees would quickly become apprentices in the consultation, education, and training work of the center, working with both individuals and institutions. The center itself, because of its contacts with a variety of institutions, could provide much of the practicum and internship required by the program. The student trainees would also have opportunities to do internship work in the systems of their choice. If a student expected to work professionally with schools, then his or her internship would take place in one or more school systems. A parish or a cluster of parishes set up according to the lateral-ministry model could be both a training site for personnel from other parishes and an internship site for those wishing to work with ministerial and church systems. From the outset of the program, students would be trained to become translators capable of intervening directly with individuals and systems and of training others to become translators.

Guidelines for Application of the People-in-Systems Model

The following suggestions constitute an attempt to summarize guidelines for readers interested in concrete applications of the people-in-systems model. These suggestions are, in the most basic sense, statements of the authors' values regarding the model and its application.

- Work collaboratively; don't do something *to* people, but engage them in a process of needs assessment and help them to plan programs to meet their needs.
- Accept the premise that effective relationship skills are essential for the effective change agent.
- Employ a sociocultural-systems view of the context of human development. Instead of focusing strictly on work with individuals, assist people to foster settings—families, organizations, and communities—that are conducive to human development.
- Emphasize a life-span developmental view of the person that stresses the active transformation of experience.
- Stress the development of a sequence of progressively complex skills for competent living, such as decision-making and interpersonal-relationship skills.
- Translate theory and research in the social sciences in such a way that it can be applied by communities to real human concerns.
- Be committed to giving the social sciences away in a systematic and thoughtful manner by educating and training communities to develop their own internal resources for the development of their members.

These guidelines relate to an approach that is one of a number of value or strategy orientations for those in the human services. Other applications of the people-in-systems model are possible. For example, treatment programs with a clearly remedial or downstream focus in such areas as chemical dependency, depression, or marital conflict may find that their clients benefit greatly from increased working knowledge and skills with respect to the social structures that are the context of their lives. Alternatively, entire social systems in crisis—families, schools, parishes, or communities—may find that the model presented here contains potential new directions for collective action with structural change as a goal.

Figure 10-2 offers examples of intervention orientations suggested by the people-in-systems model that are available to human-services workers, as well as some examples of each intervention orientation.

The people-in-systems model, with its emphasis on the social context of human experience, may suggest approaches to the delivery of services within any of the four intervention orientations suggested in Figure 10-2. In our view, it is critical that more attention be paid to upstream approaches to individuals through systematic social/psychological education (see Chapters 2 and 4–7) and training (see Chapters 3 and 8) *and* to the enhancement of social structures as contexts for human development (see Chapters 9 and 11).

Conclusion

In this chapter, we have examined some possible applications of the people-in-systems model. We are sure that you will be able to think of many others. There is no magic in the model or its applications: the parts

Approach	Individual	Social Structure
Upstream (Developmental)	Relationship-skills training Education regarding developmental events of life Education regarding the social structure of life	Family-education and support groups Consultation in building developmental climates Social planning with human- and system-development focus
Downstream (Remedial)	Counseling and psychotherapy with developmental and systems focus Remedial education in sexuality, interpersonal living, and decision making	Family therapy Crisis consultation in school systems Assisting corporate systems in making structural changes that reduce human casualties

Figure 10-2.
Possible Intervention Orientations Using the People-in-Systems Model.

of the model we have begun to implement, such as a variety of skills-training programs with populations ranging from primary-school students to residents of nursing homes, demand a great deal of work, but it is work that can lead to a strong sense of direction and hope.

In these pages, we have often alluded to the implications of the people-in-systems model for community building and community living. We believe that this topic is important enough to merit special attention, and in Chapter 11 we consider community and mutuality in the lives of people in our culture.

Chapter 10: Additional Resources

Anthony, W. A. Psychological rehabilitation: A concept in need of a method. *American Psychologist*, 1977, *32*, 658–662.

Carroll, C., Cohen, S., Lorentz, E. Maton, K., & Sarason, S. *Human services and resource networks.* San Francisco: Jossey-Bass, 1977. (See Preface and Chapters 1–4, 8–12).

Egan, G. The parish: Ministering community and community of ministers. In E. E. Whitehead (Ed.), *The parish: Community and ministry.* New York: Paulist Press, 1978, 73–90.

Gartner, A., & Riessman, F. *Self-help in the human services.* San Francisco: Jossey-Bass, 1977.

Havelock, G., & Havelock, M. *Training for change agents.* Ann Arbor, Mich.: The University of Michigan Institute for Social Research, 1976.

11

Toward Mutuality in Human Systems

Social Demoralization in a Fragmented World

In the previous chapters, we have attempted to articulate a provisional model of human development in the context of social systems. Our intent has been to focus on the *interaction* of individuals with systems as the source of development of both and to show what an approach designed to foster development through education, training, and consultation would entail. In our view, it is essential that an integrative framework of social scientific knowledge be constructed that will enable people to deal with the day-to-day reality of being human in a complex systems world.

As we noted in Chapter 1, many people experience a sense of alienation from the social systems of their lives, including their churches, neighborhoods, and families (Harman, 1977; Keniston, 1977; Nisbet, 1969). This sense of alienation—of not connecting meaningfully with systems—is typically exacerbated as one tries to deal with more complex and impersonal systems (Sennett, 1976). We suggest that social demoralization—a sense of quiet despair about one's ability to have a personal impact on the systems of one's life—is rooted in alienation (Nisbet, 1969; Sennett, 1976), since people are unlikely to be hopeful about influencing a situation in which they feel no real sense of engagement. Alienation, then, is the social phenomenon that must be effectively confronted if a rejuvenation or transformation of human systems is to become a reality.

Alienation and the Need to Be "On Guard"

Most people would probably agree that alienation is widespread in our world; indeed, as Nisbet (1969) has suggested, "alienated man" may become a symbol of the 20th century. But what will help people to comprehend and deal concretely with alienation in their own lives? What are the effects of alienation on people, and how might these effects be countered?

The Effects of Alienation

The following fantasy may help you get a feel for the concrete effects of alienation. Imagine that you are in a foreign country in which the people do not speak your language and are unable to understand anything you say. All signs, direction markers, and guideposts are written in a language you don't understand. By using hand signals, you are able to obtain the rudiments of life—food and shelter—but you meet no one capable of conversing with you. What would your reaction be? What would happen to you if this situation were to last for a period of days or weeks? Those who have traveled to a foreign country will understand immediately the emotions associated with the alienation described in this fantasy.

The basic human response to alienation is the activation of an automatic physical and psychological process we refer to as going "on guard." Caplan (1973) has described the genesis of going on guard and its results.

> Relevant messages about expectations and evaluations of an individual's behavior are not being consistently communicated, or else the individual is unfamiliar with expectations and the evaluative cues of those around him—including the signals that enable him to anticipate the friendliness or hostility of others. He is consequently never able to feel safe and valued, and his autonomic nervous system and hormonal mechanisms are continually in a state of emergency arousal, so that the resulting physiological depletion and fatigue increase his susceptibility to a wide range of physical and mental disorders [pp. 1–2].[1]

There is a close parallel between an individual in a foreign country and individuals in contemporary society (Simmel, 1971). Industrial society does not typically give people a sense of security and self-value. One of Joseph Heller's characters in *Something Happened* (1974) speaks to some extent for all of us when he says that "something did happen to me somewhere that robbed me of confidence and courage and left me with a fear of discovery and change and a positive dread of everything unknown that may occur" (p. 6). Like this character, all of us, to one degree or another, spend a good deal of time on guard because of our inability to feel secure and valued in the context of our systems and because of a feeling of being "outside"—of being alienated.

Alienation may be understood as the subjective experience of not being in solid and meaningful contact with the settings of life. It produces an on-guard (fight or flight) response that, when extended over time, leaves people vulnerable to psychological and physical problems that are essen-

[1]This and all other quotations from this source are from *Support Systems and Community Mental Health,* by G. Caplan. Copyright 1973 by Human Sciences Press. Reprinted by permission.

tially reactions to stress (Selye, 1974). People who use the bulk of their energy to remain on guard in order to survive in a complex and often unfriendly world deplete the energy they need to involve themselves in the immediate settings of their lives.

Being "On Guard" as a Source of Vulnerability to Physical and Psychological Illness

John Cassel (1973) offers the following insight based on a review of studies investigating the relationship between changes in the social context of life, such as rapid urbanization, and physical and psychological difficulties.

> In human populations the circumstances in which increased susceptibility to disease would occur would be those in which, for a variety of reasons, individuals are not receiving any evidence (feedback) that their actions are leading to desirable and/or anticipated consequences. In particular this would be true when these actions are designed to modify the individual's relationships to the important social groups with whom he interacts [p. 405].

Cassel suggests that one human cost of living in a rapidly changing, mobile, diverse, and pluralistic world is the disruption of relationship networks—the family, the neighborhood, the hometown, the parish—that causes people to become social and psychological strangers. When people are deprived of customary and reliable feedback, they are forced to go on guard. The importance of the system in which feedback is inadequate is directly related to the strength of the self-protective, on-guard response. However, constantly remaining on guard extracts a high price from a human being: " ... chronic alterations in the autonomic nervous system activity and hormonal secretions [are] associated with such activity. These, in turn, alter the homeostatic mechanisms of the organism, leading to increased susceptibility to disease" (Cassel, 1973, p. 405).

Available evidence has related disruption in social relationships to elevation in blood pressure (Scotch, 1963), to the prevalence of coronary heart disease among people with occupationally and residentially mobile life-styles (Syme, Borhani, & Buechley, 1965; Syme, Hyman, & Enterline, 1964, 1965), and to physical and emotional illness and absenteeism in first-generation industrial workers from rural mountain areas (Cassel & Tyroler, 1961). People who are unable to feel at home in their systems must remain on guard. Remaining on guard for an extended period of time is associated with generalized susceptibility to physical and psychological problems, including a chronic lack of energy (Ingalls, 1976).

Our suggestion, based on these data and on the logic and values of the model that we have presented, is that systems should become more responsive to the individuals who are their members. A *minimal* requirement for humane social living is that individuals be buffered by the immediate settings of their lives against the need to be on guard constantly. This buffering occurs whenever individuals are viewed and responded to in a manner described by Caplan:

> In such relationships the person is dealt with as a unique individual. The other people are interested in him in a personalized way. They speak his language. . . . Above all, they are sensitive to his personal needs, which they deem worthy of respect and satisfaction [1973, pp. 5–6].

Caplan goes on to suggest that support or buffering systems provide three things for their members: psychological support, assistance in dealing with tasks, and other needed resources, such as knowledge and skills. As we have indicated in previous chapters, systems tend to provide task assistance and the resources needed to accomplish tasks, but they often neglect to provide basic human support. Therefore, many systems fail to function as buffers for their members.

Beyond Buffering Systems: The Experience of Community

The concept of community has been called "the most fundamental and far-reaching of sociology's . . . ideas" (Nisbet, 1966, p. 47). However, social scientists have found difficulty in trying to agree on a definition of community. Whitehead (1977) suggests that three fundamental meanings of the term *community* can be found in the social-science literature: community as a setting with recognizable boundaries, community as a particular pattern of interaction, and community as a subjective experience of belonging.

Other analyses (Kanter, 1972; Minar & Greer, 1969; Nisbet, 1969; Sennett, 1976) suggest that the concept of community cannot be adequately understood without a social as well as a psychological perspective. In *The Psychological Sense of Community*, a thoughtful critique of American psychology's response to human needs, Sarason (1974) defined community from a sociological perspective and then from a psychological perspective. In defining the sociological view of community, he said:

> A community is a highly differentiated and configurated set of relationships, things, functions, and symbols, grounded in implicit and explicit traditions which in turn reflect geographic, economic, religious, political, and educational factors [p. 101].

In defining the psychological view of community, Sarason said:

> The perception of similarity to others, an acknowledged interdependence with others, a willingness to maintain this interdependence by giving or doing for others what one expects from them, the feeling that one is part of a larger dependable and stable structure—these are some of the ingredients of the psychological sense of community [p. 157].

The first definition describes community from the *objective* standpoint of an observer analyzing recurrent patterns of social interaction, whereas the second definition describes the *subjective* experience of community. The intensity of this subjective experience varies widely. We do not wish to suggest that the feeling of community is characterized by a high degree of emotional intensity, awareness, or intimacy. In fact, the day-to-day experience of being part of a community is likely to be taken for granted as a sense of connectedness to others with whom one has both a common history and an anticipated future (Toennies, 1961). The members of a stable neighborhood group, for example, experience a sense of connectedness over a period of years.

Whitehead argues for a *social/psychological* approach to community that includes the subjective experiences of individuals as well as an analysis of the patterns of social interaction that seem to be the origin of those experiences. Our analysis and recommendations concerning community formation at the applied level parallel Whitehead's regarding community theory and research. If the formation of communities is a viable response to alienation, then patterns of operation and interaction that result in the subjective experience of community should be developed in systems. In our view, the concept of *mutuality* in interpersonal relationships is crucial to understanding how systems can offer a basic sense of "connectedness" —of community—to their members.

Community as a Hybrid Social Form

Sociologists (see Cooley, 1909; Toennies, 1961) have pointed out important differences in the types of human systems in which we spend our lives. One type of system, the *primary group,* is characterized by emotional bonds, unspoken expectations, broad involvement of members in one another's lives, and loyalty to members even when their behavior is "out of line." The family is the classic example of a primary group. In our society, the nuclear family has primary responsibility for the social and emotional development and sustenance of its members. It is the key human system, the crucial locus of developmental challenge and support.

Perhaps the most tragic failure of our social systems can be seen in the lives of those whose experience in their primary group was a destructive one. In the words of Erikson (1958): "There is nothing so terrible as the mutilation of the spirit of a child." The spirit of a husband or wife can be similarly affected by membership in an ill-functioning primary group.

The primary group is where our capacity to love is initially shaped. This shaping can affect our ability to form meaningful and decent relationships throughout our lives. Fortunately, the effects of shaping are subject to change through development, education, and training of the type described here (see Chapters 2 and 3), and counseling and psychotherapy.

The second major type of human system, the *associational group,* is characterized by nonemotional relationships, specific expectations regarding performance, narrow involvement of members in one another's lives, and loyalty based on continued performance of duties. The workplace is the classic example of an associational group. Other examples include neighborhood councils, parent-teacher associations, political parties, and classrooms. In our society, the associational group has primary responsibility for the socialization of adults. In the associational group, our capacity to work competently and with a sense of meaning is either nurtured or destroyed. Events that take place in associational groups have a profound effect on the entire fabric of our lives.

It has been said that the productive human being is one who is capable of love and work (Fromm, 1947). If the primary group nurtures our capacity to love and the associational group strengthens our ability to work, what is the role of the social form known as community? Whitehead (1978) describes the basic function of communities.

> Some communities will incorporate several elements and expectations of primary groups; other communities will manifest some of the concerns and more formal patterns of [associational] life. All, however, meet the requirement of community—that is, they are social settings beyond the family in which group members can experience themselves . . . more completely and authentically, apart from the sometimes restricting prescriptions of their social roles [p. 388].

Community, in other words, combines the characteristics of the primary group and those of the associational group. A social system that functions as a community is one that draws on and supports its members' capacities to love *and* to work, and helps them to return to the primary and associational groups of their lives with renewed energy.

Mutuality in Interpersonal Living

In our view, the sense of belonging to groups that respond to people as individuals worthy of dignity and respect is rooted in the experience of mutuality in interpersonal relationships (see Egan, 1976). *Mutuality* refers to the ability of two people to engage in direct and non-manipulative dialogue while comprehending and accepting each other's frame of reference. Relationships based on mutuality, referred to in their pure form as "I-thou" (Buber, 1937), are lateral rather than vertical and resemble friendship rather than psychotherapy. The level at which mutuality can occur depends upon the system's mission, the interpersonal skills of its members, and the values of the system and its members. The following is an examination of three levels of mutuality.

Level One: Self-Disclosure and Empathy

The provision of basic human support, which we have already identified as a central developmental resource regardless of one's life stage, requires what we call *first-level mutuality* in relationships. In order to engage in basic mutuality, system members must have two relationship skills—self-disclosure and basic empathy—as well as the values that put these skills into action (see Egan, 1976). In other words, system members must be capable of directly sharing thoughts, feelings, and values with one another. They must be capable of accurately hearing thoughts, feelings, and values from other members' frames of reference. And the system itself must permit or encourage such relating as a value.

This first level of mutuality constitutes the minimal requirement for basic decency in human relationships, providing a foundation for constructive communication. Relationships between spouses, parents and children, employers and employees, or students and teachers that are not characterized by basic decency in their communication patterns undermine rather than support the psychological health and development of those involved.

Level Two: Challenge and Exploration

The level of communication that takes place within effectively functioning systems goes beyond basic mutuality or support. As we have indicated in previous chapters, the dynamic interplay of challenge and support leads to the development of people and systems. Challenge often takes the form of new tasks, but challenge also involves the capacity of people to invite one another to look at issues, problems, and crises from various frames of reference (Egan, 1976). Individuals must be willing to accept the invitation and be open to the challenge being made in order to attain this level of mutuality; they must be willing to explore new perspectives.

Some examples of constructive interpersonal challenge may be helpful in clarifying this second level of mutuality. Parents who are disturbed about their child's refusal to help with family duties have three basic options: ignore the behavior, vent their feelings of irritation and demand different behavior, or confront the child directly and with care—that is, invite the child to examine what he or she is presently doing and to explore more constructive options. A business manager who has become aware of racist or sexist attitudes that are interfering with effective performance by an otherwise competent supervisor has options that are parallel to those of the parent: he can ignore the racist or sexist attitudes, demand a change of attitude, or invite the supervisor to examine his or her opinions.

When the first option is taken—doing nothing—the individual loses feedback that can serve as the basis for developmental challenge. The system suffers as well, because necessary tasks are not carried out or are carried out inadequately.

The problem associated with taking the second option—essentially a power tactic—is that it elicits temporary compliance but ultimately leads to resistance and defensiveness on the part of the individual being challenged. Moreover, this type of challenge is often experienced as attack, and it is likely to solidify the individual's position rather than encourage development. The results of this apparent attack and the resistance to it tend to clutter future interactions in the setting with unfinished emotional business (Polster & Polster, 1973).

The third option—direct and responsible challenge—is the basis of deeper mutuality. It is important that this responsible challenge be carried out in the spirit of basic empathy (Egan, 1976), which entails an awareness of the other person's frame of reference. Challenge needs to be understood and experienced by people as an *invitation* to examine some aspect of their behavior. Responsible challenge, which is experienced as an invitation rather than an attack, is likely to elicit exploratory rather than defensive responses.

Since development cannot take place without adequate challenge, people who don't have a capacity for responsible challenge are unlikely to be developmental resources for others. Responsible challenge is especially critical, because the very essence of developmental change involves movement toward greater complexity and integration in the frame of reference from which each of us views our world (Flavell, 1963; King, 1977; Mischel, 1971; Perry, 1970). This movement toward complexity is enhanced when points of view are directly and responsibly challenged.

Level Three: Immediacy and Exploration

The third level of mutuality in interpersonal living has a more limited focus than the second level. At the third level of mutuality, individuals are able to challenge one another concerning aspects of their relationships that limit personal development. At this level, individuals are willing to explore themselves in the context of a particular relationship and examine events in the relationship in question.

The minister who experiences loneliness and resentment because he is kept on a pedestal by his congregation, the child who feels her own judgment being continually called into question by inflexible family regulations, the Black supervisor who is afraid to comment on her White manager's insensitivity to potentially explosive racial issues, the office worker who feels that some of the boss's demands are demeaning—all these are examples of immediate issues in relationships. By facing such immediacy issues directly and positively, individuals can open up new areas of development for themselves. By refusing to face these issues, members can block development altogether.

Immediacy issues are potent sources of developmental change because of their highly personal nature; they deal directly with the way in which one individual is experienced by another rather than with roles, tasks, or knowledge. Cooley (1922), Erikson (1968), Mead (1934), and Sullivan (1953), all of whom are significant contributors to our understanding of the concept of identity, have stressed that the development of identity is inextricably bound up in social relationships and is not, therefore, a primarily intrapersonal phenomenon. Thus, we find Cooley's "looking glass self," Erikson's definition of identity as a stable sense of who one is that is confirmed by significant people in one's life, Mead's notion of reflected appraisals as the basis of self, and Sullivan's definition of personality as the habitual interpersonal expression of self.

Our assertion that mutuality in interpersonal relationships is critical to the development of individuals and systems is based on the fact that personal development takes place within the network of interpersonal relations that form in human settings. Obviously, the depth and intensity of mutuality will differ with the type of setting: the intimacy of committed personal relationships is inappropriate in typical business relationships, but important interpersonal issues do arise in business settings. In our view, a system cannot be optimally effective in both task accomplishment and member development unless its members can deal with one another appropriately at each of the three levels of mutuality discussed here.

Mutuality as a System Characteristic

We have stated our assumption that development is inextricably bound up with experiences in the social settings that constitute the context of life. In this chapter, we have explored the alienation that is characteristic of contemporary experience in the world of systems and the personal and social costs of that alienation. Community may be considered the antithesis of alienation. In our view, mutuality, which is one basis for community, is of critical importance to the humanizing of systems. Mutuality in human systems provides a framework within which individuals can come to grips with developmental challenges and avail themselves of basic human support throughout their lives.

Level One: Basic Decency in Systems

The first level of mutuality is basic to the functioning of any system that values the integrity and development of its members. The members of a system that operates at the basic decency level of mutuality know that other members will be able and willing to understand their experience from their individual frame of reference; as a result, they don't feel as though they have to remain on guard at all times. They are able to explain their experience in direct and understandable language, which assists others in understanding them. When individuals aren't on guard constantly, the stress associated with physical and psychological problems is low, and levels of available energy are high (Cassel, 1973). Individuals who are fortunate enough to experience first-level mutuality in the important personal systems of their lives are buffered from the alienation of impersonalized institutions.

A system with the capability (values, knowledge, and skills) of operating consistently at the basic decency level of the mutuality continuum makes a substantive contribution to the development of its members. As Caplan (1973) has noted:

> The harmful effect of absent or confusing feedback in a general population may be reduced in the case of those individuals who are effectively embedded in their own smaller social networks which provide them with consistent communication of what is expected of them, support and assistance with tasks, evaluations of their performance, and appropriate rewards [pp. 4–5].

In our view, a fundamental obligation of all systems is to provide a climate of basic human decency for their members. This obligation applies to the workplace as well as to the family. Ordinarily, measures are taken to ensure that people in the workplace are not harmed by air, noise, or other preventable forms of pollution. Perhaps it is time now to consider an equally potent commitment to the psychological well-being of people in human settings. First-level mutuality in the interpersonal network of a system has effects beyond the prevention of stress-related illnesses; it is also the primary source of basic human support, which is a fundamental developmental resource (see Chapter 2). The presence of those who can be trusted to understand and accept others' experiences is a potent agent for encouraging the development of people, as the peer self-help movement has shown (Gartner & Riessman, 1977; Lieberman & Borman, 1976).

Level Two: Responsible Challenge in Systems

The second level of mutuality in systems goes beyond disclosure and empathy and involves the system's capacity to offer responsible challenge that results in exploration. We have noted the role of challenge in the developmental process (see Chapter 2). When people possess positive challenging skills, their settings become secure places where they have access to the feedback that is necessary for their continuing development. Like a human relationship, a human setting that doesn't go beyond basic decency robs its members of a rich source of developmental possibilities. The family that can confront life-style differences decently, the supervisory team that can offer performance feedback without threatening their workers' integrity, the classroom that has rules allowing students to involve themselves in evaluating educational procedures—these are all examples of settings in which responsible challenge contributes to member development and to the development of the setting itself. Positive challenge is also foundational to the next level of mutuality—relationship immediacy.

Level Three: Relationship Immediacy in Systems

When the members of a system are capable of basic decency and responsible challenge in dealing with one another, they are able to move to the third level of mutuality. At this third level, individuals are capable of dealing directly and openly with one another concerning the current state of their relationships in a way that evokes thoughtful exploration rather than defensiveness or withdrawal. Although a type of intimacy or game-free interaction (see Berne, 1964) is involved at this level of mutuality, the intensity and content of the interaction varies with the type of system; the third level of mutuality should not be confused with complete emotional sharing. *Relationship immediacy* refers to the ability of persons to talk directly about the current state of their relationship as it pertains to a common mission, whatever the depth or intensity of the relationship. Relationship immediacy in the workplace differs in many respects from the relationship immediacy of friendship or marriage.

A human system that operates consistently at this third level of mutuality offers its members a rich combination of support and challenge as it buffers them against the destructive effects of a complex and often alienating world. Such a system can form the foundation from which individuals can move with a sense of hope and potency to cope with and effectively engage the rest of their world. It provides a secure retreat from a less responsive world and challenges its members to develop the capabilities they need for effective engagement with other systems.

It has been observed that our world is alienating and threatening; it is not a place where individuals readily experience a sense of community with other human beings. Many have argued that the deepest longing of contemporary people is for this sense of community, of personal relatedness (Nisbet, 1969; Sarason, 1974). Is alienation, the lack of a sense of community, inescapably a part of a world made up of complex and interrelated systems? We think not. We maintain that the current state of affairs stems from our collective failure as a culture to devise effective systemic approaches to fostering development that are consistent with criteria of task effectiveness. Since we have concentrated a disproportionate amount of available human-services resources on remedial approaches, we have failed to significantly and deliberately affect the social structures in which people live out their lives.

Fostering Human Communities: A Fundamental Upstream Approach

People who are concerned with the development of others are faced with the task of encouraging and supporting the process of building community in human settings. Because of their centrality in the lives of everyone and their immediate availability to their members, immediate personal systems, such as the family, the school, and the workplace, have high priority in this regard; however, it is futile to focus on these smaller systems while ignoring their context.

In the following list, we offer a number of attributes of socially viable and responsive systems characterized by a sense of community. This list is offered as a suggestion of the major dimensions of community, rather than a complete taxonomy.

1. *Shared purpose.* All human systems have some reason for being; the depth or importance of such reasons varies widely. The bridge club or drinking group, as well as the family, may function as communities for their members. The basic point is that every community has a unifying activity or purpose, whether it be learning, living, working, or recreating.

2. *Mutuality in interpersonal relations.* As we pointed out earlier in this chapter, mutuality refers to the quality and depth of communication among individuals. Without some degree of mutuality, community is limited, whereas community deepens as mutuality becomes characteristic of interaction.

3. *Commitment to learning.* Every viable system has an ongoing commitment to new learning. Such openness is necessary for two reasons: the external environment is constantly changing and must be responded to, and members are constantly in a developmental process that requires new forms of challenge and support. A closed system is likely to have difficulty in maintaining itself as a community over an extended period of time.

4. *Involvement with other communities.* We live in a highly interdependent world in which social structures that are also communities are capable of becoming involved with one another. Mutual involvement is a source of development for communities and for the broader world of social systems—personal, institutional, and cultural. Effective communities accept their interdependence as a challenge.

One way in which systems become communities is by engaging collectively in the learning cycle described in Chapter 2. First, the members of a system develop the capacity to share personal concerns about the purpose or issue that brings them together and to hear others' concerns. Second, the members develop the capacity to challenge one another by presenting their points of view in ways that provoke a deepening and enrichment of individual perspectives. Finally, the members develop the capacity to behave collectively in ways that reflect their new awareness. In simple language, a system becomes a community when its members learn to talk and listen to one another, to openly share differing views with one another, to act together out of shared concerns, and to learn from the results of their collective experience.

Community that characterizes a functioning family or friendship group differs in many ways from community in a corporate system or in a classroom. A group of neighbors working together on an area-improvement project experience community in a way that differs from the experience of a cohesive self-help group for alcoholics. Moreover, the specific forms of community vary according to cultural and ethnic background. The important issue is the presence of a sense of community in people's lives, not the particular forms which a community's interactions take.

Those who are committed to human development can build on the skills of effective helping relationships—empathy, challenge, and assistance in behavioral change—to help systems function as communities at levels consistent with their purpose. What is needed, and what we have tried in a provisional way to articulate in these pages, is a cognitive map of how systems work—a map that doesn't restrict itself to the individual psychological perspective but suggests new approaches to supporting development in a social context. Such a map, or model, would help us to get upstream by making systems more comprehensible and more approachable. The professional person in the human services of tomorrow must learn to understand and affect the world of human systems and help others build and sustain systems that foster development.

Our families, schools, workplaces, communities, and governments need people who are capable of assisting them in becoming communities.

Helping systems to become communities is a complex task, but in the accomplishment of this task lies hope for the ongoing transformation of the social world as the context for the development of all people.

Chapter 11: Additional Resources

Caplan, G. *Support systems and community mental health.* New York: Behavioral Publications, 1974. (See Introduction and Chapter 1.)

Egan, G. *Interpersonal living.* Monterey, Calif.: Brooks/Cole, 1976. (See Chapters 3–8 and 10–13.)

Nisbet, R. *The quest for community.* London: Oxford University Press, 1969. (See Chapter 3 and Conclusion.)

Sarason, S. *The psychological sense of community.* San Francisco: Jossey-Bass, 1974. (See Chapter 6.)

Scherer, J. *Contemporary community: Sociological illusion or reality?* London: Tavistock, 1972.

Epilogue

A paradigm may be defined as the working model or set of assumptions that guides individuals in their activities. The model presented in these pages constitutes a "paradigm shift" for many professionals who work in the field of human development. Kuhn's (1970) work demonstrates that there is a sequence of paradigmatic revolutions—new ways of looking at the world—that underlies the progress of scientific activity. These revolutions yield breakthroughs that weren't possible under previous working models. The people-in-systems model is intended to offer a new point of view, rather than a ready-made set of programmatic answers. We believe that the task of devising, delivering, and evaluating human-service and educational programs will ultimately be enhanced by the development of working models such as this one.

We acknowledge the enormity of the task confronting those professionals who, in attempting to understand and affect the lives of others, adopt a working model that stresses sociocultural structure as the context for human development. We offer this work as a contribution to a new paradigm for those who are committed to the betterment and enrichment of all people and their systems.

References

Adler, R. (Ed.). *Television as a social force: New approaches to TV criticism.* New York: Praeger, 1975.

Alberti, R. E., & Emmons, M. L. *Your perfect right: A guide to assertive behavior* (2nd ed.). San Luis Obispo, Calif.: Impact, 1974.

Alberti, R. E., & Emmons, M. L. *Stand up, speak out, talk back.* New York: Pocket Books, 1975.

Alex, N. *New York cops talk back.* New York: Wiley, 1976.

Allen, I. The mighty monolith? *Society*, 1977, *15* (1), 11, 20–23.

Alverno College. *Competence based learning at Alverno College.* Milwaukee: Alverno College, 1974.

Andrews, E. *The emotionally disturbed family and some gratifying alternatives.* New York: Aronson, 1974.

Anthony, W. A. *The principles of psychiatric rehabilitation.* Amherst, Mass.: Human Resource Development Press, 1978.

Anthony, W. A., & Carkhuff, R. R. *The art of health care.* Amherst, Mass.: Human Resource Development Press, 1977.

Appley, F. G., & Winder, A. E. An evolving definition of collaboration and some implications for the world of work. *Journal of Applied Behavioral Science*, 1977, *13*, 279–291.

Argyris, C. *Integrating the individual and the organization.* New York: Wiley, 1964.

Argyris, C. *Increasing leadership effectiveness.* New York: Wiley-Interscience, 1976a.

Argyris, C. Theories of action that inhibit individual learning. *American Psychologist*, 1976b, *31*, 638–654.

Argyris, C., & Schön, D. A. *Theory in practice: Increasing professional effectiveness.* San Francisco: Jossey-Bass, 1974.

Ashby, W. R. *An introduction to cybernetics.* London: Chapman & Hall, 1956.

Aspy, D. *Toward a technology for humanizing education.* Champaign, Ill.: Research Press, 1972.

Aspy, D., & Roebuck, F. *Kids don't learn from people they don't like.* Amherst, Mass.: Human Resource Development Press, 1977.

Aulepp, L., & Delworth, U. *Training manual for an ecosystems model.* Western Interstate Commission for Higher Education, 1976.

Ausubel, D. *Cognitive psychology.* New York: Holt, Rinehart & Winston, 1968.

Azrin, N. H. A strategy for applied research: Learning-based but outcome-oriented. *American Psychologist*, 1977, *32*, 140–149.

Ball, G. *"Magic Circle": An overview of the human development program.* La Mesa, Calif.: Human Development Training Institute, 1974.

Baltes, P. B., & Schaie, K. W. The myth of the twilight years. *Psychology Today, 7*, 1974.

Bandler, R., & Grinder, J. *The structure of magic* (Vol. 1). Palo Alto, Calif.: Science and Behavior Books, 1975.

Bandura, A. *Principles of behavior modification.* New York: Holt, Rinehart & Winston, 1969.

Bandura, A. *Social learning theory.* Englewood Cliffs, N. J.: Prentice-Hall, 1977.

Bane, M. J. *Here to stay: American families in the twentieth century.* New York: Basic Books, 1976.

Barker, R. *Habitats, environments, and human behavior.* San Francisco: Jossey-Bass, 1978.

Barker, R. *Ecological psychology.* Stanford, Calif.: Stanford University Press, 1968.

Barnes, D., & Todd, F. *Communication and learning in small groups.* London: Routledge & Kegan Paul, 1977.

Barocas, R., & Karoly, P. Effects of physical appearance on social responsiveness. *Psychological Reports,* 1972, *31,* 495–500.

Bendix, R. Inequality and social structure: A comparison of Marx and Weber. In L. Coser & B. Rosenberg (Eds.), *Sociological theory* (4th ed.). New York: Macmillan, 1976.

Berenson, B. G., & Mitchell, K. M. *Confrontation: For better or worse.* Amherst, Mass.: Human Resource Development Press, 1974.

Berger, P. L., & Neuhaus, R. J. *To empower people: The role of mediating structures in public policy.* Washington, D. C.: American Enterprise Institute for Public Policy Research, 1977.

Berger, R. *Government by judiciary: The transformation of the fourteenth amendment.* Cambridge, Mass.: Harvard University Press, 1977.

Berkovitz, I. H. (Ed.). *When schools care: Creative use of groups in secondary schools.* New York: Brunner & Mazel, 1975.

Berne, E. *Transactional analysis in psychotherapy.* New York: Grove Press, 1961.

Berne, E. *Games people play.* New York: Grove Press, 1964.

Berne, E. *Principles of group treatment.* New York: Oxford University Press, 1966.

Berne, E. *What do you say after you say hello?* New York: Grove Press, 1972.

Bessell, H. *Methods in human development: Theory manual.* La Mesa, Calif.: Human Development Training Institute, 1973.

Blake, R. R., & Mouton, J. S. *The managerial grid.* Houston, Texas: Gulf Publishing Company, 1964.

Blake, R. R., & Mouton, J. S. *Corporate excellence through grid organization development.* Houston, Texas: Gulf Publishing Company, 1968.

Blake, R. R., & Mouton, J. S. *Building a dynamic corporation through grid organization development.* Reading, Mass.: Addison-Wesley, 1969.

Blauner, R. *Alienation and freedom.* Chicago: University of Chicago Press, 1964.

Blaxall, M., & Reagan, B. (Eds.). *Women and the workplace. The implications of occupational segregation.* Chicago: University of Chicago Press, 1976.

Blechman, E. A. The family contract game. *Family Coordinator,* 1974, *23,* 269–281.

Blechman, E. A., & Olson, D. H. The family contract game: Description and effectiveness. In D. H. Olson (Ed.), *Treating relationships.* Lake Mills, Iowa: Graphic Publishing, 1975.

Bledstein, B. J. *The culture of professionalism: The middle class and the development of higher education in America.* New York: Norton, 1976.

Blumberg, P. (Ed.). *The impact of social class.* New York: Crowell, 1972.

Blumler, J. G., & Katz, E. (Eds.). *The uses of mass communication.* Sage Annual Reviews of Communication Research (Vol. 3). Beverly Hills, Calif.: Sage Publications, 1974.

Boston Women's Health Collective. *Our bodies, our selves* (Rev. ed.). New York: Simon & Schuster, 1976.

Boulding, K. General systems theory—the skeleton of science. In D. Ruben & J. Kim (Eds.), *General systems theory and communication.* Rochelle Park, N.J.: Hayden, 1975.

Bowles, S., & Gintis, H. *Schooling in capitalist America: Educational reform and the contradictions of economic life.* New York: Basic Books, 1976.

Brim, O. Macro-structural influences on child development and the need for childhood social indicators. *American Journal of Orthopsychiatry,* 1975, *45,* 516–524.

Brim, O., & Wheeler, S. *Socialization after childhood.* New York: Wiley, 1966.

Bronfenbrenner, U. Nobody home: The erosion of the American family. *Psychology Today,* 1977a, *10* (No. 12, May), 41–47.

Bronfenbrenner, U. Toward an experimental ecology of human development. *American Psychologist,* 1977b, 513–531.

Brooks, P. R. *Officer down, code three.* Schiller Park, Ill.: Motorola Teleprograms, 1975.

Broom, L., & Selznick, P. *Sociology* (5th ed.). New York: Harper & Row, 1973.

Buber, M. *I and thou.* New York: Scribner, 1937.

Buchholz, R. An alternative to social responsibility. *M.S.U. Business Topics,* 1977, *25,* 12–16.

Buckley, W. *Sociology and modern systems theory.* Englewood Cliffs, N.J.: Prentice-Hall, 1967.

Buckley, W. (Ed.). *Modern systems research for the behavioral scientist.* Chicago: Aldine, 1968.

Bullmer, K. *The art of empathy.* New York: Human Sciences Press, 1975.

Burglass, M. E., & Duffy, M. G. *Thresholds: Teacher's manual.* Cambridge, Mass.: Correctional Solutions Foundation, 1974.

Buss, A., & Plomin, R. *A temperament theory of personality development.* New York: Wiley, 1975.

Calia, V. F. Systematic human relations training: Appraisal and status. *Counselor Education and Supervision,* 1974, *14*(2), 85–94.

Caplan, G. *The theory and practice of mental health consultation.* New York: Basic Books, 1970.

Caplan, G. *Support systems and community mental health.* New York: Human Sciences Press, 1973.

Caplan, G., & Killilea, M. (Eds.). *Support systems and mutual help: Multidisciplinary explorations.* New York: Grune & Stratton, 1976.

Caplan, N., & Nelson, S. D. On being useful: The nature and consequences of psychological research on social problems. *American Psychologist,* 1973, *28,* 199–211.

Carkhuff, R. R. *The development of human resources.* New York: Holt, Rinehart & Winston, 1971.

Carkhuff, R. R. *The art of problem solving.* Amherst, Mass.: Human Resource Development Press, 1973.

Carkhuff, R. R. *How to help yourself: The art of program development.* Amherst, Mass.: Human Resource Development Press, 1974.

Carkhuff, R. R., & Berenson, B. G. *Teaching as treatment.* Amherst, Mass.: Human Resource Development Press, 1976.

Carkhuff, R. R., & Berenson, B. G. *Beyond counseling and psychotherapy* (Rev. ed.). New York: Holt, Rinehart & Winston, 1977.

Carkhuff, R. R., Berenson, D. H., & Pierce, R. M. *The skills of teaching interpersonal skills.* Amherst, Mass.: Human Resource Development Press, 1977.

Carkhuff, R. R., Pierce, R. M., et al. *The art of helping III.* Amherst, Mass.: Human Resource Development Press, 1977.

Cassel, J. Psychiatric epidemiology. In S. Arieti (Ed.), *American handbook of psychiatry* (Vol. II). New York: Basic Books, 1973. Pp. 401–410.

Cassel, J., & Tyroler, H. Epidemiological studies of culture change. *Archives of Environmental Health*, 1961, *3*, 25–32.

Cassirer, E. *An essay on man.* New Haven: Yale University Press, 1944.

Chaliand, G. *Revolution in the third world: Myths and prospects.* New York: Viking, 1977.

Chickering, A. W. *Education and identity.* San Francisco: Jossey-Bass, 1969.

Chickering, A. W., & McCormick, J. Personality development and the college experience. *Research in Higher Education*, 1973, *1*, 43–70.

Claiborne, R. The great health care rip-off. *Saturday Review*, January 7, 1978, Pp. 10–16, 50.

Collingwood, T., & Carkhuff, R. R. *Get fit for living.* Amherst, Mass.: Human Resource Development Press, 1976a.

Collingwood, T., & Carkhuff, R. R. *Get fit trainer's guide.* Amherst, Mass.: Human Resource Development Press, 1976b.

Combs, A., Richards, A., & Richards, F. *Perceptual psychology.* New York: Harper & Row, 1976.

Commoner, B. *The poverty of power: Energy and the economic crisis.* New York: Knopf, 1976.

Cooley, C. H. *Social organization.* New York: Scribner, 1909.

Cooley, C. H. *Human nature and the social order* (Rev. ed.). New York: Scribner, 1922.

Corbett, T. H. *Cancer and chemicals.* Chicago: Nelson-Hall, 1977.

Corey, G., & Corey, M. S. *Groups: Process and practice.* Monterey, Calif.: Brooks/Cole, 1977.

Cowan, M., Egan, G., & Bacchi, M. *Instructor's manual to accompany INTERPERSONAL LIVING and YOU AND ME.* Monterey, Calif.: Brooks/Cole, 1978.

Craig, R. Lawrence Kohlberg and moral development: Some reflections. *Educational Theory*, 1974, *24* (Spring), 121–129.

Cross, K. P. *Accent on learning: Improving instruction and reshaping the curriculum.* San Francisco: Jossey-Bass, 1976.

Curran, C. A. *Counseling and psychotherapy: The pursuit of values.* New York: Sheed & Ward, 1968.

Danish, S., & Hauer, A. *Helping skills: A basic training program.* New York: Behavioral Publications, 1973.

Deci, E. L. *Intrinsic motivation.* New York: Plenum, 1975.

Dewey, J. The reflex arc concept in psychology. *Psychological Review*, 1896, *3*, 357–370.

Dinkmeyer, D., & McKay, G. D. *Systematic training for effective parenting.* Circle Pines, Minn: American Guidance Service, 1977.

Dion, K. Physical attractiveness and evaluators of children's transgressions. *Journal of Personality and Social Psychology*, 1972, *24*, 207–213.

Dion, K., Berscheid, E., & Walster, E. What is beautiful is good. *Journal of Personality and Social Psychology*, 1972, *24*, 285–290.

Dollard, J. *Criteria for the life history.* New Haven: Yale University Press, 1935.

Downs, M. *A comparison of two methods of human relations training for teaching communication skills to adults.* Unpublished doctoral dissertation, Loyola University of Chicago, 1973.

Drucker, P. F. *The age of discontinuity: Guidelines to our changing society.* New York: Harper & Row, 1968.

Drucker, P. F. *Management: Tasks, practices, and responsibilities.* New York: Harper & Row, 1974.

Durkheim, E. The normality of crime. In L. Coser & B. Rosenberg (Eds.), *Sociological theory* (4th ed.). New York: Macmillan, 1976, 458–464.

Dustin, R. Training for institutional change. *Personnel and Guidance Journal*, 1974, *52*, 423–427.

D'Zurilla, T. J., & Goldfried, M. R. Problem-solving and behavior modification. *Journal of Abnormal Psychology*, 1971, *78*, 107–126.

Egan, G. *Encounter: Group processes for interpersonal growth*. Monterey, Calif.: Brooks/Cole, 1970.

Egan, G. *The skilled helper: A model for systematic helping and interpersonal relating*. Monterey, Calif.: Brooks/Cole, 1975.

Egan, G. *Interpersonal living: A skills/contract approach to human-relations training in groups*. Monterey, Calif.: Brooks/Cole, 1976.

Egan, G. *You and me: The skills of communicating and relating to others*. Monterey, Calif.: Brooks/Cole, 1977.

Egan, G. *Change agent skills: Model and methods for the renewal of systems*. Monterey, Calif.: Brooks/Cole, in press.

Einstein, A. *The world as I see it*. New York: Covici-Friede, 1932.

Ellis, A. *Reason and emotion in psychotherapy*. New York: Lyle Stuart, 1962.

Endler, N., & Hunt, J. Generalizibility of contributions of sources of variance in the S-R inventories of anxiousness. *Journal of Personality*, 1969, *37*, 1–24, p. 20.

Erikson, E. *Young man Luther*. New York: Norton, 1958.

Erikson, E. *Childhood and society* (2nd ed.). New York: Norton, 1963.

Erikson, E. *Identity: Youth and crisis*. New York: Norton, 1968.

Fenhagen, J. C. *Mutual ministry: New vitality for the local church*. New York: Seabury, 1977.

Flavell, J. *The developmental psychology of Jean Piaget*. New York: Van Nostrand Rheinhold, 1963.

Fogelson, R. M. *Big-city police*. Cambridge, Mass: Harvard University Press, 1978.

Ford, R. N. *Motivation through work itself*. New York: American Management Association, 1969.

Ford, R. N. Job enrichment: Lessons from AT&T. *Harvard Business Review*, 1973, *51*, January–February, 96–106.

Fordyce, W. E. *Behavioral methods for control of chronic pain and illness*. St. Louis, Mo.: Mosby, 1976.

Freire, P. *Pedagogy of the oppressed*. New York: Seabury, 1970.

Frank, J. *Persuasion and healing* (Rev. ed.). Baltimore: The Johns Hopkins University Press, 1973.

Fromm, E. *Man for himself*. New York: Holt, Rinehart & Winston, 1947.

Gartner, A., & Riessman, F. *Self-help in the human services*. San Francisco: Jossey-Bass, 1977.

Gazda, G. M. *Human relations development: A manual for educators*. Boston: Allyn & Bacon, 1973.

Gazda, G. M., Walters, R. P., & Childers, W. C. *Human relations development: A manual for health sciences*. Boston: Allyn & Bacon, 1975.

Gerbner, G. (Ed.). *Mass media policies in changing cultures*. New York: Wiley-Interscience, 1977.

Gerhard, M. *Effective teaching strategies with the behavioral outcomes approach*. West Nyack, N.J.: Parker, 1971.

Gerson, E. M., & Strauss, A. L. Time for living: Problems in chronic illness care. *Social Policy*, 1975, *6*, 12–18.

Giroux, H., & Penna, A. Social relations in the classroom: The dialectic of the hidden curriculum. *Edcentric*, 1977, (Spring–Summer), 39–46.

Goldfried, M. R., & Goldfried, A. P. *Cognitive change methods.* In F. H. Kanfer & A. P. Goldstein (Eds.), *Helping people change.* New York: Pergamon Press, 1975. Pp. 89–116.

Goldiamond, I. A diary of self-modification. *Psychology Today*, 1978, *11*, 95–102.

Goldman, R. *A work experiment: Six Americans in a Swedish plant.* New York: Ford Foundation, 1976.

Goldstein, A. P. *Structured learning therapy: Toward a psychotherapy for the poor.* New York: Academic Press, 1973.

Goldstein, A. P., Sprafkin, R. P., & Gershaw, N. J. *Skill training for community living. Applying structured learning therapy.* Fairview Park, N.Y.: Pergamon Press, 1976.

Goodman, J. Values clarification: A review of major books. In J. W. Pfeiffer & J. J. Jones (Eds.), *The 1976 annual handbook for group facilitators.* La Jolla, Calif.: University Associates, 1976, Pp. 274–279.

Goodyear, R. K. Counselors as community psychologists. *Personnel and Guidance Journal*, 1976, *54*, 512–516.

Gordon, S. *Lonely in America.* New York: Simon & Schuster, 1976.

Gordon, T. *Parent effectiveness training.* New York: Wyden, 1970.

Gordon, T. *Teacher effectiveness training.* New York: Wyden, 1974.

Gordon, T. *Leadership effectiveness training.* New York: Wyden, 1977.

Gross, M. *The psychological society.* New York: Random House, 1977.

Gruber, H., & Voneche, J. *The essential Piaget.* New York: Basic Books, 1977.

Hacker, A. Safety last. *New York Review of Books*, 1977, *24* (14), 3–8.

Hales, D. *How early is early contact? Defining the limits of the sensitive period.* Paper presented to the Symposium on the Ecology of Human Development of the Society for Research in Child Development, New Orleans, March, 1977.

Haley, J. *Problem-solving therapy: New strategies for effective family therapy.* San Francisco: Jossey-Bass, 1976.

Hall, E. *Beyond culture.* Garden City, N. J.: Anchor Press, 1977.

Handel, G. Work, women, and class. *Society*, 1977, *14* (6, September-October), 82–83.

Hare, A.P. *Handbook of small group research.* New York: Free Press, 1962.

Harman, S. Implication for public policy: The role of government in the enhancement of human development in the world of work. *Journal of Applied Behavioral Science*, 1977, *13*, 458–462.

Harman, W. The coming transformation. *Futurist*, 1977, *11*, 106–112.

Harmin, M., Kirschenbaum, H., & Simon, S. B. *Clarifying values through subject matter.* Minneapolis: Winston Press, 1973.

Harrington, M. *The vast majority: A journey to the world's poor.* New York: Simon & Schuster, 1977.

Harris, M. *Cannibals and kings: The origins of cultures.* New York: Random House, 1977.

Harwood, E. The pluralist press. *Society*, 1977, *15*(1), 10, 17–20.

Haskell, T. L. Power to the experts. *New York Review of Books*, 1977, *24* (No. 16, October 13), 28–33.

Hassol, L., & Cooper, S. Techniques of mental health consultation in a preventive context. In Grunebaum, H. (Ed.), *The practice of community mental health.* Boston: Little, Brown & Co., 1970.

Havighurst, R. *Developmental tasks and education* (3rd ed.). New York: McKay, 1972.

Heath, D. *Growing up in college.* San Francisco: Jossey-Bass, 1968.

Heath, D. Presentation at the University of Minnesota Conference on Developmental Theory in Higher Education. Minneapolis, Spring, 1976.

Heath, D. Academic predictors of adult maturity and competence. *Journal of Higher Education,* 1977b, *48,* 613–632.

Heath, D. *Maturity and competence.* New York: Halstead Press, 1977a.

Heath, R. *The reasonable adventure.* Pittsburgh: University of Pittsburgh Press, 1964.

Heidegger, M. *Being and time.* New York: Harper & Row, 1962.

Heisler, W. J., & Houck, J. W. (Eds). *A matter of dignity: Inquiries into the humanization of work.* Notre Dame, Ind.: University of Notre Dame Press, 1977.

Heller, J. *Something happened.* New York: Alfred A. Knopf, 1974.

Hendin, D. *Death as a fact of life.* New York: Norton, 1973.

Herzberg, F. *Work and the nature of man.* Cleveland: World, 1966.

Herzberg, F. One more time: How do you motivate employees? *Harvard Business Review,* 1968, *46* (1), 115–124.

Hilgard, E., & Bower, G. *Theories of learning* (4th ed.). Englewood Cliffs, N. J.: Prentice-Hall, 1975.

Hillery, G. Definitions of community. *Rural Sociology,* 1955, *20,* 111–123.

Hirsch, F. *Social limits to growth.* Cambridge, Mass.: Harvard University Press, 1976.

Horn, J., & Donaldson, G. On the myth of intellectual decline in adulthood. *American Psychologist,* 1976, *31,* 701–719.

Horn, J., & Donaldson, G. Faith is not enough. *American Psychologist,* 1977, *32,* 369–373.

Howard, J. *Please touch: A guided tour of the human potential movement.* New York: McGraw-Hall, 1970.

Howell, M. C. *Helping ourselves: Families and the human network.* Boston: Beacon, 1975.

Hurvitz, N. Peer self-help psychotherapy groups and their implication for psychotherapy. *Psychotherapy: Theory, Research, and Practice,* 1970, *7,* 41–49.

Hurvitz, N. Similarities and differences between conventional psychotherapy and peer self-help psychotherapy groups. In P. S. Roman & H. M. Trice (Eds.), *The sociology of psychotherapy.* New York: Aronson, 1974. Pp. 110–120.

Hurvitz, N. The origins of the peer self-help psychotherapy group movement. *Journal of Applied Behavioral Sciences,* 1976, *12,* 283–294.

Illich, I. *Deschooling society.* New York: Harper & Row, 1971.

Illich, I. *Medical nemesis: The expropriation of health.* New York: Pantheon, 1976.

Ingalls, J. *Human energy.* Reading, Mass.: Addison-Wesley, 1976.

Ivey, A. E. Counseling psychology, the psychoeducator model and the future. *Counseling Psychologist,* 1976, *6*(3), 72–75.

Ivey, A., & Aischuler, A. An introduction to the field of psychological education. *Personnel and Guidance Journal,* 1973, *51,* 591–597.

Jackson, B. *Killing time: Life in the Arkansas penitentiary.* Ithaca, N. Y.: Cornell University Press, 1977.

Jackson, P. *Life in classrooms.* New York: Holt, Rinehart & Winston, 1968.

James, M., & Jongeward, D. *Born to win: Transactional analysis with Gestalt experiments.* Reading, Mass.: Addison-Wesley, 1971.

Janis, I. L., & Mann, L. *Decision making.* New York: Free Press, 1977.

Jones, D. *Business ethics bibliography.* Charlottesville, Va.: University Press of Virginia, 1977.

Jones, E., & Gerard, H. *Foundations of social psychology.* New York: Wiley, 1967.

Jones, E., Kanouse, D., Kelley, H., Nisbet, R., Valins, S., & Weiner, B. *Attribution: Perceiving the causes of behavior.* Morristown, N. J.: General Learning Press, 1972.

Kanfer, F. H. Self-management methods. In F. H. Kanfer & A. P. Goldstein (Eds.), *Helping people change: A textbook of methods.* New York: Pergamon Press, 1975. Pp. 309–355.

Kanter, R. M. *Commitment and community*. Cambridge, Mass.: Harvard University Press, 1972.

Kanter, R. M. *Men and women of the corporation*. New York: Basic Books, 1977a.

Kanter, R. M. Power games in the corporation. *Psychology Today*, 1977b, *11*(2), 48–53.

Kaplan, A. *The conduct of inquiry*. San Francisco: Chandler, 1964.

Kaufman, R. *Identifying and solving problems: A system approach*. La Jolla, Calif.: University Associates, 1976.

Kelley, C. Assertion: The literature since 1970. In J. W. Pfeiffer & J. J. Jones (Eds.), *The 1977 annual handbook for group facilitators*. La Jolla, Calif.: University Associates, 1977. Pp. 264–275.

Kelly, G. *The psychology of personal constructs* (Vol. 1). New York: Norton, 1955.

Kelman, H. C. Three processes of social influence. In E. P. Hollander & R. G. Hunt (Eds.), *Current perspectives in social psychology*. New York: Oxford University Press, 1967. Pp. 438–446.

Keniston, K. *All our children: The American family under pressure*. New York: Harcourt Brace Jovanovich, 1977.

Kennell, J. N., et al. Maternal behavior one year after early and extended postpartum contact. *Developmental Medicine and Child Neurology*, 1974, *16*, 172–179.

Kimmel, D. C. *Adulthood and aging*. New York: Wiley, 1974.

King, P. *What does "development" mean?* Paper presented at the American College Personnel Association Meeting, Denver, 1977.

King, S. W. *Communication and social influence*. Reading, Mass.: Addison-Wesley, 1975.

Kirschenbaum, H. *Advanced value clarification*. La Jolla, Calif.: University Associates, 1977.

Kirschenbaum, H., & Simon, S. B. (Eds.). *Readings in values clarification*. Minneapolis: Winston Press, 1973.

Klaus, M. H., Kennell, J. H., Plumb, N., & Zueblke, S. Human maternal behavior at the first contact with her young. *Pediatrics*, 1970, *46*, 187–192.

Klaus, M. J., et al. Maternal attachment: Importance of the first post-partum days. *New England Journal of Medicine*, 1972, *286*, 460–463.

Koch, K. *Wishes, lies, and dreams: Teaching children to write poetry*. New York: Random House, 1971.

Koch, K. *Rose, where did you get that red? Teaching great poetry to children*. New York: Random House, 1973.

Koch, K. *I never told anybody: Teaching poetry writing in a nursing home*. New York: Random House, 1977.

Kockelmans, J. (Ed.). *Phenomenology: The philosophy of Edmund Husserl and its interpretation*. Garden City, N. Y.: Anchor Books, 1967.

Kohlberg, L. Stage and sequence: The cognitive developmental approach to socialization. In D. Goslin (Ed.), *Handbook of socialization theory and research*. Chicago: Rand McNally, 1969.

Kolhberg, L. The development of moral stages: Uses and abuses. *Proceedings of the 1973 invitational conference on testing problems*. Princeton, N. J.: Educational Testing Service, 1973.

Kohlberg, L., & Mayer, R. Development as the aim of education. *Harvard Educational Review*, November, 1972, *42*, 449–496.

Kohlberg, L., & Turiel, E. Moral development and moral education. In G. Lesser (Ed.), *Psychology and educational practice*. Glenview, Ill.: Scott, Foresman, 1971.

Köhler, W. *Gestalt psychology*. New York: Liveright, 1947.

Köhler, W. *The place of value in a world of facts*. New York: Mentor Books, 1966.

Kraus, S., & Davis, D. *The effects of mass communication on political behavior.* University Park, Penn: Pennsylvania State University Press, 1976.

Kubler-Ross, E. *On death and dying.* New York: Macmillan, 1969.

Kubler-Ross, E. *Questions and answers on death and dying.* New York: Macmillan, 1974.

Kubler-Ross, E. (Ed.). *Death: The final stage of growth.* Englewood Cliffs, N. J.: Prentice-Hall, 1975.

Kuhn, A. *The logic of social systems.* San Francisco: Jossey-Bass, 1974.

Kuhn, T. *The structure of scientific revolutions* (2nd ed.). Chicago: University of Chicago Press, 1970.

Lakoff, S. A., & Rich, D. (Eds.). *Private government.* Glenview, Ill.: Scott, Foresman, 1973.

Lange, A. J., & Jakubowski, P. *Responsible assertive behavior: Cognitive/behavioral procedures for trainers.* Champaign, Ill.: Research Press, 1976.

Larson, Magali S. *The rise of professionalism: A sociological analysis.* Berkeley, Calif.: University of California Press, 1977.

Lasch, C. The siege of the family. *New York Review of Books,* 1977, *24* (No. 19, November 24), 15–18.

Lasch, C. *Haven in a heartless world: The family besieged.* New York: Basic Books, 1978.

Laszlo, E. *The systems view of the world.* New York: Braziller, 1972.

Laszlo, E. *A strategy for the future.* New York: Braziller, 1974.

Lazarus, A., & Fay, A. *I can if I want to.* New York: Morrow, 1975.

Lefrancois, G. *Adolescents.* Belmont, Calif.: Wadsworth, 1976.

Lessor, L. R. *Love, marriage, & trading stamps.* Niles, Ill.: Argus, 1971.

Levanthal, A. M. *The PEACE program at American University.* A report after one year's operation. Washington, D. C.: American University Counseling Center, 1974.

Levinson, D., et al. *The seasons of a man's life.* New York: Knopf, 1978.

Liberman, R. P., King, L. W., DeRisi, W. J., & McCann, N. *Personal effectiveness: Guiding people to assert themselves and improve their social skills.* Champaign, Ill.: Research Press, 1975.

Lieberman, M., & Borman, L. Self-help groups. *Journal of Applied Behavioral Science,* 1976, *12*(3).

Lippitt, G. *Visualizing change.* La Jolla, Calif.: Learning Resources Corporation/ University Associates, 1973.

Loevinger, J. *Ego development.* San Francisco: Jossey-Bass, 1976.

Loevinger, J. Panel discussion. Minnesota Personnel and Guidance Association Meeting, Minneapolis, 1977.

Luchs, E-M. *Yoga for children.* New York: Paulist Press, 1977.

Luft, J. *Of human interaction.* Palo Alto, Calif.: National Press Books, 1969.

Luijpen, W. *Phenomenology & atheism.* Pittsburgh: Duquesne University Press, 1964.

Luthans, F., & Kreitner, R. *Organizational behavior modification.* Glenview, Ill.: Scott, Foresman, 1975.

Mahon, B. R., & Altmann, H. A. Skill training: Cautions and recommendations. *Counselor Education and Supervision,* 1977, *17,* 42–50.

Marx, K. The definition of class. In L. Coser & B. Rosenberg (Eds.), *Sociological theory* (4th ed.). New York: Macmillan, 1976. Pp. 306–307.

Maslow, A. H. *Toward a psychology of being* (2nd ed.). New York: Van Nostrand Reinhold, 1968.

Mayeroff, M. *On caring.* New York: Harper & Row, 1971.

McGregor, D. M. *The human side of enterprise.* New York: McGraw-Hill, 1960.

McLuhan, M. *Understanding media: The extensions of man.* New York: McGraw-Hill, 1964.

Mead, G. H. *Mind, self, and society.* Chicago: University of Chicago Press, 1934.

Means, B. L., & Roessler, R. T. *Personal achievement skills training: Instructor's manual.* Hot Springs, Arkansas: Arkansas Rehabilitation Research and Training Center, University of Arkansas, 1976a.

Means, B. L., & Roessler, R. T. *Personal achievement skills training: Participant's manual.* Hot Springs, Arkansas: Arkansas Rehabilitation Research and Training Center, University of Arkansas, 1976b.

Meehl, P. *Psychodiagnosis: Selected papers.* Minneapolis: University of Minnesota Press, 1973. vii–xxii.

Mehrabian, A. *Tactics of social influence.* Englewood Cliffs, N. J.: Prentice-Hall, 1970.

Meichenbaum, D. *Cognitive behavior modification.* New York: Plenum, 1977.

Merton, R. K. *Social theory and social structure* (Enlarged ed.). New York: Free Press, 1968.

Miliband, R. *The state in capitalist society.* New York: Harper & Row, 1969.

Miller, G. A. Psychology as a means of promoting human welfare. *American Psychologist,* 1969, *24,* 1063–1075.

Miller, L. M. *Behavior management: New skills for business and industry.* Atlanta: Behavioral Systems, 1974.

Miller, L. M. *Behavior management: The new science of managing people at work.* New York: Wiley, 1978.

Mills, C. W. *The sociological imagination.* London: Oxford University Press, 1959.

Minar, D., & Greer, S. (Eds.). *The concept of community.* Chicago: Aldine, 1969.

Mische, G., & Mische, P. *Toward a human world order: Beyond the national security straitjacket.* New York: Paulist Press, 1977.

Mischel, T. (Ed.). *Cognitive development and epistemology.* New York: Academic Press, 1971.

Mischel, W. Toward a cognitive social learning reconceptualization of personality. *Psychological Review,* 1973, *80,* 252–283.

Mitford, J. *Kind and usual punishment: The prison business.* New York: Knopf, 1973.

Moore, M. Counselor training: Meeting new demands. *Personnel and Guidance Journal,* 1977, *55,* 359–362.

Morrill, W., Oetting, E., & Hurst, J. Dimensions of counselor functioning. *Personnel and Guidance Journal,* 1974, *52,* 354–359.

Morris, D., & Hess, K. *Neighborhood power.* Boston: Beacon, 1975.

Morrow, A. A., & Thayer, F. C. Collaborative work settings: New titles, old contradictions. *Journal of Applied Behavioral Science,* 1977, *13,* 448–457.

Mosher, R. L., & Sprinthall, N. A. Psychological education: A means to promote personal development during adolescence. *Counseling Psychologist,* 1971, *2*(14), 3–82.

Muir, W. K. *Police: Streetcorner politicians.* Chicago: University of Chicago Press, 1977.

Murphy, L., & Moriarity, A. *Vulnerability, coping, and growth.* New Haven: Yale University Press, 1976.

Murrell, S. *Community psychology and social systems.* New York: Behavioral Publications, 1973.

Murstein, B. I. *Current and future intimate lifestyles.* New York: Springer, 1977.

Neill, A. S. "Can I come to Summerhill? I hate my school." *Psychology Today,* 1968, *1*(12), 34–40.

Neugarten, B. L. *Middle age and aging.* Chicago: University of Chicago Press, 1968.

Newman, B., & Newman, P. *Development through life.* Homewood, Ill.: Dorsey Press, 1975.

Newman, R. G. *Groups in schools.* New York: Simon & Schuster, 1974.

N.I.M.H. Personal correspondence. Department of Health, Education, and Welfare, Washington, D. C., 1977.

Nisbet, R. *The sociological tradition.* New York: Basic Books, 1966.

Nisbet, R. *The quest for community.* London: Oxford University Press, 1969.

O'Banion, T., Thurston, A., & Gulden, J. Junior college student personnel work: An emerging model. In T. O'Banion & A. Thurston (Eds.), *Student development in the community junior college.* Englewood Cliffs, N. J.: Prentice-Hall, 1972.

O'Toole, J. (Ed.). *Work and the quality of life.* Cambridge, Mass.: MIT Press, 1974.

Parker, C. The new scope of counseling. *Personnel and Guidance Journal,* 1974, *52,* 348–350.

Parker, C. (Ed.). *Psychological consultation: Helping teachers meet special needs.* Reston, Va.: Council for Exceptional Children, 1975.

Parker, C. Discussant comments. *Applications of student development theory to graduate education.* Paper presented at the American College Personnel Association Meeting, Denver, 1977.

Parsons, T., & Shils, E. *Toward a general theory of action.* Cambridge, Mass.: Harvard University Press, 1951.

Patterson, G. *Families.* Champaign, Ill.: Research Press, 1973.

Patterson, G., & Gullion, M. E. *Living with children: New methods for parents and teachers.* Champaign, Ill.: Research Press, 1971.

Peck, R. C. Psychological events in the second half of life. In B. L. Neugarten (Ed.), *Middle age and aging.* Chicago: University of Chicago Press, 1968.

Perry, W. *Forms of intellectual and ethical development in the college years.* New York: Holt, Rinehart & Winston, 1970.

Perry, W. Comments, appreciative and cautionary. *Counseling Psychologist,* 1977, *6*(4), 51–52.

Peterson, R. E. *Goals for California higher education: A survey of 116 college communities.* Princeton, N. J.: Educational Testing Service, 1973.

Phillips, K. Controlling media output. *Society,* 1977, *15*(1), 10–17.

Piaget, J. *The origins of intelligence in children.* New York: International Universities Press, 1952.

Piaget, J. *The construction of reality in the child.* New York: Basic Books, 1954.

Polanyi, M. *Personal knowledge.* Chicago: University of Chicago Press, 1958.

Polster, E., & Polster, M. *Gestalt therapy integrated.* New York: Vintage, 1973.

Powers, R. *The newscasters: The news business as show business.* New York: St. Martin's Press, 1977.

Purcell, T. V. *Institutionalizing ethics into top management decisions.* Paper presented at the Association for Social Economics Meeting, September, 1976.

Radzinowicz, L., & King, J. *The growth of crime: The international experience.* New York: Basic Books, 1976.

Ramey, J. W. *Intimate friendships.* Englewood Cliffs, N. J.: Prentice-Hall, 1976.

Ramey, J. W. Alternate life styles. *Society,* 1977, *14* (5, July/August), 43–47.

Rapoport, A. Homeostasis reconsidered. In R. R. Grinker (Ed.), *Toward a unified theory of human behavior* (2nd ed.). New York: Basic Books, 1967. Pp. 225–246.

Rappaport, J. *Community psychology: Values, research, and action.* New York: Holt, Rinehart & Winston, 1977.

Raths, L., Harmin, M., & Simon, S. B. *Values and teaching.* Columbus, Ohio: Charles E. Merrill, 1960.

Raven, B. H. Social influence and power. In I. D. Steiner & M. Fishbein (Eds.), *Current studies in psychology.* New York: Holt, Rinehart & Winston, 1965.

Reddy, W. B. A bibliography of small-group training, 1973–1974. In J. W. Pfeiffer &

J. J. Jones (Eds.), *The 1975 annual handbook for group facilitators*. La Jolla, Calif.: University Associates, 1975. Pp. 264–274.

Reddy, W. B., & Lippert, K. A bibliography of small-group training, 1974–1976. In J. W. Pfeiffer & J. J. Jones (Eds.), *The 1977 annual handbook for group facilitators*. La Jolla, Calif: University Associates, 1977. Pp. 238–251.

Richardson, F. D., & Island, D. A model for training workshops and labs. *Personnel and Guidance Journal*, 1975, *53*, 592–597.

Ringler, J., Kennell, J. H., Jarvella, R., Navojosky, B. J., & Klaus, M. H. Mother-to-child speech of two years—Effects of increased post-natal contact. *Journal of Pediatrics*, 1975, *86*, 141–144.

Rockey, E. H. *Communicating in organizations*. Cambridge, Mass.: Winthrop, 1977.

Rogers, C. R. *Client-centered therapy*. Boston: Houghton Mifflin, 1951.

Rogers, C. R. *Freedom to learn*. Columbus, Ohio: Charles E. Merrill, 1969.

Rokeach, M. *The nature of human values*. New York: Free Press, 1973.

Rotter, J. *Social learning and clinical psychology*. Englewood Cliffs, N. J.: Prentice-Hall, 1954.

Royce, J. R. Psychology is multi-. In W. J. Arnold (Ed.), *1975 Nebraska Symposium on motivation*. Lincoln, Nebraska: University of Nebraska Press, 1975.

Ruben, D., & Kim, J. *General systems theory and human communication*. Rochelle Park, N. J.: Hayden, 1975.

Rubin, L. B. *Worlds of pain: Life in the working class family*. New York: Basic Books, 1976.

Ryan, W. *Blaming the victim*. New York: Pantheon, 1971.

Samuels, M., & Bennett, H. *The well body book*. New York: Random House, 1973.

Sanford, N. *Where colleges fail*. San Francisco: Jossey-Bass, 1967.

Sarason, S. *The creation of settings and the future societies*. San Francisco: Jossey-Bass, 1972.

Sarason, S. B. *The psychological sense of community: Prospects for a community psychology*. San Francisco: Jossey-Bass, 1974.

Satchell, M. How to enjoy life—up to the last moment. *Parade*, October 16, 1977, 16–18.

Satir, V. *Conjoint family therapy*. Palo Alto, Calif.: Science & Behavior Books, 1964.

Satir, V., et al. *Helping families to change*. New York: Aronson, 1975.

Satir, V., et al. *Changing with families*. Palo Alto, Calif.: Science & Behavior Books, 1976.

Scarr-Salapatek, S., & Williams, M. L. The effects of early stimulation on low-birth-weight children. *Child Development*, 1973, *44*, 94–101.

Schachter, S. *The psychology of affiliation*. Stanford, Calif.: Stanford University Press, 1959.

Schmuck, P. A., & Schmuck, R. A. *Group processes in the classroom*. Dubuque, Iowa: Brown, 1975.

Schmuck, P. A., & Schmuck, R. A. Humanistic education: A review of books since 1970. In J. W. Pfeiffer & J. J. Jones (Eds.), *The 1976 annual handbook for group facilitators*. La Jolla, Calif.: University Associates, 1976. Pp. 265–273.

Schofield, W. *Psychotherapy: The purchase of friendship*. Englewood Cliffs, N. J.: Prentice-Hall, 1964.

Scotch, J. A. Sociocultural factors in the epidemiology of Zulu hypertension. *American Journal of Public Health*, 1963, *52*, 1205–1213.

Select Committee on Nutrition and Human Needs. *Dietary goals for the United States*. Washington, D. C.: U. S. Government Printing Office, 1977.

Selye, H. *Stress without distress*. New York: Signet, 1974.

Sennett, R. *The fall of public man*. New York: Knopf, 1976.

Sevareid, E. Free press for a free people. *Society*, 1977, *15*(1), 11, 23–25.

Shapiro, S. Critique of Eric Berne's contributions to subself theory. *Psychological Reports*, 1969, *25*, 293–296.

Shaull, R. Foreword. In P. Freire, *Pedagogy of the oppressed*. New York: Seabury, 1970. Pp. 9–15.

Shealy, C. W. *The pain game*. Millbrae, Calif.: Celestial Arts, 1976.

Sheehy, G. *Passages: Predictable crises of adult life*. New York: Dutton, 1976.

Shure, M. B., & Spivack, G. *Problem-solving techniques in childrearing*. San Francisco: Jossey-Bass, 1978.

Simmel, G. The stranger. In D. N. Levine (Ed.), *Georg Simmel on individuality and social forms*. Chicago: University of Chicago Press, 1971. Pp. 143–149.

Simon, S. B. *Meeting yourself halfway: Thirty-one value clarification strategies for daily living*. Niles, Ill.: Argus, 1974.

Simon, S. B., Howe, L. W., & Kirschenbaum, H. *Values clarification: A handbook of practical strategies for teachers and students*. New York: Hart, 1972.

Skovholt, T. Issues in psychological education. *Personnel and Guidance Journal*, 1977, *55*, 472–476.

Smith, J. R., & Smith, L. G. *Beyond monogamy: Recent studies of sexual alternatives in marriage*. Baltimore: Johns Hopkins University Press, 1974.

Smith, M. *A practical guide to value clarification*. La Jolla, Calif.: University Associates, 1977.

Sperry, L., Mickelson, D., & Hunsaker, P. *You can make it happen*. Reading, Mass.: Addison-Wesley, 1977.

Spivack, G., Platt, J. J., & Shure, M. B. *The problem-solving approach to adjustment*. San Francisco: Jossey-Bass, 1977.

Spivack, G., & Shure, M. B. *Social adjustment of young children: A cognitive approach to solving real-life problems*. San Francisco: Jossey-Bass, 1974.

Sprinthall, N. A. A curriculum for secondary schools: Counselors as teachers of psychological growth. *School Counselor*, 1973, *20*, 361–369.

Sprinthall, N. A., & Erickson, V. L. Learning psychology by doing psychology: Guidance through the curriculum. *Personnel and Guidance Journal*, 1974, *52*, 396–405.

Steiner, C. *Scripts people live*. New York: Grove Press, 1974.

Stinchcombe, A. L. Social structure and organizations. In J. G. March (Ed.), *Handbook of organizations*. Chicago: Rand McNally, 1965. Pp. 142–193.

Strong, S. R. Counseling: An interpersonal influence process. *Journal of Counseling Psychology*, 1968, *15*, 215–224.

Strupp, H. H. On the basic ingredients of psychotherapy. *Journal of Consulting and Clinical Psychology*, 1973, *41*, 1–8.

Sullivan, H. S. *The interpersonal theory of psychiatry*. New York: Norton, 1953.

Susman, G. *Autonomy at work: A sociotechnical analysis of participative management*. New York: Praeger, 1976.

Sydnor, G. L., Akridge, R., & Parkhill, N. L. *Human relations training: A programmed manual*. Minden, La: Human Resources Development Training Institute, 1972.

Sydnor, G. L., & Parkhill, N. L. *Advanced human relations training: A programmed manual*. Minden, La.: Human Resources Development Training Institute, 1973.

Syme, S. L., Borhani, N. C., & Buechley, R. W. Cultural mobility and coronary heart disease in an urban area. *American Journal of Epidemiology*, 1965, *82*, 334–346.

Syme, S. L., Hyman, M. M., & Enterline, P. E. Some social and cultural factors associated with the occurrence of coronary heart disease. *Journal of Chronic Diseases*, 1964, *17*, 277–289.

Syme, S. L., Hyman, M. M., & Enterline, P. E. Cultural mobility and the occurrence of coronary heart disease. *Health and Human Behavior,* 1965, *6,* 173–189.

Szasz, T. S. *The myth of mental illness.* New York: Hoeber-Harper, 1961.

Sze, W. *Human life cycle.* New York: Aronson, 1975.

Terkel, S. *Working.* New York: Pantheon, 1974.

Thayer, L., & Beller, K. D. (Eds.). *Affective education: Innovations for learning.* Ypsilanti, Mich.: Eastern Michigan University (SIG: Affective Education Handbook Series), 1977.

Theroux, P. *The consul's file.* Boston: Houghton Mifflin, 1977.

Thomas, W. I. *The definition of the situation.* In L. Coser & B. Rosenberg (Eds.), *Sociological theory* (4th ed.). New York: Macmillan, 1976. Pp. 207–209.

Toennies, F. Gemeinschaft and gesellschaft. In T. Parson, et al. (Eds.), *Theories of society* (Volume 1). Glencoe, Ill.: Free Press, 1961. Pp. 191–201.

Toffler, A. *Future shock.* New York: Bantam, 1970.

Trist, E. Collaboration in work settings: A person perspective. *Journal of Applied Behavioral Science,* 1977, *13,* 268–278.

Turk, H. *Organizations in modern life.* San Francisco: Jossey-Bass, 1977.

Vallence, E. Hiding the hidden curriculum: An interpretation of the language of justification in 19th century education reform. *Curriculum Theory Network,* 1973/1974, *4* (1).

Vendler, H. The wonder man. *New York Review of Books,* 1977, *24* (No. 19, November 24), 10–14.

von Bertalanffy, L. *General system theory* (Rev. ed.). New York: Braziller, 1968.

Walker, R. E., & Foley, J. M. Social intelligence: Its history and measurement. *Psychological Reports,* 1973, *33,* 839–864.

Wang, J. Breaking out of the pain trap. *Psychology Today,* 1977, *11*(2), 78–86.

Warnath, C. F., & Shelton, J. F. The ultimate disappointment: The burned-out counselor. *Personnel and Guidance Journal,* 1977, *55,* 172–175.

Warren, D. I., & Warren, R. B. *The neighborhood organizer's handbook.* Notre Dame, Ind.: University of Notre Dame Press, 1977.

Watson, D., & Tharp, R. *Self-directed behavior* (2nd ed.). Monterey, Calif.: Brooks/Cole, 1977.

Weber, M. Class and status. In L. Coser & B. Rosenberg (Eds.), *Sociological theory* (4th ed.). New York: Macmillan, 1976. Pp. 313–319.

Wegner, D. M., & Vallacher, R. R. *Implicit psychology: An introduction to social cognition.* New York: Oxford, 1977.

Weiner, B., & Kukla, A. An attributional analysis of achievement motivation. *Journal of Personality and Social Psychology,* 1970, *15,* 1–20.

Weisbord, M. Organizational diagnosis: Six places to look for trouble with or without a theory. *Group and Organizational Studies,* 1976, *1,* (4).

Wertheimer, R. Are the police necessary? In E. Viano & J. Reiman (Eds.), *The police in society.* Lexington, Mass.: Lexington Books, 1975.

White, R. W. Motivation reconsidered: The concept of competence. *Psychological Review,* 1959, *66,* 297–331.

White, R. W. *Competence and the psychosexual stages of development.* Lincoln, Neb.: University of Nebraska Press, 1960.

White, R. W. Sense of interpersonal competence. In R. W. White (Ed.), *The study of lives: Essays on personality in honor of Henry A. Murray.* New York: Atherton, 1963. Pp. 73–93.

White, R. W. *The enterprise of living* (2nd ed.). New York: Holt, Rinehart & Winston, 1976.

Whitehead, E. *Notes on the need for a social psychological approach to the study of community.* Unpublished manuscript, University of Notre Dame, 1977.

Whitehead, E. *The parish in community and ministry.* New York: Paulist Press, 1978.

Widick, C. The Perry scheme: A foundation for developmental practice. *Counseling Psychologist*, 1977, *6*(4), 35–38.

Widick, C., & Cowan, M. How developmental theory can assist facilitators in the design of structured learning experiences. In C. Carney & L. McMahon (Eds.), *Exploring contemporary male/female roles*. La Jolla, Calif.: University Associates, 1977.

Widick, C., & Simpson, D. *A developmental approach to the teaching of history.* Paper presented at University of Minnesota Conference of Developmental Theory in Higher Education, Minneapolis, 1976.

Wiebe, G. D. Responses to the televised Kefauver hearings: Some social psychological implications. *Public Opinion Quarterly*, 1952, *16*, 179–200.

Williams, R. L., & Long, J. D. *Toward a self-managed life style*. Boston: Houghton Mifflin, 1975.

Wills, G. What religious revival? *Psychology Today*, 1978, *11*, 74–81.

Wilson, C. *Changing the ties that bind us: How to relate to our parents in more effective ways*. Unpublished manuscript, College of St. Benedict, St. Joseph, Minn., 1977.

Wilson, J. Q. *Thinking about crime*. New York: Basic Books, 1975.

Winikoff, B. Changing public diet. *Human Nature*, 1978, *1*(1), 60–65.

Woolridge, D. *The machinery of the brain*. New York: McGraw-Hill, 1963.

Wright, C. R. *Mass communication: A sociological perspective* (2nd ed.). New York: Random House, 1975.

Name Index

209

Subject Index